JOHN PYM
1583–1643

John Pym from an engraving by Houbraken, 1739

JOHN PYM

1583—1643

THE STATESMAN OF THE
PURITAN REVOLUTION

*

S. REED BRETT

*

LONDON

JOHN MURRAY, ALBEMARLE STREET, W.

First Edition . . . 1940

Made and Printed in Great Britain by Butler & Tanner Ltd., Frome and London

To
F. J. W.

CONTENTS

LIST OF ILLUSTRATIONS

*John Pym and his family used for Arms : Sable a Bull's
head couped Argent enclosed in a wreath Or and Azure.
But the College of Arms contains no record that either
John Pym or any of his ancestors ever proved the right to
the use of such Coat*

PREFACE

SINCE John Pym's death in December 1643, only two biographies of him have hitherto been written, namely, Forster's which was published in 1837, and Wade's in 1912. This is not the place for a detailed criticism of either of those books. Suffice it to say that since their appearance—and particularly during the century since Forster wrote—much new light has been thrown upon the general history of the seventeenth century.

First in importance, as well as in time, in this process of illumination, was the work of Dr. S. R. Gardiner, whose *History of England, 1603–1642*, and *History of the Great Civil War, 1642–1649*, have necessarily been the foundation for all subsequent study of the period. More recently, the researches of Professor Notestein, of Yale, and his collaborators, have added considerably to our knowledge of the early Stuart Parliaments. Alongside this work on the political history of the seventeenth century has gone much investigation into contemporary colonial enterprise. Professor A. P. Newton's *Colonizing Activities of the English Puritans* (published 1914) was of the highest significance in this connection. The new knowledge thus made available must reflect upon the man who, until his death during the opening months of the Civil War, was the very pivot of the struggle between Parliament and the early Stuarts. Hence, this biography is primarily an attempt to bring together the results of recent historical research so far as it affects the person and career of Pym.

Of necessity, therefore, I have drawn upon the material provided by the historians who have specialized on the early seventeenth century, especially those mentioned above, and I take this opportunity of making grateful acknowledgment of my indebtedness. A list of authorities to whom reference has been made is given in the Bibliography, and details of the references are supplied in footnotes throughout the book.

The most serious gap in our knowledge of Pym occurred, however, not in his later public career but in his early private life. This was an aspect of the subject almost entirely ignored by his previous biographers. Nor can the present biography claim to present Pym's complete portrait. What it does claim is that a thorough-going effort has been made to discover all the possible sources of information and that at least a number of points hitherto obscure have been cleared up. In this the most difficult part of my task I have been indebted less to books than to the personal kindness of individuals. The late Mrs. I. M. Pym-Shipster and Mr. Leslie R. Pym freely placed at my disposal their own stores of knowledge of the Pym family history both before and after the days of the great John. Genealogical Tables were kindly supplied by Mr. H. S. Marsham-Townshend. Mr. T. Bruce Dilks and Mr. Maurice Page allowed me to investigate a large number of Pym documents, many bearing the signature of John Pym or of his sons. These documents, now in the Bridgwater Archives, are, so far as is known, for the first time available in preparing a biography of Pym. Mr. Page further supplied the photograph of " Brymore " ; and Mr. J. Saunders has helped to clear up certain legal obscurities.

My debt to Mr. F. J. Weaver can never be sufficiently acknowledged. Without his generous encouragement and guidance the book could never have been completed or even begun. Also, his reading of the MS. resulted in many corrections and suggestions of which I have made free use.

Notwithstanding the help received, I must take full responsibility for whatever errors the book contains. I set out with no very definite views about Pym ; and such views as I had have been modified at many points as I have proceeded. Throughout I have endeavoured to present an interpretation as nearly unbiassed as is humanly possible. To what extent this aim has been achieved must be left to the reader to decide.

S. R. B.

Nuneaton,
September 1939.

Brymore House,
  showing the original porch and Pym's oak-tree

JOHN PYM
1583–1643

INHERITANCE AND YOUTH

JOHN PYM was a member of no mean family; and because the man that he became, and the influence that he wielded, were to no small degree an inheritance from the past, we must try to see what that inheritance was.

His birthplace was the estate of Brymore in the parish of Cannington near Bridgwater, Somerset. Brymore was originally part of the lordship of Rodway in the Hundred of Cannington, and at the beginning of the thirteenth century it was held by a certain Geoffrey de Bramora. Early in the reign of Henry III the estate was given to Odo, son of Durand de Derleigh, who held it for the service of half a knight's fee. Odo later conveyed Brymore to William Fitchett; and it was he who in the latter part of Henry III's reign, conveyed it to Elias Pym.[1] From this Elias, Brymore descended from father to son in an unbroken line down to the John who is the subject of this biography.[2]

To follow the story of that descent in every detail would be beside our purpose. What is essential to note is that several holders of Brymore married heiresses, so that, by the sixteenth century, the Pym estates had become very considerable. For example, a Roger Pym, who held Brymore from 1399 till 1435, married Joan, the co-heiress of John Trivet of Sidbury in Devonshire. Not the least important of the Pym marriages was that of Roger's grandson, whose name also was Roger and who also married a lady named Joan. The father of this latter Joan was John Gilbert, lord of the Manor of Woolavington (some half a dozen miles on the far side

[1] See James Savage : *History of the Hundred of Carhampton* (1830), pp. 229–31.
[2] See Genealogical Tables at end of book.

of Bridgwater from Brymore), which henceforward was called Woolavington-Pym, while her mother was Eleanor, daughter and co-heiress of William Doddesham. Joan, therefore, as the heiress of both her father and her mother, brought valuable additions to the properties of her husband, including the Manor of Cutcombe-Mohun, which belonged to the Doddeshams. In the year 1483 Roger made over all his estates—at Brymore, Woolavington-Pym, and elsewhere—to his son Alexander Pym, who was the great-grandfather of the Alexander who was the father of John. This latter Alexander added yet further properties by purchasing from Francis Throckmorton an adjoining estate at Woolavington (since called Woolavington-Throckmorton).

In short, the Pyms, through all the generations, seem to have been possessed by a land-hunger which they were willing to satisfy either by marriage or by purchase. As a result, John's father, Alexander, owned estates that were widespread, including Cutcombe-Mohun and Woolavington, of both of which places he was Lord of the Manor. These estates, as we shall see later in this chapter, he transmitted to his son John.

Alexander Pym married twice. His first wife was Elizabeth Conyers, and their daughter Catherine married William Cholmeley of Highgate. His second wife was Philippa Coles of Barton near Wincanton in Somerset. Alexander and Philippa had two children—the elder a daughter named Jane, and the younger a son John with whom we are chiefly concerned.

The exact date of John's birth is still uncertain. The date commonly accepted has been 1584, as, for example, in the *Dictionary of National Biography*, which, however, offers no authority for the statement. One of the Genealogical Tables reproduced at the end of this volume shows the date as 1583, and other similar documents tend to support this date.[1] The point is of no material significance to our narrative, and we shall assume the earlier date, 1583, as correct.

The Brymore House in which John was born dated back to the fifteenth century. It stood on rising ground facing the Bridgwater-

[1] See also p. xx (note).

Minehead road. Of that house nothing now remains except the red-brick porch which introduces a visitor into the rambling house that bears no resemblance to the home of John Pym. The only other link which the estate holds with Pym is the oak-tree which local tradition strongly affirms to have been planted by him and whose age seems to agree with this tradition.

John was a mere infant, certainly less than two years old, when his father died in January 1584-5. Shortly afterwards his mother married Sir Anthony Rous of Halton St. Dominick just over the Cornish border and not far from Saltash. There John went to live with his mother, and there he was brought up. The relationship between the Rous and the Pym families—belying what is commonly reputed to be the relationship between stepparents and their stepchildren—was intimate and cordial. Moreover, as later chapters will show, this friendliness persisted throughout the following generation. For example, Sir Anthony Rous had married before, and the second son by his first wife married John's eldest sister Jane. Also, members of the Rous family were closely associated with John's colonizing schemes.

The years spent at Halton St. Dominick were to prove critical in shaping John Pym's whole life. This was true particularly in two respects.

First, Sir Anthony was the representative, on the Devon and Cornish borders, of the Russell family. Halton St. Dominick is less than ten miles from Tavistock, and when the great Abbey at Tavistock had been dissolved in 1539 its spoils had fallen to the first Lord Russell. The head of the Russell family in John Pym's boyhood was the third Earl of Bedford, and it was the latter's estates that Sir Anthony managed. In this way young John Pym was introduced to the notice of the Earl, who evidently was favourably impressed by the boy's qualities. In later chapters we shall see that Pym, during the whole of his career, was assisted not only by the third Earl (who died in 1627), but also by the fourth Earl (who died in 1641). They supported both his colonizing and his parliamentary activities. Also, in the Short Parliament of 1640, Pym's fellow-member for Tavistock was William, Lord Russell, who in 1641 became the fifth Earl and was to be created the first Duke of Bedford in 1694.

Second, Saltash was on the coast near to Plymouth, and the Rous family was friendly with the Drakes. It was at Saltash that Francis Drake had found his wife Mary Newman. In this way young Pym, during his most impressionable years, was brought under the spell of the Elizabethan mariners and became familiar with their stories of oversea exploration and settlement. To the influence of this atmosphere upon the boy's mind may well be traced the colonizing work that he was to do when a man. Further, the supreme purpose of Drake and his school of seamen was the destruction of Roman Catholicism and all its works, particularly as Roman Catholicism expressed itself in the arch-enemy Spain. To the boy's mind, Roman Catholicism and Spain must have been almost synonymous terms. To this aspect of the subject we must return later ; but here it falls to be emphasized as a boyhood influence. It is surely no mere flight of fancy to imagine his being taken to some vantage-point in order to watch the beacon-fires which, that night in July 1588, when he was five years old, were lit to warn the country that the great Armada had been sighted off the Lizard, against which Armada Sir Francis Drake himself was that very night leading the English ships. John was only twelve years old when Sir Francis Drake left near-by Plymouth on what proved to be his last and fatal voyage. Here, then, may be traced the embryo of another of the passions of his manhood, namely, hatred and distrust of Roman Catholicism and a correspondingly mighty devotion to the Protestant Church.

Such was the youth who, only fifteen years old, was sent up to Oxford. The entry in the University Register stands as follows :

1599. 18 May. Broadgates Hall. Pim (Pym) John ; Som., arm. f. 15.

(that is, of Somerset, son of an esquire [*armigeri filius*], aged fifteen).[1] Broadgates Hall is now Pembroke College. His tutor there was

[1] Even this information does not clear up the question of the date of Pym's birth : all that it proves is that he was born on some date after 18th May 1583.

Degory Wheare, then on the threshold of a brilliant academic career. In later years Wheare was to become the first Professor of Modern History in the University of Oxford, and also the Principal of Gloucester Hall. What is perhaps more interesting for our purpose is that Wheare had matriculated at Broadgates Hall on the same day (6th July 1593) as Francis Rous, the son of Pym's stepfather Sir Anthony, and that between Wheare and Francis Rous there was a warm and life-long friendship. Of the life of Pym at Oxford nothing is known. He left the University without a degree, thence passing to the Middle Temple.

The Admission Register of the Middle Temple shows the following entry : [1]

1602. April 23. John Pym, son and heir of Alexander Pym of Brymore, Somerset, esq., decd.,

his sureties being entered as Francis Rowse and William Whitaker.

That there was an almost traditional family connection with the Middle Temple is suggested by the fact that both the father and the son of John Pym were there also, as is shown by the following particulars on the Admission Registers :

1565. July 31. Alexander Pym, son and heir of Erasmus Pyme of Canyngton, Somerset, esq.
1629. October 20. Alexander Pym, son and heir of John Pym, of Brymore, Somerset, esq.

Here again our knowledge of Pym is tantalizingly meagre. All that the Middle Temple Records can tell us is that John Pym was fined twenty shillings on 26th October 1604 and on 25th January 1604-5, and again on 16th April 1605 " for absence and being out of commons."

The purpose of this family training in the law was not professional. John Pym was never called to the Bar. Nevertheless, for a gentle-man who owned wide estates, and was frequently concerned in leases and the like, a thorough legal grounding was invaluable. For Pym in particular, knowledge of the law was to have an un-

---

[1] Information kindly supplied by the Librarian and Keeper of the Records of the Middle Temple.

suspected and unintended importance : both in his dealings with the colonies and in his relations with the King, the effect of this knowledge was constantly apparent.

About Pym's period at the Middle Temple, all that can with certainty be said is that he was still there in April 1605. This date, however, is significant because in that year the interest of the Earl of Bedford secured for him the reversion of the receivership of Hampshire, Wiltshire, and Gloucester. The details are as follows, as shown in the Calendar of State Papers (Domestic) :

1605 June 11, Greenwich. Lord Hume of Berwick to Sir Thomas Windebank. Order to Draw a grant to John Pymme, in reversion after Henry Audley, of the receivership of cos. Hants, Wilts, and Gloucester.

How long Pym had to wait before the office fell vacant we do not know ; but the following three entries in the Calendar show that he did receive it :

1613 November 6, Greenwich. Warrant to John Pymme, Receiver of Wiltshire, to pay yearly to Geo. Hungerford, 13s. 4d. per load, for eight loads of hay for the King's deer in Braydon Forest.

1614 July 9, Westminster. Grant to William Bowler of the office of Bailiff of the Hundreds of Holford, Gretton, and Kittesgate, co. Gloucester ; with certificate of John Pymme, Receiver General of the County, of his fitness for the place.

1618 September 28, Egham. John Pymme to the Lords of the Treasury. Impossibility of raising at once £2,000 by the sale of His Majesty's rent, iron, and fines on leases of disforested grounds, Blackmore and Pewsham. Can get no sale for the iron at the price required, £12. 10s. per ton, and has no offers, save for part of one forest.

It was during this period of his life that Pym married, his wife being Anne, daughter of John Hooke (or Hooker) of Stowmarsh. The exact date of the marriage is uncertain. But as Anne died in 1620 and they had a numerous family—Table 2 at the end of the book shows five daughters and four sons—it seems reasonable to suppose that the marriage took place not long after Pym secured the reversion of the Receivership in 1605. After Anne's death he never married again.

1620 was for Pym a year of double loss, for in that year his mother Philippa died also. She was buried in Halton St. Dominick, the Church Register of which shows an entry of her death. Inside the Church there is a fine tomb to her husband, Sir Anthony Rous. The rector of St. Dominick was Charles FitzGeoffrey, who, incidentally, had entered Broadgates Hall at Oxford five years earlier than Pym. FitzGeoffrey preached Dame Philippa's funeral oration, in the course of which he described Philippa as : " A comfortable helper to her loving husband [that is, her second husband], and no small support of so great a house for more than thirty years' continuance." [1] Thus at thirty-seven years of age, and before his life's main work had begun, he had lost both parents and wife and was responsible for the welfare of a large family of sons and daughters.

In brief, during the period prior to his first entry into Parliament in 1621,[2] Pym was kept busy in two directions. First, there were the duties arising from his receivership. By its means he gained financial skill and an inside knowledge of Exchequer method which were to prove invaluable in later years. Second, he had to manage the family estates. This alone, considering the extent of the estates, must have called for constant vigilance and attention, of which there is tangible proof in the numerous deeds of property-leases, bearing his signature, still in existence.[3] Indeed, there seems some reason for thinking that Pym found it impossible, at one and the same time, to carry out the duties of the receivership and to care for his private estates. This, at least, seems the only explanation of two documents, recently brought to light, which show that Pym, for a period of twenty-one years, placed the care of his property in other hands. The main text of the first of them is as follows : [4]

---

[1] *Death's Sermon unto the Living* : *delivered at the Funeral of Philippa*, late wife of Sir Anth. Rous of Halton in Cornwall, *on Eccles. 7, 2, London 1620, dedicated to John Pym, esq.*

[2] See p. 23 (note).   [3] Bridgwater Archives.   [4] Ibid.

THIS INDENTURE made the Fyfteenth day of February in the Twelueth yeare of the reigne of our souereigne lorde James . . . Betwene John Pym of Brymore in the countye of Somersett esq. of th' one parte and Humfrey Nicoll of Penvose in the countye of Cornewall esq., Willm Fraunces of Combeflorye in the said countye of Somersett esq., Robte Rous of Woolton in the said countye of Cornewall, & Diagorye Where of London gentleman of th' other parte. WITNESSETH that the said John Pym in consideracion of a competent somme of money paid unto him by the said Humfrey Nicoll, Willm Fraunces, Robte Rous and Diagorye Where & other consideracions him movinge, hath graunted bargayned solde and by these presents doth graunte bargayne and sell unto the said Humfrey Nicoll [etc.] . . . their executors and assignes all that his mannor of Brymore in the county of Somersett aforesaid . . . from the feast of St Michaell the archangell wch shall next happen & come after the decease of Dame Phillipp Rous wife of Sir Anthony Rous knight unto the end & terme of twenty & one yeares from thence next ensewing fully to be compleate & ended. YIELDINGE & payinge therefore yearelye duringe the said [*sic*] unto the said John Pym hys executors administrators & assignes the somme of Tenne poundes of lawfull money of England . . . PROVIDED allwayes that yf the said John Pym or his heires . . . shall hereafter pay . . . unto the said Humfrey Nicoll, Willm Fraunces, Robte Rous, Diagorye Where . . . . the somme of Tenne shillinges of the lawfull money of England, Then the said graunt bargayne & sale shalbe utterlye voide & of none effecte and the said terme shall cease and determyne.

Incidentally, the name of "Diagorye Where" in this deed is of some interest, for it must refer to Degory Wheare, John Pym's tutor at Oxford. Though this Indenture was drawn up in legal form on parchment, it is neither signed nor sealed, and there is no evidence that it was ever carried into effect.

Of all the greater interest, therefore, is the second document, dated 18th March 1635, revoking the uses, not only of Brymore but apparently of all Pym's properties, which it states had been granted by a document of 16th February 1614 (that is, only one day after the deed quoted above). The interpretation seems to be that the indenture of 15th February 1614, conveying the use of Brymore only, was the draft of a proposal never in fact carried out, but that by a deed of the next day (which we do not possess) Pym did convey the use of all his estates as well as of Brymore. This revoking deed of March 1635 is worth quoting at some length :

WHEREAS the said John Pym by one or more Fine or Fines . . . hath graunted conveyed and assured unto William Cholmeley,[1] Edward Wardour, and William Whitaker and theire heirs . . . All those the Mannors of Wollavyngton Pym, Wollavington Throgmorton, Brymore, Cuttcombe Rawleighe, Cuttcombe Mohan, Hawkewell, Langham and Poole in the Countie of Somerset . . . and all his Rents . . . of the Mannor of Bomson in the said Countie of Somerset. And all those messuages, lands, tennements, and heriditaments, in the said Countie of Somersett which he the said John Pym hearetofore purchased of Alexander Tilley gent, And alsoe the messuages, lands [etc] . . . of him the said John Pym scytuate . . . in Cannyngtone Cuttcombe als Cuttcombe, Exford, Luxborowe, Luccombe, Carhampton, Willetone, St. Deacows, Wollavington, Bridgwater, Huntspill, Puryton, Murlinge, Edingtone, Cosington, Shapwick, Mariscrofte, Stretcholt, Sterte, Pawlett, Stokeursey, Burneham, Cluttisham, Nettlecombe, Pethershams Marshe, Stockeland, Graunt, Otterhampton and Downend or els where in the said Countie of Somersett to diverse and severall uses behoofs as by my deede indented dated the sixteenth daie of February in the twelfth yeare of the Raigne of our late soweraigne Lord King James made betweene the said John Pym of The one parte and William Cholmeley of Highgate in the County of Middlesex, Edward Wardoure of the parishe of St. Martin in the feilds neere London Kt. then esqr. and William Whitaker of the Midle Temple London esqr. . . . NOW knowe yee that the said John Pym is resolued to revoke . . . the uses . . . concerninge all and every the said mannors, lands, [etc.] . . . And that the will and pleasure of him the said John Pym is that ymediately from henceforth all and every the use and uses . . . in the said deede . . . for and concerninge all and every the said mannors, lands, [etc.] . . . shall cease determyne and be utterly frustrate and voide.

The reason for Pym's putting his estates in use is far from clear, inasmuch as there is nothing in his known circumstances to suggest that he would need to gain any of the advantages—such as avoiding feudal burdens, or facilitating the settlement or the conveyance of

---

[1] Husband of John's stepsister Catherine Pym, who was the daughter of Alexander Pym and his first wife Elizabeth Conyers.

land—which were the common reasons for transferring lands to the use of trustees.[1]   There is nothing improbable in the suggestion, offered above, that the duties of the receivership proved too heavy to enable Pym also to manage his own large and scattered properties, and that he therefore conveyed to three friends—Cholmeley his stepsister's husband, Whitaker who had been his surety at the Middle Temple, and Wardoure—the whole of his estates to the "uses" set out in the indenture of 16th February 1614 which unfortunately we do not possess.   The three friends would thus become virtually trustees with power to administer the estates within the terms of the trust.

Similarly there is no certainty as to Pym's reasons for revoking the use in 1635.   By that year he was even busier than he had been twenty-one years earlier, for he was fast becoming absorbed by the colonizing work of the Providence Company.[2]   That he would wish to resume the active administration of his properties at such a time, when he necessarily lived mostly in London, is highly improbable.   A more likely explanation is the reverse one, namely, that he revoked the use so that the estates would fall back into his complete control and could therefore be disposed of in some other way, for example, by sale or mortgage.   Such a disposal of any considerable parts of his properties would explain the large sums that he was able to invest in the Providence Company and also the penniless condition of himself and his family at the time of his death.

These explanations, though only conjectural, have at least the virtues of simplicity and of fitting the facts of the rest of Pym's life.   Whatever the explanation, the fact seems beyond dispute that for twenty-one years, February 1614–March 1635, Pym did not administer his own properties.

One incidental, but considerable, value of the deed of revocation is the list which the deed gives of the Pym estates.   There can be no doubt that the Pyms were among the great landowners of the west country (see map opposite).

[1] See *Cheshire's Modern Real Property*, 4th edition, pp. 47–9.
[2] See below, Chapter VI.

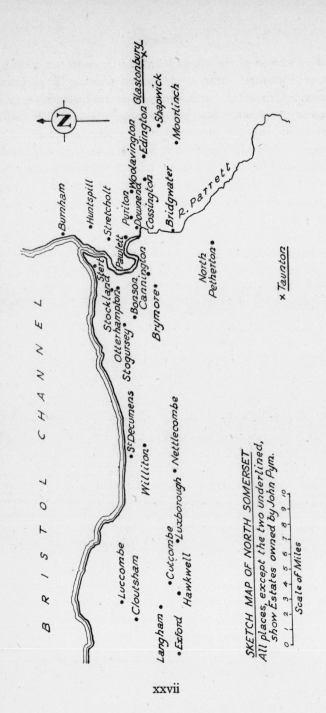

SKETCH MAP OF NORTH SOMERSET

All places, except the two underlined, show Estates owned by John Pym.

Scale of Miles
0 1 2 3 4 5 6 7 8 9 10

BRISTOL CHANNEL

Burnham
Huntspill
Stretcholt
Puriton Woolavington
Downend Edington Glastonbury
Cossington Shapwick
Bridgwater Moorlinch
Pawlett
R. Parrett
Stert
Stockland
Otterhampton Bonson
Stogursey Cannington
Brymore
St Decumens
North Petherton
Williton
x Taunton
Luccombe
Cloutsham
Nettlecombe
Langham Cutcombe Luxborough
Exford Hawkwell

xxvii

This account of the life of John Pym prior to the opening of his parliamentary career is, we must recognize, disappointingly meagre. The most painstaking researches, including those by descendants of other branches of the Pym family, have failed to reveal anything else of consequence. Many details about both himself and his family remain mysteriously obscure. For example, though the Pyms lived and died at Brymore for four hundred years, no trace is to be found either of a register of their deaths or of their burial-places. The only hint of their place of burial is contained in the will of John Pym's grandfather Erasmus : [1]

Erasmus Pimme, of Brymmore, Somerset, esq., Will dated Sep. 13, 1575 ; proved Feb. 7, 1582 [1582-3], by Alexander Pimme. To be buried in the Trinity Isle of the par. Church of Cannington, where Philip Pimm and others of my ancestors heretofore have been buried. To William Pimme, my son, £200, and an annuity of £20 out of my Manors in Somerset and Devon, my Manor of Langham and Poole, Somerset, only excepted. The residue of all my goods, etc., to my son Alexander Pimme, Exor.

It is as though the race of the Pyms had lived and then ceased to be. Similarly of John Pym himself : there is no indication of how he spent his time (other than in the duties of the receivership), or of what friends he made, between 1605 and 1621. We have to be content with the few facts outlined.

Having thus sketched in what is known of the youth and family life of John Pym, we pass to the part that he played in a larger sphere. Before doing so, it will be well for us to try to understand the national issues that were at that period at stake.

[1] MS. document at Somerset House. Printed in *Abstracts of Somersetshire Wills copied from the MS. collection of Rev. Frederick Brown*, 4th series (1889).

Part I

THE RULE OF KING JAMES

CHAPTER I

THE HISTORICAL SCENE

THE business of a statesman is to see further ahead than most of his contemporaries. Nevertheless the mind of a statesman, like the mind of anyone else, is moulded largely by the ideas of the previous generation, the ideas, that is, which prevailed when he was a child. Hence, though we may agree that John Pym was " one of the greatest statesman of that or of any age ",[1] if we are to interpret rightly the work of his mature years, we must first examine the conditions—political, religious, and social—which surrounded him in youth and in early manhood.

The period of thirty-eight years which separated the year 1583, when he was born, and the year 1621, when he first took his seat in the House of Commons, was divided into two nearly equal parts by the death of Elizabeth, and the consequent accession of James I, in 1603. It will be convenient to bear this division in mind as we study the influences which moulded the character of Pym and which prepared the way for the constitutional struggle in which he was to play the leading part.

The year of his birth, 1583, began, in several respects, a period of severe crisis in English history.

On 10th July of the following year William I of Orange perished at Delft by the hand of an assassin. William had supplied the necessary quality of leadership to the Netherlands, resistance to the Spaniards, and a price had long been placed upon his head by Philip II of Spain. The resulting position of the Netherlands was rendered the more perilous by the death of the Duke of Anjou in June of the same year. In 1581, the Seven United Provinces, after declaring their severance from Spain, had offered the sovereignty

[1] J. A. R. Marriott : *Life and Times of Lord Falkland*, p. 2.

3

to Anjou, who had gladly accepted it. Though his overlordship had not brought to the Provinces the material resources that they had hoped—for France had refused to support him—his rank had given to their cause, at least for a time, a certain prestige abroad and a rallying-point at home. So serious was their situation that they could ill afford to lose even a sympathizer. The death of William, following that of Anjou, affected the politics of England scarcely less than those of the United Provinces. The Provinces had proved themselves to be the bulwark of Protestantism against Roman Catholic Spain. If the Spaniard succeeded in suppressing his rebel subjects in the Netherlands, he would certainly use his position there as a base of operations against England towards whom, during the quarter of a century since Elizabeth's accession, his antagonism had steadily been growing more and more intense. The gallant people, " thus bereft of their native leader and the only foreign prince who was committed to their defence ",[1] looked an easy prey to the relentless maw of their enemy. The dismay which thus filled England within a few months of Pym's birth was reflected both in her foreign and in her domestic politics.

Abroad, Elizabeth was about to take a step almost without parallel in her long reign. Notwithstanding her antipathy to war-like action, and to the expense which such action entailed, she realized that the cause of the Provinces and of England was one and the same ; and, after long negotiations and haggling about terms, in August 1585 she made a Treaty with the Provinces and began to send detachments to their aid. The expedition, under the command of the Queen's favourite, the Earl of Leicester, proved a dismal failure in a military sense. It had, however, served the useful purpose of enheartening the Dutch at the moment of crisis and of stiffening their resistance long enough for them to discover in Maurice, the son of William, a new leader worthy to succeed his father and capable of organizing their continued resistance to Spain.

The death of Anjou had raised another issue which affected England. Anjou had been the heir to the French throne which

[1] Black : *The Reign of Queen Elizabeth*, p. 316.

then was occupied by his elder brother Henry III, who was thus left as the sole representative of the House of Valois. The next heir to the throne was Henry, King of Navarre, a representative of the House of Bourbon. Navarre was a Protestant, and Roman Catholic France might therefore at any time have to decide whether a heretic could be recognized as her king. If Henry of Navarre should ascend the throne—as in fact he did in 1589—the balance of power in Europe might be radically changed, and England particularly might have to reconsider her whole foreign policy.

The boyhood of John Pym was thus a period of acute stress in the foreign affairs of the country. Though the defeat of the Armada in 1588 removed immediate anxiety from English politics, there was no certainty that in another year or two a new danger would not threaten, or that in the future England would be as fortunate as she had been in the past.

Within England, the murder of William of Orange increased the public anxiety for the safety of the Queen. In October 1584 the Council drew up the Bond of Association : its signatories undertook to pursue to death any person in whose interest a plot should be made against the life of the Queen. The Bond, copies of which were circulated over the country and signed by all sorts of folk, became the focus of an outburst of loyalty towards Elizabeth. During the remainder of her reign, though not infrequently there were sharp clashes between Elizabeth and her parliaments and people, and though towards the close of her reign the aged Queen seemed a survival from a former day, she retained undiminished the loyalty of the nation. In what proportions the glory of the reign should be shared between the Queen and the statesmen whom she gathered around her can never with certainty be decided. What matters is that her subjects looked to her as the fount and symbol of English prosperity and security. In this atmosphere the last generation of her reign was reared. Like his contemporaries, John Pym grew up accustomed to the idea of intense loyalty to the Crown because the wearer of the Crown, preferring the welfare of the people to any personal advantage, was worthy of allegiance.

The other dominant factor in domestic politics during the latter part of the reign was religion. In a very real sense all the issues of the reign were religious—or, at least, ecclesiastical—issues. This was true of the war against Spain, and of the relations with Mary of Scots and with France ; and the influences which brought those political issues to a head, both at home and abroad, brought the more strictly religious issues to a head also. The Roman Catholic issue was brought to a head by the execution of Mary Stuart in February 1587 and by the defeat of the Armada in 1588. These two events greatly reduced the political power of Roman Catholicism in England ; and henceforward it was Puritanism rather than Roman Catholicism with which the Government concerned itself.

Puritanism was the very antithesis of the Tudor system of government. There were various sections of Puritans, with correspondingly various ideas about Church forms and organization ; yet all alike insisted that " church and state were separate and distinct corporations : the church was a voluntary association of believers whose aims and ideals were entirely spiritual, whose bond was the acceptance of a common creed, and whose only head was Christ ".[1] The Presbyterians would have gone even further than this and would have subordinated the secular government to the will of the Church. This idea that within the political state was a spiritual State which not even the monarch could touch was one which no Tudor monarch—and certainly not Elizabeth—would have tolerated. It was a claim which not even a Roman Catholic would have made. Consequently, as Elizabeth's reign proceeded, the Puritans became increasingly the object of royal displeasure ; and when in 1583—the year of Pym's birth—Whitgift became Archbishop of Canterbury, a strong attack was launched against Puritanism.

Whitgift, while Master of Trinity and Regius Professor of Divinity at Cambridge, had been an implacable enemy of Puritanism. In the very year of his consecration, Whitgift issued his Six Articles which decreed, among other things, that the Crown possessed supreme ecclesiastical power, that nothing in the Prayer Book was contrary to Scripture, and that all the Thirty-nine Articles were

[1] Black : *The Age of Elizabeth*, p. 153.

6

in accordance with Scripture. With these Six Articles every clergyman was to declare his agreement. The almost immediate effect was that two hundred ministers, refusing to pledge themselves to these beliefs, were suspended. In the same year also, Whitgift reconstituted the Court of High Commission which became the instrument for enforcing uniformity of belief and practice. The general effect of the new policy was to intensify and to embitter the religious controversy. Each side defined its views with increasing hardness, and each tended to become increasingly extreme. In 1589 Richard Bancroft, who in the next reign was to become the leader of the High Church party, boldly proclaimed " the divine right of episcopacy and the apostolic succession of the English bishops ". A Statute of 1593 enacted that those who refused to attend Church or who questioned the Queen's ecclesiastical authority should be liable to imprisonment or banishment or, if they returned without the Queen's permission, even death. Though this statute was directed mainly against certain sectaries—since the bulk of the Puritans were still members of the established Church— it indicates that the attitude of the Government was hardening. A few individuals were executed under its provisions, and others made their escape to Holland. Here is a suggestive anticipation of the Pilgrim Fathers who, in the next reign, forgathered in Holland. Not less significant, in view of subsequent events, was the fact that Parliament and even the Privy Council were growing more Puritan. Few intelligent and educated young men, brought up in such a time, could help taking one side or the other in this paramount subject of religion. Time was to show that there was no uncertainty about which side John Pym had taken.

Reference to the Pilgrim Fathers is a reminder that the year 1583 was a notable year also in the history of the American colonies. Five years previously the Queen had granted to Sir Humphrey Gilbert a patent " to discover and possess . . . heathen lands not actually possessed of by any Christian prince or people ". The result was the Newfoundland expedition of 1583 which ended disastrously and involved the death of Gilbert himself. In April of the following year, Walter Ralegh—Gilbert's half-brother—

obtained from the Queen a patent to "plant" America with English settlers. Ralegh, the month after receiving his patent, sent out a party to explore the coast of Florida. In 1585 Ralegh (now Sir Walter) sent out his first body of settlers, Sir Richard Grenville being in command. The settlers, however, were so soon disillusioned about their prospects that the next year they took advantage of a visit from Drake and accompanied him back to England. A second expedition, despatched by Ralegh in 1587, ended more tragically : the naval war against Spain in 1587 and 1588 meant that no ships could be spared the infant colony ; and when ships went out in 1590 no trace of the settlers was to be found. Though John Pym was too young to have any connection with these expeditions overseas, they were preparing the way for a work which was to be one of the formative influences of his life. A later chapter will show that Pym became one of the leading figures in the colonizing of the Island of Providence in Central America and of Connecticut on the mainland of North America, and that this activity brought him into intimate relationship with some of the men with whom he was associated also in the constitutional struggle with James I and Charles I.

This constitutional struggle under the early Stuarts, like the other matters already summarized, had its roots away back in the reign of Elizabeth. The crux of the struggle was finance. From the beginning of her reign, Elizabeth had suffered from financial stringency. As the reign proceeded, the stringency became more and more acute. In part this was due to economic world conditions, namely, the decline in money-value which in turn was due to the large-scale influx to Europe of the precious metals from the Spanish possessions in America. This rapid decline was then a new phenomenon. Its causes were a mystery to Elizabethan Englishmen who, in true English fashion, expressed their disapproval of what they did not understand by blaming the Government. After the murder of Orange in 1584, expeditions to help the Netherlands, and preparations against a Spanish invasion of England, involved increased expenditure. This combination of higher expenditure with lower value of income meant that the Queen and her ministers were constantly at their wits' end for funds to meet their day-to-day needs. All manner of expedients had to be tried. Some of the Crown lands were sold—a dangerous precedent to be justified only by the most acute national exigency. Loans were raised, and benevolences were imposed upon the wealthy. All these items were ominous shadows of coming events. The need for a John Hampden and a John Pym to champion the rights of Parliament against irregular financial expedients evidently had its origin earlier than the Stuarts.

In one direction, royal financial irregularities were a blessing in disguise. For Members of Parliament, by expressing their discontent and by struggling towards redress, were learning to forge weapons—namely, a rudimentary corporate sense, and the establishment of certain precedents of parliamentary supremacy in matters of finance—that were to prove invaluable when the main struggle was engaged against James I and Charles I.

The fact was that parliamentary power, as it came to be understood under the Stuarts, was of recent growth. The general Tudor principle was that it was the King who governed, Parliament being only a consenting or consulted party. At certain epochs—for example, during the Reformation Parliament of Henry VIII—the consent and the consultation had been real; yet even at such times, with only rare exceptions, the initiative had rested with the monarch. That this was the position under Elizabeth is indicated by the brevity of the active life of her parliaments, which did not average more than three weeks for each year of her reign. Even while Parliament was in session, certain topics were excluded from its purview. An attempt to debate foreign policy or the succession to the throne was certain to evoke a sharp rebuke from the Queen. As the reign proceeded, Parliament became restless under these restraints, and Elizabeth, intuitively sensing when her subjects were seriously moved, knew unerringly when to make concessions and how to deepen her people's enthusiastic affection as she did so. Nothing illustrated more strikingly this growing restlessness of Parliament, and the Queen's skilful method of meeting its wishes, than did the vigorous protest of her last parliament against monopolies—an incident all the more significant for our purpose because monopolies were to be one of the causes of bitter contention between Charles I and the parliamentarians headed by Pym. The granting to particular individuals of the sole right to manufacture or sell specified articles (for which privilege the beneficiaries paid substantial sums to the royal exchequer) was, during the latter part of Elizabeth's reign, one of the expedients adopted for providing royal income. When the 1601 Parliament was informed of the numerous fresh monopolies granted since the end of the previous parliament, there was a prolonged and acrimonious debate which not all the tactics of the Queen's ministers could either sidetrack or suppress. There was evidence of widespread popular support for the Parliament's demands. The Queen, accurately sensing the situation, thus addressed Parliament : [1]

This I count the glory of my crown : that I have reigned with your loves. This makes me that I do not so much rejoice that God hath made me to be a queen as to be a queen over so thankful a people . . . That my grants should be grievous to my people, and oppressions privileged under our patents, our kingly dignity will not suffer it. . . . I was never so much enticed with the glorious name of king or royal authority of a queen as delighted that God hath made me His instrument . . . to defend this kingdom from peril, dishonour, tyranny and oppression.

The immediate effect of this queenly condescension was an outburst of loyalty both to the throne and to the person of Elizabeth. The incident illustrates perfectly the growing force of public opinion that Elizabeth's successor would have to face and the improbability that anyone who was not a Tudor would know how to deal with it. This question of monopolies was like many other questions in the reign of Elizabeth : it had been asked but not answered. The answer was to be fought out during the years that followed.

Thus the elements of most of the great issues in which Pym was to play the leading part existed already during the closing period of the reign of Elizabeth. This was the youthful, formative period of the lives of Pym and his contemporaries. By the time that the

---

[1] Quoted, A. F. Pollard : *Political History of England*, VI, 475.

Queen made her gracious concession to the 1601 Parliament, Pym was eighteen years of age and therefore nearing man's estate. It will be remembered that in 1599 he had gone to Oxford, and in 1602 had entered the Middle Temple. He can hardly have been ignorant of the events of 1601. Nor can he have been unmoved by the death of the Queen on the morning of 24th March 1603. Though there was continuity in the political issues before and after 1603, there was a profound difference in the way those issues were handled. For the Queen's successor was not a Tudor but a Stuart.

The legacy that James I inherited from his predecessor did not consist solely of embarrassments. In certain respects it conferred advantages also. Both at home and abroad there was the prospect of a long period of peace. The religious question and the succession question, both of which for many years had threatened confusion to the Queen's government and disruption to the State, were settled beyond dispute. The vigorous policy of Elizabeth in Ireland, though harsh in character and the source of much future bitterness, had for the moment left that country more peaceable than it had been for many years. The reign of Elizabeth had seen also the end of strife between England and Scotland : with the conversion of Scotland to Protestantism—though it was Protestantism of a different type from that of England—the long tradition of a Franco-Scottish alliance against England had gone for ever. This relatively new policy of peace between England and Scotland was immensely strengthened by the accession of James : for, though the two countries remained in government and in law as separate as they had ever been, the fact that their two crowns were now worn by the same head meant that war between them was unthinkable. Also, on the sea, and beyond the sea, new and ever-expanding outlets for English energy were provided by enterprises in seafaring and colonization. In her relations with foreign Powers, too, England was more secure than she had been since the heyday of Wolsey : Spain was no longer to be feared ; in matters of commerce, England's most formidable rivals were passing into decline —the Italian and German states owing mainly to the shifting of the centre of trade from the Mediterranean to the Atlantic, and Flanders owing to the religious policy of Spain ; moreover, the two most enterprising continental states—namely, France under Henry IV and the Netherlands—were friendly towards England. When all these elements are considered together, it is probably safe to say that England was in a sounder condition—united at home and secure abroad—than at any previous time in her history. To the government of the country James brought certain personal qualifications. He possessed a keen wit ; his private life was clean ; also for eighteen years he had ruled Scotland, and the experience thus gained ought to stand him in good stead in dealing with the larger opportunities and problems which opened out before him when he came to England in 1603.

To this picture of the pleasant prospect which awaited James, there was a less pleasant reverse side. The advantages, summarized above, had corresponding and complementary disadvantages. For example, while it is true that the religious issue had been settled, in the sense that Protestantism had decisively supplanted Roman Catholicism as the religion of the State and of the great majority of the people, the particular type of Protestantism most in favour was not conducive to a strong monarchy. In spite of all the efforts of Elizabeth and of Whitgift, Puritanism had continued to grow until " Puritanism in the wider sense—the Puritanism which asked for a further reformation of doctrine and ritual than Elizabeth had been willing to allow—was the creed of the greater part of the members of the Church of England ".[1] Moreover, of the Puritan members of the Church of England, many were Calvinists. James had already experienced, among the Presbyterians of Scotland, the attitude of Calvinism towards monarchy ; Andrew Melville, when Moderator of the General Assembly of the Church of Scotland, had once told James that he was not a king but only a member of Christ's Kingdom and was, indeed, only " God's silly [that is, weak] vassal ". Small wonder that James commented later : " A Scotch presbytery agreeth as well with monarchy as God and the Devil." And small wonder that when James left Presbyterianism

[1] J. R. Tanner : *English Constitutional Conflicts of the Seventeenth Century*, p. 10.

behind him in Scotland he had no intention of encouraging it in England. From the time of the Hampton Court Conference in 1604—within a few months of the beginning of his reign—James identified himself with the High Church party whose bishops proclaimed the doctrine of the Divine Right of Kings. Herein lay a cause of dissension in the State, of dissension that would be all the more serious because Parliament was becoming increasingly Puritan and Calvinist.

The reverse side of the picture of peace with the continent was no more pleasant for James than that of conditions at home. Because the English people had no longer any need to fear a foreign enemy, they were free to give their attention to domestic problems that had long been shelved. Not the least of these problems was the relation between King and Parliament. We have seen that Elizabeth had considerable difficulty in restraining her parliaments, and that even she sometimes had to bow to the storm and make concessions. During the first thirty years of her reign, opposition to the Queen's government, whilst she was grappling with the difficulties of national defence, was branded as unpatriotic ; and during the closing fifteen years this attitude largely continued through the force of tradition, though the reason for it had ceased. The death of Elizabeth snapped that tradition, and James had to face Parliaments whose feelings, long pent-up, were likely to express themselves in terms of explosion.

Similarly, the unity which characterized the nation at James' accession, though of good augury for the nation, was not without its embarrassments for James. The national unity of the closing years of Elizabeth had expressed itself in a common loyalty to the Queen. The personal character of the monarch was thus a decisive factor in the State. Of this, the reign of Elizabeth had afforded striking evidence. Even her personal foibles, though they might lower her subject's estimate of her as a woman, yet served to throw into high relief her greatness as a queen. The Elizabethan Age was not a mere name, for it had been Elizabeth's leadership which had provided the stimulus to national greatness whether in seamanship, expansion overseas, economic prosperity, or a blossoming literature. Elizabeth's successor, no matter who he might be, would have a difficult task to maintain the lofty tradition which she had set ; and what would have been difficult for anyone would be impossible for James. Of all the long line of English monarchs, James I is the only one of whom it can be said without exaggeration that he lacked all the personal qualities necessary for a king. So marked was the contrast between James I and his own Stuart fore-bears that the theory has been seriously advanced that he was not the son of Mary Stuart and Darnley but was a changeling.[1] What-ever the truth about the ancestry of James, he was without any trace of kingly dignity in person or conduct. " A big head, slob-bering tongue, quilted clothes, and rickety legs " : this description which Macaulay gives of him may be an exaggeration, but it is only an exaggeration of the impression left by James upon his contemporaries. Though deeply learned in certain branches of knowledge, particularly in theology and in the theories of govern-ment, the only practical effect of this erudition was to make him conceited and therefore unreceptive of advice from others. He had no gift for choosing wise counsellors, and no tact in dealing with individuals, whether friends or opponents. Like George I, James was a foreigner and incapable of appreciating the intricacies of English government ; but unlike George I he lacked the good sense to trust ministers who could govern for him. This was the man whose lot it was to be monarch in one of the most fateful crises of English history.

The result was tragedy both for James and for England. For once, at least, Macaulay stated the bare truth :

It was no light thing that, on the very eve of the decisive struggle between our Kings and their Parliaments, royalty should be ex-hibited to the world stammering, slobbering, shedding unmanly tears, trembling at a drawn sword, and talking in the style alternately of a buffoon and of a pedagogue.

The nature of this " decisive struggle " was of necessity determined largely by the particular expression of royalty with which Pym and his fellow-parliamentarians had to deal.

[1] G. R. Francis : *Scotland's Royal Line.*

14

It was not intelligence, in the narrow sense of the word, that James lacked. Often he displayed a nimbleness of wit that was disconcerting to his courtiers. Indeed, his wit became a snare to him, so that he mistook craftiness for statecraft. "Hence the skill in outwitting people, the sly ways of temporizing, the studied deceit and cunning which he formed gradually into a system under the misused name of king-craft, and in which his whole idea of government consisted." [1]

James' theories of government were formally set out in his treatise *The True Law of Free Monarchies*, published in 1598. The essence of these theories is that, since God, not man, appoints the monarch, it is to God alone that the monarch is responsible. It therefore follows that the monarch is not bound by man-made law. Further, the monarch is the source of all authority in the State, and to him all his subjects—of whatever rank—owe an absolute obedience since he is God's representative in the State. A monarch, on his side, must recognize that his duty is to rule in the interests of his subjects. This, however, does not justify rebellion against a king who does not so rule. If a monarch betrays his trust, that is a matter between himself and God who ordained him. Hence, rebellion against a God-ordained ruler is always sinful. A tyrant may be God's appointed chastisement of a nation ; and the proper cure for tyranny is that the nation should give itself, in patience and prayer, to a purer life.

In one sense there was nothing very novel about these ideas. The Tudors had never tolerated any rival authority in the State, and, for the most part, they had tried to govern in what seemed the interests of their subjects. What was novel about James' theory was that it was given formal expression. No Tudor would ever have dreamed of provoking a challenge to his supremacy by formally claiming absolute power. Henry VIII was content to make Parliament the vehicle of his momentous ecclesiastical changes ; and Elizabeth knew when to acknowledge herself in the wrong. So long as the Tudor monarchs enjoyed the reality of

---

[1] J. R. Tanner : *English Constitutional Conflicts of the Seventeenth Century*, p. 94.

power they cared little for its theory. " The Stuarts were never content to let sleeping dogs lie. They demanded not merely the practical recognition of a right, but the theoretical acceptance of a dogma." [1] James I, both in theory as expounded in this *True Law* and in practice as shown in his relations with Parliament, perfectly illustrated the truth of this generalization. Otherwise expressed, James I was a doctrinaire : he was acquainted with the letter of the Tudor's power but had no appreciation of the spirit whereby the Tudors had tempered the letter in its practical interpretation. The inevitable result was a clash between James and his people ; and James, utterly sincere in his beliefs, never understood the point of view of his opponents and was genuinely hurt by their contumacy.

The Commons with which he had to deal was not the relatively unimportant body that its predecessors of the Middle Ages had been. Those classes in the nation whom it represented were no longer to be despised by their rulers. The Tudors had deliberately followed a policy of counteracting the power of the ancient baronage by increasing the influence of the smaller gentry and of the traders.

The Tudor rule was essentially educative. It left the people ready, as they had never been before, to take upon their shoulders the high responsibilities of self-government. In Parliament, in Council, as ministers and magistrates the flower of the middle classes had been steadily trained for the work to which they would presently be called. [2]

Outside Parliament, the trading element especially had been growing more influential through the wealth that had come to them from the increased trade with Europe and overseas. When James came into conflict with the Commons he would find that he was dealing with a body that knew what it wanted and knew also how to achieve it.

Nor was the conflict long in coming. Elizabeth died on 24th March 1603 ; by 20th June 1604 relations between King and Parliament had become so strained that on that day the House of

---

[1] J. A. R. Marriott : *The Life and Times of Lord Falkland*, p. 21.
[2] Marriott, op. cit., p. 14.

Commons discussed its famous, and lengthy, *Apology*. After declaring :

what grief, what anguish of mind hath it been unto us . . . to find and feel by effect your gracious Majesty (to the extreme prejudice of all your subjects of England, and in particular of this House of Commons thereof) so greatly wronged by misinformation,

the *Apology* went on to assert the established privileges of the Commons.

And, contrariwise, with all humble and due respect to your Majesty our sovereign lord and head, against these misinformations we most truly avouch, first, that our privileges and liberties are our right and due inheritance, no less than our very lands and goods. Secondly, that they cannot be withheld from us, denied or impaired, but with apparent wrong to the whole state of the realm. Thirdly, that our making of request in the entrance of parliament to enjoy our privilege is an act only of manners, and doth weaken our right no more than our suing to the King for our lands by petition.

Accordingly the *Apology* made certain complaints :

First, the freedom of persons in our election hath been impeached. Secondly, the freedom of our speech prejudiced by often reproofs. Thirdly, particular persons noted with taunt and disgrace, who have spoken their consciences in matters proposed to the House, but with all due respect and reverence to your Majesty.

The King's *True Law of Free Monarchies* and the Commons' *Apology* enunciated flatly contrary views ; and the political history of the reigns of James and Charles was the unavoidable consequence. Within little more than twelve months after the beginning of James' reign, therefore, the stage on which Pym was later to play the lead was already set. For what was to happen on that stage both sides must bear some share of blame. On occasion the Commons were narrow-minded and obstinate. But, when every allowance has been made, the chief blame in handling the situation must rest with the King.

Changes in the balance of power were rendered inevitable by the growth of wealth and intelligence and by the decline of the influence of the old nobility ; but it was largely due to the king that the transition took the form of revolution instead of evolution. . . . By generous conduct, the king could at any moment have cancelled the accumulated store of discontent and hostility.[1]

All the main questions, which were to become issues between Charles I and Parliament, were raised during the opening years of James I. The fundamental issue was James' claim to rule by Divine Right. Every struggle between James and Parliament, no matter what the immediate practical cause of the dispute, was a particular example of the King's claim to rule without interference and of Parliament's challenge to that claim.

The most intense struggles occurred over matters of finance. James began his reign at a financial disadvantage. Elizabeth's legacy to him was a debt of £400,000 ; and the Crown income from regular sources was certainly too small to meet the minimum demands upon it. Moreover, James' reckless extravagance made demands far beyond the minimum. During his reign in Scotland he had lived under a sense of constant poverty. He seemed to imagine that in England he could, by comparison, enjoy endless wealth. Elizabeth's normal, peace-time expenditure was in the neighbourhood of £220,000 yearly. By 1607 James was spending £500,000, and Elizabeth's legacy of debt of £400,000 had grown to £735,000. The greater part of this difference was due to extravagance in the gifts he made to courtiers and favourites and in the maintenance of his own household. In order to try to make good the increasing deficiency, James adopted many irregular expedients for raising money—impositions (that is, customs-duties on classes of goods not included in regular tunnage and poundage), benevolences and forced loans, the sale of offices and honours, and grants of monopolies.

Whether these expedients would be successful would depend largely upon whether the King could rely upon the law-courts to enforce them against recalcitrant subjects. The first round in the contest went to the King. The Exchequer Judges, arguing a case of impositions in 1606, declared that the King " guideth all under God by his wisdom, and this is not to be disputed by any subject ".

---

[1] G. P. Gooch : *English Democratic Ideas in the Seventeenth Century*, p. 60.

Unfortunately for James, the most truculent opponent of his claims was Coke, his own Lord Chief Justice. Coke's experience, both parliamentary and legal, was of long standing. As far back as 1593 he had been Speaker of the House of Commons, and in 1594 he had been made Attorney-General. The latter event was notable because Coke secured the office in spite of the competition of Francis Bacon (who will figure prominently later in our story), and for long afterwards the two men remained keen rivals. After acquiring a high legal reputation in several important trials, Coke rose to be Lord Chief Justice in 1613. If James imagined that this would buy Coke's support for royal illegalities he made a serious mistake. Coke was an unflinching champion of the " Rule of Law ". He maintained the view that the King could not make law without Parliament. Hence no man could be punished unless he had committed an offence against the law. The details of Coke's resistance to James prior to 1621 are not our present concern. What does concern us is the significance of that resistance. Coke must not be regarded as a self-sacrificing heroic patriot. He " was an ambitious, pushing lawyer, a bully, and in his early days a sycophant ". Nevertheless " only one thing was dearer to Coke than promotion and power, and that was the Common Law ".[1] The antagonism between Bacon and Coke

was not accidental or personal only : they represented opposing tendencies in thought and action. Bacon was by far the greater man, for in him the philosopher included both the lawyer and the statesman ; and thinking after the manner of a philosopher he advocated a large reform of English law. Coke, on the other hand, with a mind fanatically narrow, was possessed with a profound veneration for the law as it stood and he was convinced that it was not by change and reform, but by the following of precedents that the liberties of England were to be defended. . . . Thus Coke represented a rigid conservatism—the conservatism of constitutional liberties as they were ; Bacon represented reform— but reform carried out by a philosopher king wielding sovereignty unlimited and half-divine.[2]

[1] G. M. Trevelyan : *History of England*, p. 391.
[2] J. R. Tanner : *English Constitutional Conflicts of the Seventeenth Century*, pp. 41–2.

The climax of Coke's resistance to James was reached in 1616 when he refused the King's request that judgment should be suspended against the Bishop of Lichfield who was charged with holding— by royal authority—a church-living *in commendam*, that is, with receiving the emoluments of a vacant living while a suitable successor was (theoretically) being looked for. As a result, Coke was dismissed from office the same year. The decline of Coke was accompanied by the rise of his rival, Bacon, who in March 1617 was made Lord Keeper, and in January 1618 Lord Chancellor. For the moment, James had the upper hand and could rely upon a Bench of subservient judges. But his triumph was short-lived. Coke's views were not lost upon at least some others of his profession. Moreover, in 1621 Coke again entered Parliament (as Member for Liskeard), where he was one of the leaders of the Commons, along with Pym, Hampden, and Wentworth, against James' illegalities.

Hitherto Parliament had opposed the claims of the King by assertions of its own, appealing to common knowledge for their truth ; but the antagonist who now confronted James was still more formidable. The true ruler of the Kingdom was not the King but the Law, to which the King was subject ; and what the Law declared was not a matter of assertion but a matter of fact.[1]

The immediate reason for summoning Parliament was financial stringency. Three years previously, solvency had been restored to the royal finances through their reorganization by Lionel Cranfield, who, having begun life as an apprentice and having become a merchant through his own capacity and enterprise, had been introduced to the notice of the King. In 1613, James appointed Cranfield surveyor-general of customs. The effect of the new surveyor's handiwork at once became apparent. In all directions there were drastic economies ; so much so that by 1618 there was actually a balance on the right side of the King's accounts. But, however successfully the King might " live of his own " in ordinary times, any extraordinary call upon his exchequer would drive him to summon a parliament. Such a call was threatened in that year,

---

[1] G. P. Gooch : *English Democratic Ideas in the Seventeenth Century*, p. 55.

1618, when the Thirty Years' War broke out between the Roman Catholics and the Protestants of the Empire. It was difficult to see how England, the leading Protestant Power of Europe, could keep out of the war if it continued for any length of time, especially as the Protestant Prince immediately concerned was Frederick, the Elector Palatine, husband of James' daughter Elizabeth.

James was in a difficult position. He was a man of peace and, since the very outset of his reign, had consistently based his foreign policy upon friendship with Spain. To cement such friendship, he was anxious to arrange a royal marriage between the two countries. The success of his scheme might well depend upon his attitude to the religious struggle. For Philip III of Spain also was interested in that struggle, partly because his country was traditionally the champion of Roman Catholicism and partly because, being a Hapsburg, he had family affinities with the Emperor Ferdinand II. James, therefore, had given no encouragement to his son-in-law Frederick when the latter, early in 1619, had asked advice about accepting the crown of the Protestant Kingdom of Bohemia, for the acceptance of the crown would inevitably involve the Bohemians in war against the Roman Catholic Emperor from whom they were determined to win their independence. Nor, when Frederick assumed the crown, and war broke out on the accession of the Emperor Ferdinand II later in the same year, would James take up arms in Frederick's support, though he allowed English volunteers to serve Frederick in the Palatinate. Philip III, having lulled James into an attitude of neutrality, in August 1620 sent 24,000 Spanish troops from the Netherlands to overrun the Palatinate. A little later, on 29th October, the Bohemians were routed by the Imperialists at the Battle of the White Hill outside Prague. Frederick had thus lost both his inherited lands in the Palatinate and his new Kingdom of Bohemia. Even James was moved to anger by these events, not least by the knowledge that he had been duped by the Spaniards through their ambassador Gondomar. Soon it became known that James had at last determined to act for the support of the Palatinate, and a benevolence was raised for the equipment of an expeditionary force. The response, however, was disappointing, the total sum produced being less than £35,000 ; and it was mainly this failure which led to the summoning of Parliament for January 1621.

With such a background of personal issues and of circumstances, at home and abroad, the Parliament of 1621 was likely to be of more than ordinary consequence.

CHAPTER II

PYM'S POLITICAL APPRENTICESHIP

James I's Third Parliament, 30th January 1621–6th January 1622

BETWEEN Pym's first entry into the House of Commons in 1621 and his death in 1643 he sat in seven parliaments. In all but the first he was Member for Tavistock. But he began his parliamentary career, in the 1621 Parliament, as Member for the little Borough of Calne in Wiltshire, his fellow-Member being John Ducket.[1]

Along with him in the Commons sat a number of men whose names would soon be familiar to every household in the land. First, there was Sir Thomas Wentworth, who had sat in the Addled Parliament of 1614 as one of the Members for Yorkshire and who was representing the same county again. Little did either Wentworth or Pym guess how closely or how strangely their political careers were to be linked together. Wentworth, although nine years Pym's junior, had already had some political experience as a Member of the Council in the North, and he was also a well-known figure about the Court. This did not mean that he was a Court favourite, for his haughty manner, and his intimacy with the Puritan Archbishop Abbot, won him more enemies there than friends. Nevertheless, if he was not generally liked, he was respected as a wealthy gentleman, influential in his own county, well-informed and alert of mind.

[1] Pym is commonly stated to have been Member for Calne in the 1614 Parliament. No evidence of this Membership exists. Gardiner stated it as a fact in Volume II of the first (1883) edition of his *History*, but corrected it in the Preface to Volume III and deleted it from the next edition of Volume II. Nevertheless (evidently through a lapse of memory) in his article on Pym in the D.N.B. (1896) he repeated the statement.

Another notable Member, also like Pym a newcomer to Parliament, was John Hampden, a native of Buckinghamshire and Member for the borough of Grampound in Cornwall. Hampden's character will sufficiently reveal itself through the part he played in later events which we shall have to follow. His naturally retiring disposition made him slow to act as a leader until the excesses of the King challenged his political principles and left him no alternative. This point had not been reached in 1621. Consequently we do not find Hampden ranged in this Parliament along with Pym in attacking abuses.

The importance of the presence of Sir Edward Coke in the House has been emphasized already and will become more apparent as the story of the Parliament unfolds itself.

Sir John Eliot, who was later to be a close ally of Pym and Hampden against Charles I, was absent from this parliament, though he had sat in the previous one of 1614.

The formal opening of Parliament took place on 30th January, when James addressed the Houses asking for supplies of money, and asking all the more confidently, he stated, because he had not received any grants from them for ten years—a strange and naïve basis of appeal—and because recent economies would ensure that the money granted would not in future be wasted. The King further promised to support the cause of Protestantism and of his daughter Elizabeth, and her husband, the Elector Palatine. "I will leave no travail untried," said he, "to obtain a happy peace. But I have thought it good to be armed against a worse time, it being best to treat of peace with a sword in my hand " [1]—words that have a curiously modern ring. Parliament gave to the King the benefit of any doubts it may have entertained about his sincerity. If James had been prepared to carry out the implications of his speech, there is every reason for believing that Parliament, content to let bygones be bygones, would have co-operated with him gladly. A few days were all that were necessary to test James' sincerity and to give the Commons the opportunity to exemplify what their temper would be if abuses were not redressed.

[1] *Proceedings and Debates in 1621* (E. Nicholas), I, 9.

Freedom of Speech

The debates of the first day on which the House met for business (5th February) were sufficient to show that the matters on which Members were most sensitive were those of religion and of the Commons' privileges.

Sir Charles Perrot started the ball rolling by his motion that, in order to discover whether any of their number were recusants, the House should receive communion at St. Margaret's. The result was a spate of oratory against Roman Catholics. Sir Robert Phelips waxed particularly warm on the theme. Perrot had evidently touched a matter very near to the surface in the Members' convictions.

The House then turned to consider the cases of several Members of the 1614 Parliament who, after the dissolution of that parliament, had been summoned before the Council and imprisoned in the Tower for speeches they had made in the House. The 1621 House, therefore, anxious not only to secure redress of what was past but also to safeguard themselves against attacks in the future, requested that the King should recognize their right to freedom of speech. Mr. Secretary, Sir George Calvert, intervened to try to divert the Commons' attention ; but the Commons, resolute that the issue should not be evaded, referred the question to a committee of the whole House. On 15th February, the Committee reported to the the House its recommendation that a bill should be introduced forbidding the imprisonment of Members for speeches delivered in the House. Thereupon Calvert rose to remind the House, by the King's command, that the King had already given his assent to the Speaker's request—made at the beginning of every parliament —for freedom of speech. The Commons' readiness to accept this reminder as making a Bill unnecessary is a further proof of their goodwill towards the Crown. Pym in his Diary thus summarizes the effect of Calvert's intervention : " This speech set an end to that matter and from that time all other Propositions concerning liberty of speech were laid aside." [1] It was largely as a sign of gratitude for the royal promise that the Commons voted two subsidies, that is, about £160,000.

[1] *Commons' Debates, 1621* (Ed. Notestein, Relf, and Simpson), IV, 55.

On the same day as the Commons received the Report concerning freedom of speech (15th February), a Bill was introduced to promote " the keeping of the Sabbath, otherwise called Sunday ". It was during the debate on this Bill that Pym delivered his maiden speech in the Commons. The *Book of Sports* which James had issued in 1618 permitted " our good people " who had attended divine service to engage in Sunday archery, dancing, maypole-display, and the like ; and the new Bill, which forbade dancing on Sunday, seemed to be plainly directed against this royal permission. So, at least, it was interpreted by a young barrister named Shepherd. Not content with a reasoned argument against the Bill, Shepherd indulged in both sarcasm and invective, declaring that not only had James allowed dancing on Sunday but that David had bidden men praise the Lord in a dance, and hence that the supporters of the Bill were defying both King James and King David. As a final effort, he declared that the promoter of the Bill was a disturber of the peace and a Puritan. The Commons, indignant that such epithets should be thrown at any of its Members, ordered Shepherd to leave the House. Next day, 16th February, the House gave its consideration to the subject in a long and weighty debate. Pym has a long note of it in his Diary and, in particular, a note of his own speech : [1]

He that first spoke [that is, Pym] begun thus : It is at all times a burden to my modesty to speak in this honourable Assembly. At this time it doth more oppress my disposition to speak against one whoe is yet (thowgh suspended) a Member of the Howse. This Gentleman, as I conceave, hath committed fower great faults yet not faults all of one nature but ariseinge each above other by fower remarkable steps of Gradacion. The first is the perticular fault against that worthy Member of this Howse who preferr'd the Bill. The second, a generall fault against all the Justices of Peace. The third, against the whole bodye of this High Courte, which is the representative-bodye of the Commons. The fowrth, as I may call it *generale generalissimum*, against the flourishinge estate of the Kingdome. All theis appeare stamped in his owne words.

---

[1] *Commons' Debates, 1621*, IV, pp. 62–5 ; also *Commons' Journals*, I, 524, i ; and *Proceedings and Debates*, I, 51–2.

Then follows, in Pym's characteristic fashion, an elaboration of each of the points enumerated. The fourth, the offence against the State, he explained under two headings :

(1) By seekeing to bring us into the ill opinion of the Kinge, whose favour and good opinion begetts our greatest hope of the prosperitie and reformacion of the Kingdome. This he endeavoured to bereave us of, saying that we went about to make a lawe in the face of his Majestie opposite to his Royall judgment declared in printe. Secondly, as he would devide the Kinge from us soe would he devide us among our selves, exasperatinge one party by that odious and factious name of Puritans ; Or at least wuld make the world beleive we were devided, which as it may breede in the Common adversarie boldnes to attempt soe it may nourish among us ieolsye and suspicion in defence of our selves. And it hath beene often seene that small seedes of Tumult and sedition growe upp into great dangers, even to the overthrowe of States. . . .

And if it be agreeable to the order of the Howse (which is practised in other Courts) That the meanest give their opinion first, I shall match his fower faults with fower punishments. In the heate and eagernes of his speech, perceiveing the dislike of the Howse, He protested he would speake, And if he did otherwise than became him, his person and his estate would answere it. I will distreigne him (thowgh moderately) by both his pledges, His person by Imprisonment dureing pleasure, His estate by the Fine of £100. And I thinke him worthy to be expelled the Howse and excepted out of the Generall Pardon.

Finally, after other observations had been made on Shepherd's speech, the House declared its judgment :

Sentence. Concerninge the punishment, there [sic] divers opinions. But the most concurred that the Sentence should be such as might rather expresse forgivenes than punishment, That this should be one of our workes of Charitie against the Communion. Therefore the Fine, Imprisonment, Exemption out of the Pardon were left out, And the sentence consisted only of his expulsion.

Soe he was called in and received his iudgment upon his Knee at the Barr, was dischardged the Howse, and a new Writt awarded.

This speech is worth quoting at some length as being a fair sample of Pym's speeches, expounding and applying fundamental principles, and marshalling his arguments in a logical formation. Further, in two respects at least the subject-matter of this maiden speech is of particular interest as foreshadowing principles from which he never swerved down to the very day of his death more than twenty years later. First, there was his indignant resentment against the unfortunate Shepherd in that he had applied to Members of the Commons "that odious and factious name of Puritans". This expressed a conviction which Pym consistently upheld. Not only did he never join any of the extremist sectaries; he never even associated himself with the Puritanism of some of his closest parliamentary colleagues. At the end of his career, as at the beginning, he was a staunch adherent of the English Church as it then stood.

The second significant note in the speech was the insistence that "the greatest hope of the prosperity and reformation of the Kingdom" depended upon the favour and the good opinion of the King. Over and over again this note appears in Pym's speeches. The suggestion that such declarations were mere hypocrisy lacks all foundation. Pym was manifestly sincere in his loyalty in 1621; and no incident in his career can be pointed to as marking a decline in that loyalty. We are bound to conclude that when, for example, even Clarendon was moved to write [1] that, during the Short Parliament of 1640, Pym mentioned the King "with the most profound reverence and commendation of his wisdom and justice", Pym meant exactly and sincerely what he said. So staunch was Pym's allegiance to the King and the kingship that, as will be shown more fully later, it is safe to predict that, had Pym lived, he would never have been a party to the execution of Charles I or to the establishment of a republic. At least, there is peculiar significance in his 1621 reference to the King as the source of the nation's prosperity.

That the rest of the House shared Pym's views was shown by the sentence imposed upon Shepherd, and also by the further resolution to delete whatever clauses of the Bill were contrary to the King's Declaration of Sports. It is remarkable that, in spite of the King's

[1] Clarendon's *Great Rebellion*, Book II, section 68.

treatment of earlier parliaments and in spite of an interval of ten years during which he had ruled without any parliament at all (except the Addled Parliament of 1614), this Parliament of 1621 was so loyal at the outset that James had the direction of affairs easily in his own hands. If he lost this loyalty, the fault would be no-one's so much as his own.

Only three days after the expulsion of Shepherd, the Commons were led to consider another question which also was to provoke the intervention of Pym. On 19th February, William Noy called the attention of the House to monopolies and the abuses arising from them. Reference has been made already to the consummate tact with which Queen Elizabeth had conceded to her last parliament the abolition of monopolies. James I's need of money, especially during the long intervals between parliaments, has led to a revival of monopolies as a method of raising revenue for the royal exchequer. Three monopolies in particular were the objects of the Commons' attack, those, namely, for inns, ale-houses, and gold and silver thread.

The person around whom the storm concerning monopolies chiefly raged was Sir Giles Mompesson. He was Member for Great Bedwin, a Wiltshire borough. Incidentally, this must have meant that both Mompesson and his works were familiar to Pym whose receivership had included Wiltshire and who himself was Member for Calne in the same county. Mompesson had suggested to James that commissioners should be appointed to grant licences to inns. In theory, the idea was sound : it was highly desirable that both the general conduct of inns and the prices they charged should be under supervision. Accordingly, in 1617, Mompesson and two others were nominated to the commission. The next year, a similar monopoly was granted to other persons for licensing ale-houses. During several years the rapid growth in the numbers of ale-houses had been causing anxiety, partly because they encouraged drunkenness and partly because they were resorts of robbers. There was much to be said for bringing them also under control. The practical difficulty was that an earlier Act of Parliament had made the Justices responsible for licensing ale-houses. The new monopolists, therefore, though unable to grant licences, were empowered to supervise the conduct of the ale-houses and to see that the keepers of undesirable houses were punished. The monopoly of the manufacture of gold and silver thread was of a different nature. In order to encourage the manufacture of such thread in England, a patent had been granted as early as 1611. Finally, after various modifications of the patent, in 1618 the King had taken over the monopoly himself and had pensioned off certain gentlemen who had sunk capital into it, including Sir Edward Villiers, brother of the rising favourite, George Villiers, Earl of Buckingham.

These were only some of the many monopolies which had been created under James. Their revival had reawakened the old mistrust both of the system itself and of the abuses which it encouraged. Accordingly, when Noy broached the subject he was but saying what nearly everyone was thinking, and there was an outburst of support. Noy directed his attack immediately against the referees, that is, the lawyers and others who had been members of the committees appointed by the Government to investigate the desirability of any proposed monopoly before a patent was granted for it. Noy's motion was that the referees should be examined by the House. In this he was at once supported by Coke, who had now returned to the Commons as Member for Liskeard. Since the referees had been appointed by the Crown, an enquiry into their conduct would virtually be a questioning of the King's ministers, and thus the thin end of the wedge of ministerial responsibility. Though this particular proposal was not adopted, the House resolved itself into Committee to examine the patent for inns.

There was no need for the Commons to summon any outsider to explain his conduct in this connection, since the individual primarily responsible was Mompesson, who was a Member of their own House. From all parts of the House came evidence of his malpractices. He had made extortionate charges for licences granted to inn-keepers, had used threats to a justice who had refused a licence to an undesirable inn, and had employed agents who induced unlicensed inn-keepers to give them shelter and then had given information against them. Some thousands of such offences by Mompesson and his satellites became known to the Committee.

Examination of the working of the patent for ale-houses revealed that the chief offender was a certain Sir Francis Michell, who had used his office as a Justice in order to enrich himself from those who applied for licences. The anger of the House rose danger-ously as the list of his known offences lengthened, and many punishments were suggested as befitting his crimes. Finally, Coke's motion was carried : Michell was sent to the Tower and deprived of his office of Justice. In so dealing with Michell, who was not a Member of their House, the Commons were cer-tainly exceeding their privileges. The immediate effect of their action was to scare Mompesson, who accordingly confessed to the House the error of his way and begged for mercy. The Committee, however, continued its investigations, and on 27th February Coke reported officially to the House the evidence collected by the Committee. There followed a heated debate in which Pym took part, though the *Commons' Journals* contain only a very condensed record of his speech.[1] That same day Pym was appointed to the Committee to examine further into Mompesson's conduct. On 6th March Pym was appointed along with Cooke, as assistants to Hakewill, to make further examinations into the matter of Mom-pesson's Concealments. Next day there occurred an interesting little episode. According to the *Journals* for 7th March, Mr. Hakewill "Desireth some other, learned in the Law, may be joined with him, Mr. Cooke and Mr. Pym being now his assistants, who are no lawyers ".[2] Seven additional members were accord-ingly appointed to the Committee.

Meantime evidence had been accumulating concerning Mom-pesson's iniquities in the matter of the patent for gold and silver thread. Among other things, it was revealed that base metal had been mixed with gold and silver. The Commons, after a con-ference with the Lords, issued a writ for his arrest. Officers were sent to arrest him, but Mompesson maintained his slipperiness to the end. By means of a trick, he escaped under the very

[1] *Commons' Journals*, I, 530, i.   [2] Ibid., p. 543, ii.

noses of the officers and fled from the country, never to be apprehended.

The Commons next turned their attention to the referees. As early as 8th March the Commons demanded an enquiry into their conduct. King James, sensing danger in this attack upon his servants, tried to resist; but at last even he saw the wisdom of giving way before the Commons' persistence. This he did by an indirect method : in order to save his referees, he sacrificed Mompesson. Pym, in his Diary for 26th March,[1] thus records the final promulgation of judgment :

The Speaker in the name of the Commons, demanded Judgment, which was pronownced by the Lord Cheife Justice, Speaker of the Lords Howse, in this manner :

That the Lords spirituall and temporall, having dulye examined and wayghed the Offences and Oppressions of Sir Gyles Mompesson, knight, Did Award and adiudge the said Sir Gyles to be degraded of the order of Knighthood, the Forme and Ceremony of his Degradation to bee performed in such sort as shalbe thowght fitt by the Lords Commissioners for the Earle Marshalls office, if he be apprehended, reserveinge the Dignitie of his wife and children. That he showld stand perpetually outlawed dureinge his life, All his goods to be forfeited to the Kinge and the Proffitts of his Lands duringe his life. That he showld stand forever dissabled to beare any office, to give any testimonye, to be of anye Jury, Assize, or to execute any Commission. That he shall, if he be taken, remayne Imprisoned during his life And be Fyned and Ransomed, which Fyne is Taxed at £10,000. That he showld never come neare the Courte of the Kinge or Prince Or any of the Courtes of Westminster. That he showld be excepted out of the Generall Pardons And to be forever reputed a Person infamous.

Four days later the King revoked by proclamation the patents for inns and for gold and silver thread.

The Commons, in recognition of these concessions, dropped their attacks upon the referees. For the moment the King had won a tactical victory. But only for the moment. Already a fortnight earlier, on 14th March, a petition had been presented to the Commons charging the Lord Chancellor Bacon with bribery.

---

[1] *Commons' Debates, 1621*, IV, 200–1.

The details of the charges against Bacon and of his trial are not our present concern since we have no record that Pym took any part in the proceedings. The latter were not unduly protracted. On 1st May, Bacon was deprived of the Great Seal, and on 3rd May he was sentenced to a fine of £40,000, to imprisonment in the Tower during the royal pleasure, to expulsion from Parliament, and to exclusion from Court. Though, for some reason, Pym was silent during the trial, the condemnation of the King's minister was a precedent of which he was to make full use later, notably against Buckingham and Strafford.

About the same time, however, Pym did intervene in another case, namely, that of Floyd. Floyd was an aged Roman Catholic barrister and a prisoner in the Fleet. On 30th April the Commons were informed that when the defeat of the Protestant Elector Palatine at Prague became known in the Fleet, Floyd showed an unfeigned joy. There was nothing on the Statute Book of England to make such joy a criminal offence. Even if there had been, Floyd was not a Member of Parliament, and therefore the Commons had no right to proceed against him. But the King's refusal to support his daughter Elizabeth and her husband Frederick the Elector, and his refusal to let Parliament debate the subject, had left the Commons in such a touchy mood that they eagerly seized this trifling occasion to relieve and to demonstrate their feelings. The House examined numerous witnesses who related stories, embellished with circumstantial details, of Floyd's disparaging remarks about the unlucky Elector and his wife. During the debate which followed this examination, the House grew increasingly heated, the Members vying with one another in suggesting punishments which they considered appropriate to the aged Floyd— whipping at the cart's tail, branding, cutting out his tongue, lopping off nose and ears, and the like. According to the *Commons' Journals*, Pym's contribution to the debate was not much more edifying than the rest : " To whip him, except within some reasonable time he pay £1,000 fine ".[1] Finally the House agreed that Floyd should be pilloried three times, should ride from pillory to pillory

[1] *Commons' Journals*, I, 602, i.

on a bare-backed horse, his face towards its tail and with a paper in his hat declaring his offence, and should pay a fine of £1,000.

For once at least King James proved himself a better guardian of liberty than did the Commons. James challenged them to prove that they had jurisdiction over anyone not a Member of their House or that they could condemn anyone without being able to examine witnesses against him on oath. The result was long negotiations between the Commons, Lords, and King. In the conference with the Lords, Pym was one of the Commons' representatives. Finally, the Commons recognized that the right to act as a law-court rested with the Lords. The latter, partly to save the dignity of the Commons, raised Floyd's fine to £5,000, ordered him to be whipped and to suffer a life imprisonment. The King, at the instance of Prince Charles, remitted the whipping. It seems clear that, in this instance, Pym's anti-Romanist convictions led him into an attitude no more sound or tolerant than that of most of his fellow-Members.

One item in the course of these proceedings had raised an interesting point concerning the relationship between the Lords and the Commons. The Commons had ordered the examination of papers contained in a trunk belonging to Floyd. The trunk was then sealed up. When Floyd's case came before the Lords, they sent to the Commons for the trunk. Thereupon ensued, on 18th May, a debate in the Commons about whether the trunk should be sent. Pym delivered a typical speech which he summarized as follows in his Diary : [1]

Against the delivery of the Trunk were theis Objeccions [all made by Pym] : (1) That wee showld discreddit the Evidence uppon which ourselves had proceeded if nowe we showld send those papers to the Lords as matters needfull for the cleering of Floyds offence uppon which we had given judgment with perusall of those papers. (2) That the Lords have not used to give sentence uppon any Commoner for any publique cryme not Concerninge the priviledges of their Howse but by Relacion from the Commons. That therefore we owght not to doe any thing which may further them in makeinge a President contrary to our owne priviledges. (3) As we had received the Kinges pleasure whereby we had hitherto

---

[1] *Commons' Debates, 1621*, IV, 361 ; also *Commons' Journals*, I, 624, ii.

forborne to open the Trunke, Soe wee showld not deliver it to be opened by others.

To this summary he adds the comment : " Notwithstandinge, the Howse Order'd that the Trunke showld be delivered "—which shows, incidentally, that even Pym, with all his cogent argument, was not always able to sway the House.

Meanwhile, another matter had arisen, also involving dealings with the Lords. This concerned a charge of corruption levelled against a Member of the Commons ; and once more Pym took his full share in exposing and punishing it. Sir John Bennett, Member for Oxford University, was Judge in the Prerogative Court which dealt with certain cases of wills, and which therefore was an ecclesiastical court. Charges were raised against Bennett that he had extorted money from those who had business in his court. The Members of the Commons were much exercised as to the procedure to be followed ; and on 20th April the question was debated at length,[1] the House being anxious not to forgo its rights of dealing with its own members. The question was whether the House should allow the Lords to judge the case while Bennett was still a Member of the Commons, or whether the Commons should hold a preliminary enquiry and then, if satisfied of Bennett's guilt, should expel him so that the Lords could then deal with him freely.

As might be expected, on such a question of principle involving the honour and privileges of the House, Pym had decided views. His speech expounded them succinctly :

Mr. *Pymme*, concerning the interest this House hath in this judgment, saith that the two Houses of Parliament were anciently but one, but being divided, the power was divided also ; the power of inquisition was left to this House, that of judgment was left in most cases to that of the Lords, but in some cases this House is not barred :—That the power of execution is in us with the Lords : —That we should reserve this power of inquisition in this business wholly to ourselves. God hath said of himself, that he is the searcher of all hearts, and therefore it is no derogation for us to be inquisitors. As for the end whither this judgment tends, every

[1] *Commons' Journals*, I, 583, i ; *Proceedings and Debates*, I, 179–285.

offender oweth a triple debt, namely, first a debt to the King ;
secondly, to the party ; thirdly, and to the Poor ; and this judgment tendeth to the satisfaction of all these three debts.[1]

Next day, Pym was one of the twelve Members added to the already
existing Committee to consider the case further. The case was
long drawn out and had not been settled when Parliament was
dissolved in January 1622. Finally the Star Chamber took cog-
nizance of the case and, in November 1622, imposed upon Bennett
a fine of £20,000, ordered his imprisonment during pleasure,
and declaring him to be perpetually debarred from office.

While the foregoing events were taking place, another cause of
difference between King and Parliament was smouldering, namely,
the King's foreign policy. The crux of this policy still was the
King's attitude towards the belligerents in the Thirty Years' War.
We have seen that one reason for summoning Parliament had been
the King's need of money to equip an expeditionary force for the
Palatinate. The Commons' grant of two subsidies on 15th February—in response to Calvert's request for £500,000 to support
30,000 men—had been made apparently on the assumption that
further grants would be forthcoming as the need arose. James,
however, instead of prosecuting the war with a vigour that would
have roused popular enthusiasm and have brought forth further
parliamentary grants, continued to dally with the idea of buying-
off the Spaniards by means of a marriage alliance. Consequently
when, in April 1621, James intimated that the two subsidies were
exhausted, the Commons ignored the hint and continued to occupy
themselves with grievances.

James, resenting both the Commons' failure to grant supplies
and their independent tone in the cases of Mompesson, Floyd, and
Bennett, decided to give himself a rest from them. On 28th May
the Commons received a message from the King to conclude their
business within a week in preparation for an adjournment.

Mr. Secretary saith that his Majesty hath commanded him to
signify to this House that this House must have a recess. His
Majesty's reasons are, the season of the year ; the ordinary govern-

[1] *Proceedings and Debates*, I, 283.

ment of the country, which his Majesty thinketh suffereth much in the absence of the Governors, the Justices of Peace and Deputy Lieutenants of the Counties.[1]

The Commons, taken by surprise, and fearing that the adjournment would become a prorogation or a dissolution, gave vent to feelings which hitherto they had suppressed. Next day Sir Edwin Sandys is reported as roundly declaring :

He seeth the House is full of two passions, grief and fear ; and, for his own part, he was never so full of either :—That the country is in a dangerous taking : our religion is rooted out of Bohemia and Germany, and rooting out of France, unless God doth miraculously defend us.[2]

During the debate on 30th May, Sir Robert Phelips used language even bolder :

He knoweth not whether he shall ever be of this House again or no, and therefore will now speak freely his conscience : . . . that (since the reformation of religion) the Papists were never more impudent and daring than now ; and, if it please not his Majesty to have some care of it, it will grow shortly to an equal balance, which are the greater number of Papists or Protestants. . . . If we consider [the Commonwealth's] wants and grievances, he thinketh, the Parliament was the only physician to cure the desperateness of the disease. In this it pleased his Majesty to say that, if he had known them, he would have remedied those grievances of our hearts ; but in the way of this gracious offer of remedy it hath pleased his Majesty (for causes best known to himself) not to divert, but to retard the same.[3]

That same day Pym intervened twice. The first time was in the morning when he followed Sir Thomas Wentworth in urging that the Commons should adopt a more moderate attitude and should make the most of the week remaining to them.[4] During the afternoon he spoke again to lay before the House the alternative courses open to it in order to get through as much business as possible.

---

[1] *Proceedings and Debates*, II, 110.   [2] Ibid., p. 121.
[3] Ibid., p. 123–4.   [4] *Commons' Journals*, I, 631, ii ; 632, i.

On 4th June, which was to be the last day before the recess, a scene, apparently in strange contrast to recent events, was enacted in the Commons. Just as the sitting was about to end, Sir John Perrot rose. As he had roused the House during its first day's debate, so he was to rouse it on its last before adjournment. Reminding the Members of the King's expressed determination at the beginning of the session to help to recover the Palatinate by treaty or by force, he urged that they should declare their readiness to support, with lives and estates, the cause of God and of the King's children. The House received Perrot's suggestion with enthusiastic acclamation ; and a long, formal resolution was quickly prepared, part of which ran as follows :

The Commons assembled in Parliament, taking into their most serious consideration the present estate of the King's children abroad, and the general afflicted estate of the true professors of the same Christian religion professed by the Church of England and other foreign parts . . . with one heart and voice do solemnly protest that, if his Majesty's pious endeavours by treaty, to procure their peace and safety, shall not take that good effect he desireth . . . then they shall be ready, to the uttermost of their powers, both with their lives and fortunes, to assist him.[1]

Once more, as the resolution was read to them, the Commons cheered wildly. The King and his ministers were quick to appreciate the significance of the Commons' declaration. Sir Edward Cecil, after listening to Perrot's speech, echoed the general conviction : " He thinketh this declaration is come from Heaven, and believeth that it will work better effects with our enemies than if we had ten thousand soldiers on the march." [2] The King, anxious that the Commons' words should not be lost upon nations abroad, ordered the resolution to be translated into several European languages and distributed.

Though we have no record that Pym took a leading part in these events, they are worth including in our story as showing that the Commons, however resentful of the infringement of their political rights, were yet willing to support the King in order to

---

[1] *Proceedings and Debates*, II, 172.   [2] Ibid., pp. 169–70.

secure the victory of Protestantism. This was entirely in keeping with Pym's own convictions and with the principles which were to inspire all the parliaments of which he was a Member until the outbreak of the Civil War.

Incidentally, Pym's comment in his Diary for 4th June,[1] is worth noting : "His Majesties answere was full of waight and deserves to be spoken in noe other than his owne words." In view of the bitter debates which had preceded the adjournment of that day, this additional proof of Pym's freedom from all prejudice against the King is of peculiar interest.

On 4th June, then, Parliament stood adjourned until 14th November. During the recess, though public business was in abeyance, the King's dealings with certain individuals were to have effects not only when this parliament reassembled but in parliaments that were to follow. On 16th June, the Earl of Southampton, Sir Edwin Sandys, John Selden, and others, were placed under arrest, no charge being specified. If James' object had been to dissipate the atmosphere of goodwill in which Parliament adjourned, he could hardly have chosen a more certain method : he had placed in confinement a Member of each House —presumably for words or actions during the debates—together with John Selden who apparently had expressed opinions, distasteful to the Court, on Floyd's case. That these men were soon released made matters but little better : Parliament would certainly remember the incident when it reassembled ; and John Selden, though not then a Member, was largely responsible for drawing up the famous Protest at the end of the 1621–2 Parliament, for proceedings against Buckingham in 1626, and for the Petition of Right in 1628.

On the other hand, several notable promotions took place in both Church and State. First, Dean Williams of Westminster, who had shown himself a zealous supporter of the King, was raised to the Bishopric of Lincoln and, immediately afterwards, was given the office of Lord Keeper in succession to Bacon (Lord St. Albans). Second, Laud was raised from the Deanery of

[1] *Commons' Debates, 1621,* IV, 413.

Gloucester to the Bishopric of St. David's. Interest in these appointments is increased by the fact that the two ecclesiastics concerned were soon to be open enemies. The third promotion, though of a different kind, was not less notable nor, from the King's point of view, less deserved : it was the elevation of Cranfield to the peerage as a Baron. Cranfield, throughout the session, had shown a tact in dealing with the Commons that was equal to the ability he had already shown in straightening the King's finances. Before Parliament reassembled in November, he had become Lord Treasurer, and a few months later was raised a step higher in the peerage with the title of Earl of Middlesex. It was an astonishingly rapid rise, both in office and in rank, for a merchant's apprentice.

During the recess, the King's attention was occupied chiefly by affairs on the continent. The Elector Frederick, after the Battle of the White Hill, was a fugitive, finally taking refuge at the Hague. Thereupon the Protestant Princes of the Empire, considering his cause hopeless, disbanded the troops which they had gathered together in his defence. Shortly before Parliament had been adjourned, James had sent Lord Digby to Vienna to try to negotiate with the Emperor on Frederick's behalf. Digby was instructed to offer that Frederick would renounce Bohemia and make submission for the past, in return for the Emperor's pardon. If the Emperor refused these terms, James threatened open war for the restoration of the Palatinate. Digby was fatally handicapped by three factors. First, the Emperor, uncertain which way the fortunes of war might turn, prolonged the negotiations and avoided a definite answer. Second, Frederick himself refused to abandon the war, thus rendering all negotiations abortive. Third, James continued to hope that peace might be maintained on the basis of a Spanish marriage. During the protracted negotiations, the war was continuing and Frederick's plight was becoming increasingly desperate. All that remained to him was the Lower Palatinate which was held precariously by the English volunteers under Sir Horace Vere. At the end of October 1621, Digby returned to England. James, deeply moved as he listened to Digby's story, determined to take action. £30,000 were borrowed and sent to the Elector, and Parliament, whose date of meeting had been postponed, was summoned for 20th November. When the King's determination became known, the nation was swept by a wave of enthusiasm. It was in these circumstances that Parliament reassembled.

Digby at once laid before the Houses his views on the situation. Digby was a statesman working on sound political principles and with clear ideas for their fulfilment. He explained what the King had done to secure peace and, this having failed, urged adequate measures of war. Digby's estimate was that this would cost no less than £90,000 for a year. The Commons, however, though enthusiastic for war, were not to be rushed unduly. On 22nd November, before proceeding to debate the vote of supplies, the House was reminded by Sir Dudley Digges of the imprisonment of Sandys at the beginning of the recess. Calvert, the Secretary of State, tried to calm the House by the assurance that Sandys' imprisonment had not been due to any words uttered in the House. Even so, the Members were not satisfied until Calvert agreed that his explanation should be entered on the Clerk's book.

It was on the 26th that the great debate on supplies for the war opened. During that day and the next, a long succession of speeches was made on the subject. While there was general agreement in favour of active intervention, there were strong expressions of distrust of a Spanish alliance. The policy of sending immediate help to the Palatinate was supported by Secretary Calvert, young Sir Thomas Wentworth, Sackville, and Rudyerd. On the other side, fiery speeches were delivered by Phelips, Coke, Perrot, and Digges. Thomas Crow expressed the sense of this second group, and of many others in the House, when he declared that before they voted supplies they must know who was their enemy. During the second day's debate, Pym delivered the first of three speeches whose statesmanship won immediate recognition by all parties alike, and not least by the King. Having elaborated, in the form that was to be typical of his orations, the pros and cons of granting supplies for the war, he brought his speech to an end in the following terms : [1]

Nowe in this Proposition to mainteyne a Warr in the Pallatinate against the power and purse of the Kinge of Spaine, And yet to keepe peace in other places, wee were called to hazard and expence and debarred from the hope of proffitt which howe Easily by the benefitt of our shippinge might be made uppon the dispersed Coastes of that Princes Dominions, The reigne of Queene Elizabeth yealds sufficient testimonye. Upon which premisses his opinion was not to agree to anie contribucion for the support of that Warre uppon this Proposicion. Yet that things might be kept upright for the present, and the Kinge might have more tyme eyther to accomplish his desired peace, Or elce to declare a Warre in such a manner as may Yeald a hope and Commodity reciprocall to the charge, Hee moved that somewhat might bee added to our former free guift in the same kind without anie mencion of the Warr. And the better to Encouradge and Enable the people in the payment thereof, wee showld labour nowe to end the Session And to carry downe with us those good Lawes which are prepared for the Establishment of Religion and releife of our Greivances.

In the course of his speech Pym had moved : "An oath of Association to be devised, for the defence of the King's person, religion, etc., and this to be taken by all before they be admitted to any place of government in the Commonwealth." [2] Here is a clear instance of the principle noted in the previous chapter, namely, that the men of Pym's generation were living under the influence of the Elizabethan environment of their youth. This suggested association was plainly on the lines of " The Association " of 1584. Equally Elizabethan in idea was the implication which ran throughout Pym's speech that the pursuit of recusants was intended not as a persecution of their religious beliefs but as a measure for the security of the State ; so also was the insistence that England's real enemy was Spain.

Finally, the House agreed that a small supply should be granted to meet the immediate needs of the Palatinate, the precise amount being determined in committee, and that the committee should

[1] *Commons' Debates, 1621*, pp. 442–3 ; also *Commons' Journals*, I, 647, ii.
[2] *Commons' Journals*, I, 647, ii.

further agree upon a petition for the execution of the existing laws
against Papists.

When the " Great Committee " met next day (28th November)
Pym delivered another weighty speech which he thus summarizes
in his Diary : [1]

Sir Robert Phillips . . . concluded with a motion for a Sub-
Committee to frame the Peticion to his Majestie for the redresse
of theis mischeifes and Execution of the Lawes against Recusants.
It was Replyed by another [that is, Pym] that it was not Yet
readye for a Sub Committee to whome the frame and order onely
was to be referred.   But the Materialls of the Peticion was to bee
prepared by this Greate Committee.   And as all his wishes did
concurre to the good speed of this worke, Soe would he conferre
towards it some part of his advice, in doeing whereof hee hoped
to be excused if in the clamor and tempest of Publicke danger he
did not observe the whisperings of his owne fortune.   That wee
delivered the like Peticion in the begining of the Parliament and
by his Majesties answere might perceive that his Royal disposition
was not as yet bent toward that which wee desired.   Not that his
Zeale in Religion was less, But that he doth not thinke a severe
execution of the Lawes to be at this tyme the waye of advantage
of Religion ; herein lyes the principall part of our labour to winne
the Kinge, for hee is the first mover, from whence all the pros-
peritye of this and other affayres of Parliament must be derived.
Haveinge spoken this by waye of Introduction, He propownded
three generall parts : The first conteyneing divers motives to worke
upon the Kinges affeccion.   The second, matters of fact to be
presented to his Judgment.   The third, some wayes by which we
may best make Use of both for the accomplishinge our desire in
the Matter of Religion.

Two factors which we have noticed already in Pym's political
philosophy express themselves clearly in this speech.   First, the
deep and obviously sincere respect in which he holds the King.
Second, the emphasis which he places upon religion as the key to
the nation's grievances.   This second factor appears even more
pointedly in the fuller account of his speech which included the
following paragraph : [2]

[1] *Commons' Debates, 1621*, Vol. IV.
[2] *Proceedings and Debates*, II, 228–30.

He would now have it made known to the King, that the Pope hath blown over the fire of the *Romish* religion into this Kingdom, and that the Popish party here are as tinder ready to take fire : —That it should be told the King how the Papists flock to the Spanish Ambassador's : which is a thing in foreign parts not permitted, and whereof all are very jealous, even in Kingdoms where all are of one and the same religion. He would have us beseech the King that there may be a commission from his Majesty to some men (whereof he would have us desire that some might be of this House and some of the Upper House) to see the Laws here of England duly executed against Papists. And he would have these things offered to the King by some honourable Members of this House.

It was hardly to be expected that the King would receive kindly the news of Pym's speeches. Both the plea for an association in his speech of 27th November, and his peroration on 28th, were tantamount to suggesting that individual citizens and Parliament must unite to carry out laws that the King had neglected. James showed his displeasure by ordering that Pym should deliver for his Majesty's examination a written copy of the speech of 28th November. Pym replied that " he had written no part of that speech, before he uttered the same, and had not any notes or memorials thereof but such as were retained in his mind ".[1] He therefore desired his Majesty that

it would please you to accept his relation thereof by speech, in which manner it was originally propounded. . . . But having received from your Majesty a second and more strict command, in dutiful obedience thereunto he humbly beseecheth your favour-able acceptance of the declaration following ; wherein sincerely and ingenuously (though, perchance, to his own disadvantage) he hath set down as much as he can remember of the occasion and matter, and especially of his intentions in that speech.

There follows at considerable length—occupying nine pages in *Proceedings and Debates*—Pym's account of his speech which, referring to himself, he concluded :

As he never consented to any thought contrary to his duty, but in all his motions did labour to advance the confidence and

[1] *Proceedings and Debates*, II, pp. 230–2.

love of your people to your Majesty, and those other honourable ends, for which this Parliament was summoned, without any declination to private respects ; so will he ever, according to the obligation of his conscience and duty, wholly resign himself to your Majesty's service, with sincerity and the utmost endeavour of his person and estate, to obey your royal will, and with humility and modesty to submit himself to your pleasure.

This dutiful conclusion was likely to impress the King less than the elaborate and forthright argument of the speech itself. There is small wonder if, after Pym's boldness in offering to voice his convictions in person before the King, and after actually delivering them in the form of this written speech, the King regarded Pym as the most dangerous of his opponents. Nor is there less wonder if the Commons regarded him as their most stalwart and effective champion.

The debate concluded by the Commons' granting a subsidy for the support of troops in the Palatinate (recusants being assessed at double the standard rate),[1] and by the appointment of a sub-committee to draw up a petition for presentation to the King. Of this committee Pym was voted a member.

On 3rd December the committee presented to the Commons the terms of the Petition which it recommended. It was a lengthy document. After referring to the devilish doctrines of Popery and to the increasing boldness of the English Papists, who were encouraged by their expectation of the Spanish marriage, the Petition urged upon his Majesty " ten remedies for these grave evils ", including :

1. The formation of a league of Protestant States.

2. The appointment of a commission to superintend the enforcement of the laws against recusants.

3. The marriage of the Prince to a Protestant.

This is the sum and effect of our humble declaration, which (no ways intending to press upon your Majesty's most undoubted and regal prerogative) we do, with the fulness of our duty and obedience, humbly submit to your princely consideration.[2]

In this form the Petition was sent to James.

[1] Ibid., p. 244.
[2] Ibid., p. 265, and *Commons' Journals*, I, 655.

James was far less impressed by the Petition's profession of humility than he was by what he not unnaturally regarded as the insolence of its demands. He was at Newmarket, and on 3rd December, wrote to the Speaker a letter which was read to the House next day.[1] Its salient sentences were :

These are therefore to command you to make known in our name unto the House, that none therein shall presume henceforth to meddle with anything concerning our government or deep matters of State, and namely, not to deal with our dearest son's match with the daughter of Spain. . . . You shall resolve them in our name, That we think ourself very free and able to punish any man's misdemeanours in Parliament as well during their sitting as after ; which we mean not to spare hereafter, upon any occasion of any man's insolent behaviour there that shall be ministered unto us.

The House was aghast at the peremptory tone of the King's reply. Realizing that to allow the claims of that reply to pass unchallenged would mean the end of their independence and privileges, yet not wishing to act hastily, the Commons adjourned until the next day, having first ordered the recall of the twelve messengers whom they had sent with the Petition to the King. Next morning, deeply sensitive to the seriousness of their proceedings, the Commons debated the situation. Once again Pym threw his weight on the side of moderation : the *Commons' Journals* contain the following terse note on his speech : [2]

Mr. Pymme : To cast Balm, to heal the Wound ; and not to make it wider.

After much discussion, the House appointed a committee to draw up a further Petition which should explain to the King the meaning of the first Petition and the purpose that the House had in sending it. Then, refusing to transact any further business until their privileges were assured, the Commons adjourned.

On 8th December the explanatory Petition was passed by the Commons. In this connection the *Commons' Journals* for that day have a curious note : [3]

---

[1] *Commons' Journals*, I, 658.   [2] Ibid., I, 659.   [3] I, 661, i.

The last petition agreed upon yesterday being found, by the Clerk, to be defective in the latter part and therefore left ungrossed ; Mr. Pymme and some others, having perused it, and reformed it in a paper, the old and new were read over by Mr. Pymme : But the House not allowing it, divers gentlemen were appointed to retire to the Committee chamber, to perfect the same : Which accordingly was done ; and being brought back, and twice read by the Clerk, was ordered to be ingrossed with the residue.

The tone of the new Petition was very different from that of its predecessor. It began by beseeching the King

that the loyalty and dutifulness of as faithful and loving subjects as ever served or lived under a gracious sovereign may not undeservedly suffer by the misinformation of partial and uncertain reports, which are ever unfaithful intelligencers.

A copy of the original Petition was at that point inserted in order that his Majesty might use " the clearness of [his] own judgment" upon it. Then, after acknowledging the King's prerogatives to choose a wife for the Prince and to decide upon peace and war, the Petition referred, in carefully chosen phrases, to the crux of the issue between King and Commons :

Whereas your Majesty's letter doth seem to abridge us of the ancient liberty of Parliament for freedom of speech, jurisdiction and just censure of the House, and other proceedings there, wherein (we trust in God) we shall never transgress the bounds of loyal and dutiful subjects ; a liberty which, we assure ourselves, so wise and so just a King will not infringe, (the same being our ancient and undoubted right and inheritance, received from our ancestors, and without which we cannot freely debate nor clearly discern of things in question before us, nor truly inform your Majesty) . . . we are therefore now again inforced humbly to beseech your Majesty to renew and allow the same, and thereby take away the doubts and scruples your Majesty's late letter to our Speaker hath brought upon us.[1]

In spite of the humility, amounting almost to subservience of the opening sentences of the explanatory Petition, there was no mistaking the firmness implicit in its closing requests. Twelve messengers—in the main, those who had previously been entrusted

[1] *Proceedings and Debates*, II, 293.

47

with representing the Commons to the King—were despatched to Newmarket with the Petition. In order not to raise further difficulties, none of the leaders in the debate was included in their number.

The King received the deputation on 11th December. This was the famous occasion on which, as soon as the Members were introduced, James called out : " Bring stools for the ambassadors ! " It was a true word said in jest, for it preceded an interview between a king and representatives of another party claiming sovereign power. James showed himself friendly towards the deputation, and then sent them back with another letter which was read to the Commons on 14th December.[1]

Both the manner and the matter of James' answer were entirely characteristic of the writer. The long argument meandered about disjointedly ; and yet here and there it paused to drive home shrewd thrusts at its opponents. He pointed out—what was undeniably true—that

the beginning of this miserable war, which hath set all Christendom on fire, was not for religion, but only caused by our son-in-law his hasty and rash resolution, following evil counsel, to take to himself the crown of Bohemia.[2]

Moreover, James declared that his request for supplies for an army no more entitled the Commons to decide how the war should be conducted than it would entitle a merchant from whom he might have borrowed money for the same purpose. After referring to the question of religion, the King's letter concluded :

And although we cannot allow of the style, calling it your ancient and undoubted right and inheritance, and would rather have wished that ye had said that your privileges were derived from the grace and permission of our ancestors and us (for most of them grow from precedents, which shows rather a toleration than inheritance), yet we are pleased to give you our royal assurance, that as long as you shall continue to contain yourselves within the limits of your duty and respect to us (as we assure ourself you will do), we will be as careful to preserve your lawful liberties and privileges, as ever any our ancestors were, nay, as to preserve

---

[1] *Proceedings and Debates*, II, pp. 317–27.   [2] Ibid., p. 321.

our own royal prerogative ; so as your House shall only need to beware to trench upon the prerogative of the crown, which would enforce us, or any just King, to retrench them of their privileges, that would pare his prerogative and flowers of the crown. But of this, we hope, there shall never be cause given.

Having received the King's letter, the Commons postponed consideration of it until the next day. The debate then showed that almost everyone in the House recognized the justice of the King's claims on policy. But equally the House was not willing to allow his claims about its privileges to pass unchallenged. It had no intention of being like a merchant, lending money but having no voice in how it was used. The unanimity among Members showed that the King had overstepped the bounds of discretion in claiming that the Commons' privileges were not of right or of inheritance but proceeded from the King's grace. Nevertheless, the tone of the debate was by no means unfriendly towards the King. In the end, the House decided to go into committee to consider the whole question of its privileges.

As soon as the King heard of this decision, he wrote to Secretary Calvert disclaiming any intention of infringing the privileges of the Commons. But, comprehensive though this disclaimer seemed to be, it was couched in general terms and did not specify what the Commons' privileges were. Now that the matter had been raised, the Commons were not disposed to abandon it until their rights had been defined and recognized. On the morning of 18th December, therefore, a committee was appointed to draw up, in the form of a Protestation, a statement of the Commons' liberties. The committee immediately got to work, and in the afternoon presented the result of its labours to the House. The introductory sentences of the Protestation sufficiently indicate the purport of the whole : [1]

That the liberties, franchises, privileges and jurisdictions of Parliament are the ancient and undoubted birthright and inheritance of the subjects of England ; and that the arduous and urgent affairs concerning the King, State and the Defence of the Realm, and

---

[1] *Proceedings and Debates*, II, 359.

of the Church of England, and the making and maintenance of laws, and redress of mischiefs and grievances which daily happen within this realm, are proper subjects and matter of counsel and debate in Parliament : and that in the handling and proceeding of those businesses every Member of the House hath, and of right ought to have, freedom of speech, to propound, treat, reason and bring to conclusion the same.

Unlike the former Petitions, this was not to be sent to the King. It was to be entered upon the Journal of the Commons : the King could then take notice of it or not, just as he might think fit. So, after the committee's draft had been read several times, the famous Protestation was duly recorded. Next day the House adjourned until February.

For several days James brooded over events, undecided about his course of action. Then, on 30th December, he suddenly sent for the Commons' Journal to be brought to Whitehall, and there, as the Council and Judges watched, he tore out the page on which the offending Protestation was inscribed.

Not content with this, James decided to deal with the individuals whom he regarded as chiefly responsible for the Commons' obduracy. Coke had already (27th December) been committed to the Tower, where a few days later Phelips and Mallory also were imprisoned. The reason for Mallory's imprisonment remains a mystery. Nor is it clear why Pym received different treatment from the others : he was not imprisoned but was merely ordered to confine himself to his London house.

That the King could again meet the Parliament whose Journal he had mutilated, and whose leaders he had imprisoned, was impossible. On 6th January Parliament was dissolved.

After the dissolution, the order for Pym's confinement remained in force for more than three months. Then Pym put in a plea of ill-health, the effect of the plea being seen in a Privy Council minute : [1]

At the Court at Whitehall, the 20th of Aprill 1622. Whereas John Pym, esquire, was heretofore by his Majestie's Commaund

---

[1] *Acts of the Privy Council of England* (1621–23), p. 199.

confined to his house here in London, the Lord Keeper of the Greate Seale and the Lord Chamberlen did this day signifie that the said Pym, haveing by his peticion made humble suite to his Majestie for enlargement from that restraynte, the rather in respect of his health being thereby much impaired, his Majestie is thereupon graciously pleased that he may for his health sake repaire to any of his houses in the country, provided that he remayne confyned within a reasonable compasse of the same untill further order.

Even then, though his place of residence had changed, his movements were scarcely less restricted than before. This is proved by three documents : [1]

1622, May 23, Whitchurch Hants—Jo. Pym to Lord Cranfield —Refers to Lord Cranfield's favourable conduct to him during the King's displeasure—Is about to take further means to get the King's grace and pardon, and asks Cranfield to admit his brother Chomly to solicit and advise with him.

1622, June 2, Greenwich. A fair copy of a Licence apparently prepared for King's signature—John Pym, Esq., by our late commandment was restrained from going abroad from his house without our leave ; he is one of the commissioners employed these last three years in a Special Commission in our service concerning the disafforested lands of Pewsham and Blackmore forests ;—the others having appointed a meeting, found Pym's presence necessary. Licence to Pym to attend that meeting ; he is not to go further from home than 50 miles, and to return thither within 14 days after he begins his journey, subject to his further restraint until we shall be pleased to give order for his further liberty and enlargement.

1622, August 20—Same to same [i.e. Pym to Lord Cranfield]— According to the King's pleasure, he has attended the service of the forests of Blackmoor and Pewsame ;—puts him in mind of his promised mediation with the King for the discharge of his restraint.

These extracts have a double interest for us. First, they give some information about Pym's movements after the close of the 1621 Parliament ; evidently he still was a Commissioner for Customs, and his knowledge was regarded as indispensable to the Department. Incidentally, we may note the coincidence that the

---

[1] *H.M.C.*, 4th Report, pp. 305-12.

second and third of the extracts relate to his services in connection with the same properties as he himself had written about some four years earlier.[1]   Second, they throw a sidelight upon Pym's relations with Cranfield, the Lord Treasurer.   Cranfield's career had had more than one point of contact with Pym's.   Thus, in 1605 Cranfield had been appointed Receiver of Customs for Dorset and Somerset.   That was also the year in which Pym had secured the reversion of the Receivership of Hampshire, Wiltshire, and Gloucestershire.   Hence, not only would Cranfield collect the customs from Pym's home county, but also his customs district would adjoin that of Pym.   Further, in 1613 Cranfield was appointed Surveyor-General of Customs.   That happens to be the year for which we possess the first documentary proof of Pym's being in possession of his receivership.   In 1613, therefore, Cranfield became the head of the State Department under which Pym was a commissioner.   After holding various other offices, Cranfield, in September 1621, was made Lord Treasurer, having been raised to the peerage as Baron Cranfield in July of that year, and becoming Earl of Middlesex in September 1622.   As Lord Treasurer he was in charge of all financial administration, and so was still Pym's official superior.   It was therefore natural for Pym to address Cranfield both on the subject of his service in connection with the forests and on that of his position of restraint.   Yet the tone of the letters suggests that Pym was writing to a former colleague at least as much as to an official superior ; and the last extract implies that Cranfield had already interceded with the King on his behalf.   It would be interesting to know whether Cranfield's mediation succeeded and, if it did, how much longer Pym remained under surveillance.   Whatever the exact issue, a later chapter [2] will show reason for believing that Pym did not forget Cranfield's good offices and that the time came when he found the opportunity to show his gratitude ; for we have no evidence that Pym joined with his parliamentary associates in supporting the impeachment of Middlesex in April 1624.

For the purpose of our story, the third parliament of James I

[1] See above, p. xxii.   [2] See below, p. 63.

had two significant results. First, within its brief life Pym, at a single stride, had won recognition as a leader not merely for readiness of speech but even more for soundness and moderation of judgment. Second, the Parliament had ended in a deadlock between King and Commons. The dissolution prevented the issue from being decided, but that the next parliament would take up the challenge was inevitable. Would James ever call another parliament ? Gondomar, the Spanish Ambassador—than whom no one was more intimate with the King's intentions or had more influence over them—gleefully expressed his conviction :

It is certain that the King will never summon another Parliament as long as he lives, or at least not another composed as this one was. It is the best thing that has happened in the interests of Spain and the Catholic religion since Luther began to preach heresy a hundred years ago.[1]

There was one flaw in this argument of Gondomar. Parliament had been dissolved without passing the Subsidy Bill, and James would no more be able to exist indefinitely without supplies after the Parliament than before it. Further, James, who by upbringing and conviction was at bottom a staunch Protestant, could not remain for ever indifferent to the plight of his daughter Elizabeth and her husband the Elector. Moreover, if anything went awry with James' policy of a Spanish marriage, there would no longer be any reason why he should not throw himself wholeheartedly on to the Protestant side in the war. Thus two of the chief items at dispute—the marriage and the war—between James and Parliament would be removed, and another parliament might then be summoned with some confidence.

Our next chapter will show events following, in the main, this course.

[1] Quoted by Gardiner, Vol. IV, p. 265, from Simancas MSS. 2558, f. 7, 11.

CHAPTER III

PYM IN THE BACKGROUND

James I's Last Parliament, 1624–5

TWO years were to elapse between the close of James I's third parliament and the opening of his fourth (January 1622–February 1624). During the interval, affairs abroad underwent a change amounting almost to a transformation. This change concerns us in so far as it provided the circumstances in which the new parliament should meet.

The first factor in the change was that the opening stage of the Thirty Years' War came to an end. In September 1622 the troops of the Catholic League, led by Tilly, overran the Upper Palatinate and seized its capital, Heidelberg. In January 1623, the Roman Catholic Maximilian of Bavaria was given the title of Elector Palatine for the remainder of his life and was made responsible for the government of the Palatinate, King James' daughter Elizabeth and her husband Frederick, the Elector Palatine, were thus in a sad plight : already they had lost their adopted Kingdom of Bohemia ; now they were cut off from their original home in the Palatinate. Henceforward they were homeless wanderers.

It was largely because of these circumstances that the related question of the Spanish marriage advanced to a fresh and final stage. In May 1622, Gondomar, the Spanish ambassador to the Court of King James, had been recalled to Madrid in order that marriage terms might be drawn up. These terms had stipulated such large concessions to the Roman Catholic household of the Infanta in London, and for the education of her children, as to make the consent of the English Court and Parliament impossible. Negotiations resulted in some modification of these demands,

though by this time the Spanish Court had privately made up
its mind not to complete the marriage. It was at this point that
Prince Charles decided to carry out the project—mooted before
Gondomar had left England—of visiting Madrid in person, and
of there paying his court to the Infanta. It was not the charms
of the Princess—whom he had never seen—which induced the
Prince to use his own endeavours towards the achievement of the
marriage : his chief motive was to urge the return of the Palatinate
to Frederick as one of the conditions of the marriage.

The person who was to accompany the Prince to Spain was the
Duke of Buckingham. During some six years Buckingham's
influence had been paramount with the King in whose favour he
had risen with meteoric rapidity. Born in 1592, Buckingham
was the second son of a Leicestershire gentleman named Villiers
and, like his father, had been christened George. It is not without
interest that when, at eighteen years of age, he had gone to France
to learn the language and to become more familiar with the ways
of the world, he travelled with Sir John Eliot who was to become
one of his most deadly enemies. In August 1614 Villiers was
introduced to King James who, vastly impressed by the young
man's presence and charm of manner, gave him a place at Court.
From that moment Villiers never looked back. January, April,
and August were his lucky months. In August 1614 he entered
the royal service ; in April 1615 he was knighted ; in January
1615–16 he was promoted to be Master of the Horse ; in April
1616 he was invested with the Order of the Garter ; in August
1616 he was made Viscount Villiers and was granted land valued
at £80,000 ; in January 1616–17 he was created Earl of Buckingham, in the following January Marquess of Buckingham, and in
January 1618–19 Lord High Admiral, though he had no experience
of seafaring or of administration. The highest honour within
a monarch's power to confer upon a subject was conferred upon
the favourite in May 1623—during his stay in Madrid—when he
was created Duke of Buckingham. Villiers did not belong to a
family of any political significance, and the early stages of his rise
were due solely to the personal pleasure which King James found

in his new favourite, especially after the disgrace and fall of his old favourite the Earl of Somerset in the early part of 1616. Nevertheless, as time went on, his constant attendance upon the doting King made the support of the favourite a necessary means of influencing royal policy. Consequently, Buckingham became not merely the power behind the throne but, more accurately, the power before the throne. What was of even greater consequence for the future was that Buckingham's influence was paramount not only over King James but also over Prince Charles. Hence it was natural that Buckingham should accompany the Prince to Spain.

Setting off incognito, as John and Thomas Smith, on 18th February 1623, the pair reached Madrid, via Paris, on 7th March. The details of all their adventures and misadventures are beyond our purview ; but the final outcome of their escapade will materially affect our story. Briefly, in spite of all the Prince's promised concessions to the Infanta and to her co-religionists, the Spanish Court could not be induced to lend its influence for the restoration of the Rhine Palatinate to its rightful Elector. While negotiations were still pending, on 18th September, Charles sailed from Santander, and on 5th October he landed at Portsmouth. In large measure, the failure of the visit had been due to the arrogance of Buckingham who had mightily offended the Spaniards. Yet, however skilled the diplomacy of Charles and of Buckingham might have been, the end would almost inevitably have been the same : such concessions to Roman Catholicism as the Spaniards demanded could never have been granted by James or endured by the English people ; nor could the Spaniards have been reasonably expected to insist on the restoration of the Palatinate, for such a policy, if carried to its logical conclusion, might well have produced war between Roman Catholic Spain and the Roman Catholic Empire in the interest of the Protestant Elector—a position too absurd to be seriously contemplated.

The English people did not conceal in which direction their sympathies lay : Prince Charles was everywhere greeted with wild enthusiasm because he had returned without the Infanta ; in London particularly, according to the accounts of eye-witnesses, the scenes of festivity were unprecedented. There were " bonfires in the streets of London and a special anthem at St. Paul's : ' When shall I come out of Egypt, and the house of Jacob [Jacobi] from amongst the barbarous people.' " [1]

Negotiations, continued after the Prince's return, could make no difference to the result, and by the end of November the Spanish marriage scheme was virtually at an end.

The Prince and Buckingham, piqued by the failure of their journey, and even more by the conviction that they had been deliberately duped by the Spaniards, completely reversed their former policy. Buckingham in particular was moved to this decision by his enjoyment of temporary popularity. War against Spain, in the interest of the Protestant Elector and of the English Princess his wife, became the instant demand of the Prince and of Buckingham. The King, unable to refuse anything to his favourite Buckingham or to " Baby Charles," yet equally unable to advocate a war which his soul abhorred, was utterly bewildered. Buckingham, knowing that a war policy would be popular in the country, urged that a parliament should be summoned. To this extent James yielded, and on 28th December he commanded that writs for a parliament should be issued. Such were the circumstances in which the fourth, and last, parliament of the reign of James I was elected.

This parliament met on 19th February 1624. It contained all the opposition leaders of the previous parliament, including Pym who now for the first time represented Tavistock in Devon, together with two valuable additions, namely, the lawyer Selden and Sir John Eliot. The latter had been a member of the brief Addled Parliament of 1614, but not of the 1621 Parliament. Though his previous parliamentary experience was thus scanty, he stepped at one stride into the position of champion, by common consent, of the rights and privileges of the nation's representatives in Parliament. Even Pym, though he did much valuable work during the Parliament, was eclipsed for the time as a leader of debate. The friendship struck up between Eliot and George Villiers during their youthful stay abroad had continued after their

[1] John Nichols : *The Progresses of King James I*, IV, 928-9.

return ; and after the Marquess of Buckingham had became Lord High Admiral of England, he appointed Eliot to be Vice-Admiral of Devon. But Eliot combined with lofty principles a staunch devotion to duty from which no personal favours could make him swerve. When it became evident that Buckingham was replacing the King as the real ruler of England, and that Buckingham was thoroughly, even criminally, incompetent, the favourite had no more implacable enemy than his former companion and subordinate.

The King's speech at the opening of Parliament reflected exactly the bewilderment of his mind. Making no effort to provide leadership, in the shape of a clearly defined policy, either of war or of peace, he promised that the Secretary and Buckingham should explain the course of affairs with Spain. He then concluded : [1]

> When you have heard it all, I shall entreat your good and sound advice, for the glory of God, the peace of the kingdom, and weal of my children. Never king gave more trust to his subjects than to desire their advice in matters of this weight ; for I assure you ye may freely advise me, seeing of my princely fidelity ye are entreated thereto. . . . For matter of Privileges, Liberties, and Customs, be not over curious, I am your kindly King. . . . God judge me I speak as a Christian Prince, never man, in a dry and sandy desert, where no water is, did thirst more in hot weather for drink, than I do now for a happy conclusion of this parliament. I now hope, after the miscarriage of the last, that this may prove happy. . . . You shall never find me desire anything of you but what shall tend to the common good and weal of the kingdom.

James' treatment of his previous parliament and of its leaders might well make him anxious about the happiness of the new one. Events would show that he had not heard the last of the subject.

On 24th February, Buckingham addressed the two Houses. His account of the duplicity of the Spaniards, and his implied demand that England should rely not upon the favour of Spain but upon her own strength in order to secure the rights of the Protestant Palatinate [2] won the ready sympathy of his audience.

---

[1] *Parliamentary History*, I, 1372. [2] *Lords' Journals*, III, 220.

The debates in both Houses during several following days testified to the popularity of Buckingham and to the widespread demand for war against Spain. Of Pym's part in the debates we have only the meagre accounts of the *Commons' Journals* : [1]

(Monday, 1st March) *Mr. Pymme* :—against Continuance of any Treaty for the Match or Palatinate.—To pray a Conference with the Lords, about a Message to the King about it.

(Tuesday, 2nd March, supporting a motion by Digges) *Mr. Pym* : To have the Committee have in Charge, to give thanks to the Prince his Highness.

Digges' Motion of the same day had been :

To have Thanks given to the Lords, for their desire of good Correspondence with, and then to desire them to join with, us, to give Thanks to the Prince : and to desire him to give Thanks to his Father, for calling this Parliament, and to desire him also, that public Thanks be given to God by the whole Kingdom.

A Petition expressing the sentiments of the Houses was, on 5th March, presented to James who made a reply characteristic of his mood : [2]

You give me your advice to break off both the Treaties, as well concerning the Match as the Palatinate ; and now give me Leave, as an old King, to propound My Doubts, and hereafter to give you My Answer.

First, it is true, that I, who have been all the Days of My Life a Peaceable King, and have had the Honour in My Titles and Impresses to be stiled *Rex Pacificus*, should without Necessity imbroil Myself in War, is so far from My Nature . . . that. . . . I should be loth to enter into it.

And I must likewise acquaint you, that I have no small Hopes given Me of obtaining better Conditions for the Restitution of the Palatinate. . . .

Sure I am I have had the least Help in Parliaments of any King that reigned over you these many Years. . . .

This being My Case, to enter into a War without sufficient Means to support it, were to show My Teeth, and do no more.

In the mean Time, I heartily thank you for your Advice, and will seriously think upon it. . . .

[1] I, 675, i ; 725, i.   [2] *Lords' Journals*, III, 250.

I will deal frankly with you. Shew me the Means whereby I may do what you would have Me ; and if I take a Resolution, upon your Advice, to enter into a War, then yourselves, by your own Deputies, shall have the disposing of the Money ; I will not meddle with it ; but you shall appoint your own Treasurers.

This answer of James showed that the ground which he and his parliament held in common on matters of foreign policy was narrower than might have been supposed. The subsequent debates served to intensify the difference : Parliament, thinking in terms of Elizabethan policy, was all out for war against Spain, and was willing to grant certain supplies for this purpose ; the King's concern was for the restoration of the Palatinate to his daughter and her husband Frederick, and he wished for supplies not only for this but also to meet his general needs. On 15th March the King suggested six subsidies and twelve-fifteenths as a suitable grant to enable him to make effective war in the Palatinate. Four days later, when the question of subsidies was being debated in the Commons, there was widespread and sharp opposition, led by Eliot, both to the granting of the enormous sum for which the King had asked and to the policy of land warfare on the continent. Even the King's ministers did not venture to urge the full amount. Finally, the Commons granted less than half the amount for which the King had asked : instead of six subsidies and twelve-fifteenths they granted three subsidies and three-fifteenths.

In the course of this debate, Pym had intervened with a speech which the *Commons' Journals* thus briefly summarize : [1]

Mr. Pym :—Have gone some degrees from our Danger.—Fears a Relapse—To have the Propositions of the Chancellor Exchequer revised.—Limitations of Time, for the Ease of the Subjects.— First to conclude the general Question, that, if the Necessity shall require, we will yield to this Demand.

The concluding sentence of this summary shows Pym as continuing the moderate course which he had followed during his first parliament. He had no desire to hamper the King. Rather,

[1] I, 741, ii.

in spite of the treatment he had received at James' hands at the close of the previous parliament, he was willing to trust the King with whatever supplies might seem expedient, always provided that the need for them was established. Perhaps it was his almost excessive moderation which explains why he played a less prominent part in his second parliament than he had in his first. Eliot's boldness of speech was much more to taste of the House. It may be, too, that Pym was less interested in foreign affairs than he was in matters of privilege and finance. Even this explanation is only partially satisfactory, for the other two questions—namely, monopolies, and the impeachment of Lord Treasurer Middlesex—which chiefly engaged Parliament's attention, involved just these issues, yet in neither of them did Pym play a leading part.

Monopolies, as we have seen, had engaged the attention of the previous parliament which had successfully attacked the monopolists Mompesson and Michell. The time that had elapsed since that previous duel had allowed both the King and the two Houses to cool their tempers and to modify some of their extreme demands. When the matter was again raised, in the 1624 Parliament, a commendable spirit of compromise was shown by both sides. A declaratory Act was passed stating that monopolies : [1]

are altogether contrary to the laws of this realm, and so are and shall be utterly void and of none effect. . . . Provided also . . . that any declaration beforementioned shall not extend to any letters patents and grants of privilege for the term of fourteen years or under, hereafter to be made, of the sole working or making of any manner of new manufactures within this realm, to the true or first inventor and inventors of such manufactures.

This, commented Professor Maitland, " is the greatest victory of the commons during the reign of James." [2] The Monopoly Act was notable in another respect, namely, that, with the exception of two subsidy Acts in the 1621 Parliament, it was the first Statute to be passed since 1610. Pym's contribution to the passage of

---

[1] 21 and 22 Jac., I, Cap. iii.
[2] *The Constitutional History of England*, p. 261.

the Act was not very noteworthy. The *Commons' Journals* of 26th February thus report his speech of that day : [1]

Mr. Pym, to have it committed.

A committee was accordingly set up, Pym himself being a member.

Scarcely less important than the abolition of monopolies, as a precedent for the future, was the impeachment of Lord Treasurer Middlesex, the outline of whose career we traced in an earlier chapter.[2] His chief crime was that he had incurred the antipathy of Prince Charles and of Buckingham. The financial reforms and economics of Middlesex had saved the royal exchequer from bankruptcy and then had enabled James to rule without continual recourse to parliamentary aids. Middlesex not unnaturally regarded the projected Spanish war with displeasure as being likely to undo within a few months all the beneficial effects of his financial reforms which had needed years to complete. Prince Charles in particular was incensed against the Treasurer who, after the visit to Madrid, had remarked that " the Prince ought to submit his private distaste therein to the general good and honour of the kingdom." Buckingham's animosity against Middlesex is also easy to understand. Clarendon relates [3] that the Lord Treasurer :

had in truth gained so much credit with the King (being in truth a man of great parts and notable dexterity) that during the duke's absence in Spain he was not only negligent in issuing out such sums of money as were necessary to the defraying those illimited expenses, and to correspond with him with that deference he had used to do, but had the courage to dispute his commands, and to appeal to the King, whose ear was always inclined to him, and in whom he began to believe himself so far fastened that he should not stand in need of the future support of the favourite. . . . The duke no sooner found the Parliament disposed to a good opinion of him, and being well assured of the Prince's fast kindness, than he projected the ruin of this bold rival of his.

In pursuing his " bold rival ", Buckingham had no difficulty in stirring up the jealousy which Middlesex had provoked against himself by his rapid rise from a nonentity to a great official, and of the enmity which his economics had aroused.

[1] I, 719, ii.   [2] See above, p. 20.   [3] *Great Rebellion*, I, 42, 43.

On 15th April Middlesex's impeachment was begun. The consensus of his various enemies left no doubt about the verdict which finally was pronounced by the Lord Keeper in the following terms : [1]

The High Court of Parliament doth adjudge : that Lionel, Earl of Middlesex, now Lord Treasurer of England, shall lose all his Offices which he holds in this Kingdom, and shall be made for ever hereafter uncapable of any Office, Place, or Employment, in the State and Commonwealth.

And, That he shall be imprisoned in The Tower of London during the King's Pleasure.

And, That he shall pay unto our Sovereign Lord the King the Fine of Fifty Thousand Pounds.

And, That he shall never sit in Parliament any more.

And, That he shall never come within the Verge of the Court.

The staunchest sympathizer of Middlesex during his trial had been King James who, if we again follow Clarendon,[2] warned Buckingham in terms of remarkable prescience :

" By God, Stenny, you are a fool, and will shortly repent this folly, and will find that in this fit of popularity you are making a rod with which you shall be scourged yourself." And turning in some anger to the Prince, told him that he would live to have his bellyful of Parliaments,[3] and that when he should be dead, he would have too much cause to remember how much he had contributed to the weakness of the Crown by this precedent that he was now so fond of.

The fact was that no one was so well able as the King to understand the services which Middlesex had rendered to the country's finances.

We may wonder whether a similar understanding explains the silence of Pym throughout the impeachment proceedings. So far as existing records show, Pym did not once intervene. It is surely fair to infer that Pym's experience at the Exchequer enabled him to appreciate both the value of Middlesex's work and the personal

[1] *Lords' Journals*, III, 383.   [2] *Great Rebellion*, I, 44.

[3] " Parliament impeachments " in the first published text, but " Parliaments " in Clarendon's original MS., now in the Bodleian.

venom which was moving the Treasurer's enemies, and that he therefore refused to associate himself with the vendetta.   There is also the strong possibility that Pym was personally indebted to Middlesex, perhaps for intervention with the King when Pym himself was under the royal displeasure at the close of the 1621–2 Parliament.[1] Whatever the true explanation of Pym's silence, here is yet another example of the absence of animus in Pym against either the King or the King's favourites as such.   Our subsequent study will show that his opposition to the King—even to Charles I—was severely restrained, and that he opposed the King's ministers only when he believed them incompetent or a menace to the freedom of the nation.

That Pym was less prominent as a leader of debate in the 1624 than in the 1621 Parliament must not be interpreted to mean that he was either idle or a nonentity.   Though the House was in session only from 19th February till 29th May 1624, the records show that Pym was a member of more than thirty committees, and was busy behind the scenes in a variety of other ways.   Whatever the reason for his being more in the background than was his wont, either before or after, he still retained the confidence of his fellow-Members, and he was building up parliamentary experience which would be invaluable in the days ahead.

On 29th May 1624, Parliament was prorogued until 2nd November ; but before the latter date a further prorogation took place until 26th February ; and before that date there was yet another.   On 27th March 1625 King James I died, and this automatically brought the dissolution of Parliament.

There can be no mistaking the significance of the reign.   All the great issues which were to produce the conflict of arms between Parliament and Charles I had already been raised under James. The question fundamental to all the others, namely, Divine Right, had been broached as early as the Hampton Court Conference of 1604.   Control of finance, responsibility of ministers, direction of foreign policy, and freedom of speech (each of which was only a particular instance of the general issue of Divine Right)—these had

[1] See above, p. 51.

all provoked acute disputes during James' reign. And these disputes would continue into the next reign to provoke friction and, finally, civil war.

Nor was this the only significance that James I's reign had, for the purposes of our study. Though parliaments had been far from regular during the reign, if judged by twentieth-century standards, they had been frequent enough to allow the formation, for the first time in English history, of regular parliamentary groups—" parties " would perhaps be a misleading term, as conveying the idea of the later Whigs and Tories—with known policies and recognized leaders. These groups also would continue into the next reign, and so would their leaders ; and not the least notable of those leaders would be John Pym.

Part II

THE RULE OF KING CHARLES

CHAPTER IV

THE DUKE OF BUCKINGHAM

Charles I's First Parliament, June–August 1625, and Second Parliament,
February–June 1626

THE new king had some admirable characteristics. His manner was full of kingly charm ; he faithfully carried out the routine duties of his office ; he was devoutly religious. His personal courage was never called in question, and at the end was demonstrated superbly by his calm dignity in the face of his judges and executioners. Perhaps most notable of all, for the time in which he lived, was his faithfulness to his queen.

Yet along with these estimable traits, Charles I combined two others which would have been fatal to successful kingship in any age, and were the more certainly so in the circumstances which he inherited. One was his inveterate habit of double-dealing. He appears to have acted on the belief that, as the divinely appointed king, he need have no moral scruples in dealing with those who tried to thwart his will. Pledges and counter-pledges repeatedly, and almost consistently, broken, ultimately resulted in convincing his opponents—who included not a few former friends —that no confidence could be placed in his promises and therefore that there could be no settled peace for England until he was removed. His other fatal weakness was the inability to choose advisers on any basis except that of personal like or dislike ; and there was no guarantee that the affection of Charles—any more than that of his father—was a reliable guide to an individual's wisdom as a minister of state. The two people to whom especially Charles gave his confidence were his favourite the Duke of Buckingham and his Queen Henrietta Maria.

The Duke of Buckingham—perhaps the supreme evil genius in the career of Charles I—has already entered our story. The Prince and the Duke had returned from Spain intent upon avenging themselves for what they regarded as the duplicity of the Spaniards. The turn of circumstances played directly into their hands. In 1624, Cardinal Richelieu became the virtual ruler of France. In May and June of that year his vigorous and adroit policy expressed itself when France intervened in the Thirty Years' War by joining an alliance of Protestant States, which included Holland and Denmark, against the Roman Catholics. That a Cardinal of the Roman Catholic Church should throw the influence of Roman Catholic France on the side of the Protestants was proof that his motives were not religious. His sole object was to support the enemies of the Hapsburg rulers of the Empire and of Spain with whom France was traditionally at feud. To this alliance, England was later added, the basis of England's adhesion to France being that Prince Charles should marry Henrietta Maria, sister of Louis XIII. After prolonged negotiations a marriage treaty was ratified on 12th December 1624. Its main, though secret, condition, upon which the French insisted, was that the English penal laws against Roman Catholics should be suspended. On 1st May 1625—that is, a month after his accession, and six months before the meeting of his first parliament—King Charles was married by proxy to the French princess. She landed in England in the middle of June. The new queen was then barely fifteen years old and was not likely to have much influence over a husband ten years her senior. But as the years passed, especially after Buckingham's death, the Queen's influence steadily grew until the King habitually sought her advice upon all political issues of any consequence. A worse-equipped counsellor could hardly have been found. Henrietta Maria had grown up from babyhood in the French Court where the monarch was an autocrat, so that she had no understanding of the meaning or methods of parliamentary government. Here, then, was a germ of serious trouble ahead for the King and for Parliament as well as for the Queen herself.

More immediately, the French marriage produced reactions which will materially affect our story. First, the Protestant stalwarts in England—including John Pym—did not welcome a Roman Catholic princess from France any more warmly than they would have welcomed the Roman Catholic Infanta from Spain. The installation of Roman Catholic worship at the royal palace, and the concessions made to Roman Catholics in the country, would be a fruitful cause of friction between the Puritan Parliament and the King. The second reaction, though it did not produce results until after the close of Charles' first parliament, was to be not less important. The French Huguenots, knowing that the policy of the new minister Richelieu was to strengthen the central government of France, believed that he would reduce the considerable privileges which they enjoyed under the terms of the Edict of Nantes of 1598. In particular, the Huguenots feared that they would lose the right to fortify themselves in certain strongholds, of which La Rochelle was the chief. Their wise course seemed to be to strike before Richelieu was too firmly entrenched in power. They therefore seized the opportunity provided by the diversion of Richelieu's attention abroad, in order to break into revolt. On 17th January 1625—two months before the death of James I—the Huguenot leader Soubise seized six of Richelieu's warships which were lying in the small Breton port of Blavet. This was yet another reason, in the eyes of staunch Puritans, against the French marriage ; for it would mean that Protestant England would be in alliance with a Roman Catholic Power that was at war against its Protestant subjects. These were not propitious circumstances for the opening of the first parliament of a new reign.

Parliament met on 18th June 1625. The plague was raging in the city ; nevertheless Parliament sat at Westminster. Charles did not neglect the opportunity of reminding the Members, in his opening speech, that the war in Europe, for which he would need their support, had been entered upon by their advice.[1]

---

[1] *Lords' Journals*, III, 436, i.

I pray you to remember that, this being my first action, and begun by your advice and intreaty, what a great dishonour it were both to you and me, if this action, so begun, should fail for that assistance you are able to give me.

The Commons, however, proved unresponsive to this mode of appeal. They had not forgotten the attempt of James I to infringe their liberties and to intimidate their spokesmen, and they would begin with James' son as they meant to continue. Under their former leaders—Eliot, Pym who again sat for Tavistock, and Coke—as well as Sir Thomas Wentworth and John Hampden, they would demand tangible concessions in return for grants of supplies.

From the outset of the session, Pym's activity was much in evidence. On 21st June, Sir William Strode brought forward a motion for a day of fast, and Pym further proposed that the fast should be a national one.[1] The former part of the motion was carried, but not Pym's addition. Pym was then chosen as one of a committee of nine to draw up a Petition to the King that the Commons' resolution might be carried into effect.[2] Next day Pym was appointed to a committee on an Act to punish divers abuses committed on " the Lord's Day called Sunday ".[3]

One incident deserves mention at this point because, though Pym was not directly involved, it had indirect results which did very much concern him. The question at issue was that of the disputed election of no less a person than Sir Thomas Wentworth. Wentworth had been returned, along with Sir Thomas Fairfax, as Member for Yorkshire. His opponent, Sir John Savile, petitioned the House, claiming that a number of his supporters had been prevented from voting by the action of the Sheriff in declaring the poll closed. The House, led by Eliot, was strongly sympathetic towards Savile, and the election was promptly quashed. The immediate result was that Wentworth returned to Yorkshire to contest the vacant seat and was elected unanimously. The more far-reaching result was that the antagonism between Went-

---

[1] *Commons' Journals*, I, 798, i.   [2] Ibid., p. 799, i.
[3] Ibid., p. 800, i.

worth on the one hand and Eliot and his party on the other would seem to date from this dispute. The incident is an apt illustration of the gulf that separated the two men. There cannot be much doubt that Wentworth's original election was irregular. To Wentworth, this outward form mattered little so long as the more efficient Member (which happened to be himself!) was returned. To Eliot, the interference with the just liberty of the electors was incapable of defence. This also was the essence of the impeachment of Wentworth which Pym was to lead nearly sixteen years later.

The first struggle in the Parliament arose over the question of supply. The needs of the royal exchequer were beyond dispute : large promises had been made to the King of Denmark and to Count Mansfeld so that they might maintain armies against the Empire ; money would have to be found to equip an English fleet against Spain ; and there were other, and by no means negligible, expenses inseparable from the beginning of a new reign. All told, the Government would need the very considerable sum of about £1,000,000. Yet, though the King and his ministers asked for generous grants, especially for the prosecution of the war on the continent, they offered no precise statement either of their foreign policy or of the amount of money that it would require. This vagueness intensified the fears of the Puritans who were reluctant to grant large subsidies without knowing how they were to be used. On 30th June, during the debate on supply, Phelips expressed a general feeling when he declared : [1] " There is no engagement ; the promises and declarations of the last Parliament were in respect of a war : we know yet of no war nor of any enemy." Phelips moved the grant of two subsidies (about £140,000), and this was passed. Such an utterly inadequate supply was clear proof of the Commons' distrust of the King and his ministers.

Further, and more serious, proof was shortly forthcoming. On 5th July the question of tunnage and poundage was brought forward. For two centuries the first parliament in each reign

[1] Gardiner : *Commons' Debates in 1625*, p. 31.

had granted these customs duties to the new king for life. Phelips again came to the fore ; and, after a prolonged debate, it was decided to make the grant to Charles I for one year only. Even this grant never became operative, for the Bill embodying it was so long delayed in the Lords that it never passed through all its stages. Thus the King was left without the usual supply wherewith to meet even his ordinary expenses. What was of even greater consequence was that, in the first parliament of the reign, indeed within a few weeks of Charles' accession, the Commons had shown their lack of confidence in the King ; and thus was engendered the condition of mutual suspicion in which Pym and his fellows, in later parliaments, would have to work.

Though money was the immediate cause of friction, the root cause was religion. This had been illustrated, even before the debate on tunnage and poundage, by Montague's case which, like nearly every other religious question, drew Pym into the fray. The case had begun in James I's reign. Dr. Richard Montague was a scholarly man and rector of the parish of Stamford Rivers in Essex. One of his parishioners there was in possession of a book entitled *The Gag for the New Gospel*, written by a Roman Catholic to show that the English Church was essentially Calvinistic. Montague determined to rebut the contention, and in 1624 he published a pamphlet called *A New Gag for an Old Goose*. In order to defeat his opponent, Montague used arguments which to-day would be regarded as " High Church " and which the seventeenth-century Puritans declared to be Romanist. Accordingly, in the last parliament of James I, Pym had declared that Montague's book was " full fraught with dangerous opinions of Arminius, quite contrary to the Articles established, in five several points ".[1] Thereupon Pym had been appointed to a committee of five which was to bring the book to the notice of Archbishop Abbot of Canterbury. Abbot sent for Montague and advised him to revise his book so as to " be occasion of no scandal or offence ". The Archbishop mis-read his man. Montague, instead of accepting the advice, went to James who, relishing as

[1] *Commons' Journals*, I, 789, i.

usual a doctrinal argument, finally declared : " If that is to be a Papist, so am I a Papist." The King further permitted Montague to publish another book with the title *Appello Caesarem*. This latter book was duly completed, and was approved by James who, however, died before its publication, so that the book finally appeared with a dedicatory note to Charles I.

The Commons were not likely to allow the matter to rest there. The book was referred to a committee of which Pym was a member, and which produced its report on 7th July.[1] " The committee held this second book as factious and seditious tending manifestly to the dishonour of the late king, and the disturbance of both church and state." Whatever the justice or injustice of this finding—and to claim that the book was " to the dishonour of the late king " who had so heartily approved it was manifestly absurd—the Commons had no power to take action against a man because of his religious opinions, and they therefore suggested a conference on the subject with the Lords. The Parliament was nearly at an end before further action was attempted, and then Montague was reported to be in bed ill. In the meantime, Charles had tried to shield Montague by appointing him as one of his chaplains. The matter was still in abeyance when the Parliament was dissolved. The next parliament renewed the attack on Montague, and later in this chapter we shall need to revert to the subject.[2] At this point, Montague's case is significant as affording yet another illustration of the susceptibility of the Commons to all matters affecting religion and of the acknowledged leadership of Pym in all such instances.

While these events had been taking place, the plague had continued its increasing ravages in the city where the deaths were numbering up to two hundred a week. The Members were living in constant dread, and there was frequent talk of ending the session. Many Members left the House and returned to their homes. By the end of June only about sixty remained to do the business of Parliament. On 11th July the Houses were informed that Parliament would that day stand adjourned and

[1] Ibid., pp. 805–6. [2] Page 80 below.

would meet again at Oxford on 1st August; and there, on the appointed day, the new session opened.

No evidence exists to show that Pym took a prominent part in the debates at Oxford. This is the more remarkable because the subject which chiefly engaged the Commons' attention during the Oxford session was the attack on Buckingham in which, when the attack was revived during the following parliament, Pym took a very active part. Because of Pym's later share in the impeachment, we must trace the beginnings of the process at Oxford.

With every day that passed, the Commons' antagonism became focussed more and more sharply upon Buckingham as the King's evil genius. Even the King and his minister could not remain blind to this personal antagonism; and on 8th August, Buckingham met the Commons in Christchurch Hall to clear himself of suspicion and to explain the royal policy. He brought from the King a promise that the recusancy laws would be carried out; he claimed that all his own actions had been carried out with the approval of the Council of War or the Privy Council; and he appealed for supplies to enable the King to prosecute the war vigorously. The debate that followed showed that once more the Commons remained unconvinced. Unfortunately for Buckingham, there was to hand an argument which neither he nor the King could gainsay. In pursuance of the alliance with France, made during the closing days of James I, a squadron of English ships, under the command of Admiral Pennington, had been hired to Richelieu to help in the war against Spain. Hardly had the arrangement been made when, as we have seen, the Huguenots of La Rochelle revolted against Richelieu's government. If Richelieu were to use the English ships against the Rochellois instead of against the Spaniards, the indignation of the English people would know no bounds. Consequently, Pennington was frequently given contradictory orders from home so as to negative his usefulness. By the time that the Commons were debating Buckingham's speech, some of the ships were home again. They brought stories of the naval mismanagement and, what was worse, of the fear that certain English ships still in French hands were to be used against La Rochelle. Such reports were not likely to prejudice the Commons in Buckingham's favour. As the debate on his speech proceeded, the Members' animosity grew fiercer. Finally, Buckingham was for the first time mentioned by name as responsible for the failure abroad. "The Duke of Buckingham is trusted and [the fault] must needs be either in him or his agents"—thus Sir Francis Seymour. Phelips followed up the attack by declaring : "It is not fit to repose the safety of the kingdom upon those that have not parts answerable to their places."

Charles, realizing that the longer the Parliament sat the more obstinate its opposition would become, determined upon a dissolution. On 12th August 1625 he dissolved the first parliament of his reign. Neither the events of the Parliament nor the occasion of its dismissal was a happy augury for the rest of the reign. The abrupt dissolution intensified rather than diminished the King's difficulties : he was still without parliamentary supply to meet either his ordinary needs or his commitments abroad—even the Bill granting tunnage and poundage for one year had not been passed—so that another parliament in the near future would be unavoidable ; and that parliament, when it met, would be embittered by the treatment meted out to its predecessor.

It was mainly this lack of financial supplies which led to the outstanding event of the interval between the first and the second parliaments of the reign. Buckingham thought he saw a way of replenishing the Exchequer. This was to be no other than a repetition of Drake's plundering expedition against the Spaniards. Buckingham himself was to go as ambassador to the Hague in order to form a League with Denmark and the north German princes which was to supplement the Anglo-Dutch alliance. The fleet was to be commanded by Viscount Wimbledon, formerly Sir Edward Cecil, grandson of Elizabeth's Burleigh. From the outset the expedition suffered from every possible handicap. Cecil himself was brave enough, but lacked any experience of the sea. The navy had been so neglected that only nine royal ships could be mustered, these being supplemented by seventy-three pressed merchant vessels. The contractors were swindlers who supplied the ships with rotten stores of all kinds. The fleet left Plymouth on 8th October 1625 to attack Cadiz and to capture the Plate treasure ships. Reduced to the briefest terms, the story of the expedition is that lack of capable leadership, and inefficiency in crews and equipment, resulted in complete failure : instead of a rapid attack on Cadiz itself, other objectives were aimed at until the Spaniards had had time to reinforce the garrison ; and meanwhile the Plate ships had slipped unseen into port. To crown the disaster, many of the English ships proved unseaworthy, and pestilence broke out among the crews. By the middle of November the expedition turned homewards.

No more fatal stroke for Buckingham could have been devised. Nothing would so surely rouse the bitter anger of the English people as a proof of the inefficiency of the navy, particularly in an expedition against a Spanish port ever to be associated with the fame of Drake. From the King's point of view the disaster would have a further serious result, namely, that, while the expedition had added to his financial embarrassment, the Spanish treasure fleet, which was to have replenished the Exchequer, had eluded capture. Buckingham had even failed in Amsterdam to raise money on the Crown jewels. Only one other solution remained : a new parliament must be summoned. Conditions less auspicious for the meeting of a parliament could hardly be imagined. As if to make Buckingham's discomfiture doubly sure, on 5th September 1625, Richelieu, with the help of English and Dutch ships, had crushingly defeated the Huguenot leader Soubise, and La Rochelle lay at his mercy.

The second parliament of Charles I met on 6th February 1626. Buckingham had tried to rob the opposition of its sting by having some of its leaders—including Phelips, Coke, and Wentworth—pricked as sheriffs so that they would be ineligible for election to the Commons. He was to find that the bitter antagonism that he had to face was too profound and too widespread to be frustrated by excluding individual leaders. Moreover, no opposition could be regarded as leaderless while it included Eliot and Pym. The records of the Parliament leave no doubt that from the very first day of parliamentary business Pym was the generally recognized leader of that large body of Members who regarded themselves as the champions of political and religious freedom. The *Commons' Journals* show that, during the four months of the Parliament, he was appointed to nearly fifty committees; and though some of these were for specific purposes and may have met only once or twice, others—like that dealing with Buckingham's impeachment—must have involved frequent and prolonged meetings. What was true of Pym's work behind the scenes was true equally of his activity in the House itself: in this 1626 Parliament, as never before, he showed himself a master of vigorous, cogent reasoning, exactly suited to the Members who now formed the bulk of the Commons. It was not an accident that the recognized leaders of the Commons were no longer lawyers but were landowning gentlemen intent not on arguing fine points of the law or on making a reputation that might bring professional promotion but on establishing the liberty of the people whom they represented and the security of the land in which they had a personal stake. Sir Robert Phelips of Montacute, Somerset; Sir John Eliot of Port Eliot, Cornwall; Sir Thomas Wentworth of Wentworth Woodhouse in the West Riding of Yorkshire; and John Pym himself, a list of whose properties we have already seen—all these are notable examples of the leadership of landowning gentry. Even Sir Edward Coke, though one of the most brilliant legal lights—perhaps *the* most brilliant—of the day, was now shorn of his offices and sat, or had sat, in the 1625 Parliament, rather as a Norfolk squire than as a lawyer. That Coke, Wentworth, and Phelips were, as sheriffs, excluded from this particular parliament did not alter the composition of the Commons as a whole: it merely left Pym and Eliot as the unchallenged leaders who would see to it that the House did not suffer unduly through the absence of some of its champions.

Religion and the Duke of Buckingham were once more the topics which chiefly engaged Parliament's attention. On 10th February, the first day of real parliamentary business, Pym started the ball rolling by moving [1] that the Committee on Religion " may also consider of certain other Articles, set down last Parliament, but not put into (the) Petition : or any thing else concerning Religion ". Of this committee, Pym was made a member. The same day he was appointed also to a committee of six to examine every Saturday the Clerk's entries in the *Commons' Journals*.[2] That day, Eliot called boldly for an enquiry into the failure of the Cadiz expedition. The King's minister had asked for supplies : Eliot demanded that the accounts of the subsidies voted by the previous parliament should first be produced. A committee was accordingly set up and, in the course of its investigations, it gathered much information damaging to the reputation of Buckingham, the Lord Admiral. To this subject we shall have reason to return.

Meanwhile, the Committee on Religion was busying itself with Richard Montague. The bishops, when consulted by the King on the subject of Montague's books, had found that, though the books contained some matters that might be disputed, there was nothing in them fundamentally contrary to the doctrines of the English Church. Charles, however, wisely withdrew his former contention that a royal chaplaincy barred the Commons from discussing the case. Finally, Pym reported the findings of the committee.[3] These were elaborated under five articles in which, point by point, the contents of Montague's books were proved to conform to the Roman, and not to the English Church. The author had even dubbed his opponents as " Puritans ". The committee therefore asked that Montague might be punished. Before the committee's report could be considered by the Lords, the session was at an end, and for the moment Montague was free. The end of the matter was that two years later Charles raised Montague to be Bishop of Chichester. The main interest which the case has for us is that it shows once again the religious position of Pym, for the report of the committee bears the stamp of his mind. He stood foursquare for the orthodox doctrines

[1] *Commons' Journals*, I, 817, ii. [2] P. 818, i.
[3] Rushworth, I, 209–12.

of the Church of England. If, on the one hand, he held Popery to be anathema, on the other he regarded the name of Puritan as an insulting epithet.

During the remainder of the session it was upon Buckingham that the attention of the Commons was focussed. A recital of all the details of his impeachment would be irrelevant to our study of the career of John Pym : we must limit ourselves to the outstanding events which marked the main process. Eliot, in his speech of 10th February, had plainly indicated the general antagonism towards "those we trust", though being careful not to mention a name. On 10th March, matters were advanced a step further when the King, through the Treasurer Weston, asked for an immediate grant of supply. During the ensuing debate, one of the Members, a certain Dr. Turner, summarized in the form of six questions the outstanding evils which, according to "public fame", sprang from the Duke and his government : it was the Duke who was to blame for the failure at Cadiz, for the nation's impoverishment, for the bad government, and for the increase of recusancy.[1] About this bold reference to Buckingham, there were two items of significance. First, it made no pretence of being founded on anything more definite than common rumour. This fact the Commons realized, and forthwith they proceeded to regularize the position by resolving :[2] "That Common Fame is a good ground of proceeding for this House, either by enquiry, or presenting the complaint (if the House finds cause) to the King or the Lords." Second, it propounded a doctrine that was to become one of the bases of the British Constitution, namely, that the King's ministers were responsible to Parliament. Charles' appreciation of the significance of this attack was plainly shown by his message to the Commons : " This is such an example as he can by no means suffer, though it were to take inquiry of one of the meanest of his servants, much less one so near himself." The House, however, was not deterred, and Sir William Walter subsequently moved in the Commons a resolution to the effect :[3] " That the cause of all the grievances, was, for that (as was said

[1] Ibid., p. 219.   [2] Ibid.   [3] Ibid.

of Louis XI King of France) all the King's council rides on one horse."

Once again it was Eliot who, on 27th March, gave a decisive turn to events. That day, during a further debate on supply, he delivered a smashing attack on the Government by declaring that the series of disasters which the nation had lately suffered had left the people unwilling to contribute further to the Exchequer, and that these enterprises were " fixed on the person of the Lord General, who had the whole command both by sea and land ".[1] As if to leave no doubt what the consequences to the minister might be, he reminded his hearers of two precedents : Hubert de Burgh in the reign of Henry III, and De la Pole, Earl of Suffolk in the reign of Richard II, had both been ministers whom the Commons distrusted and whom the King therefore had to remove from office before supplies were granted. As the struggle over both of these ministers had developed into revolt, Eliot's allusions were particularly pointed. Two days after this speech, the Commons, waiting upon the King at Whitehall by royal command, had to listen to the King's astonishing declaration :[2] " Remember that Parliaments are altogether in my power for their calling, sitting, and dissolution ; therefore, as I find the fruits of them good or evil, they are to continue or not to be." This may have been a sound statement of previous constitutional practice, but it was singularly tactless at that particular juncture. The day following (30th March), the Commons were summoned to hear Buckingham's explanation of his past policy and actions. His long speech was an attempt to show that he had acted always by the King's command or by the advice of the Council, and that many of the projects that he had fostered had been carried out only by large contributions from his private purse. Perhaps the most singular feature of his speech was not its contents but its effect : the Commons, instead of being moved to a reply, merely ignored it and continued with their programme of business as though the speech had never been delivered. The comprehensive attack which the Commons were later to deliver against

[1] Ibid, pp. 220-2.   [2] Ibid., p. 225 ; *Parliamentary History*, II, 60.

Buckingham was sufficient proof that their silence was not due to lack of material. The simple explanation appears to be that they disbelieved the whole story that he had told. The form in which the Commons asserted their rights as against the King's declaration of constitutional doctrine was a Remonstrance in the following terms :

It hath been the ancient, constant and undoubted right and usage of Parliaments, to question and complain of all persons, of what degree soever, found grievous to the commonwealth, in abusing the power and trust committed to them by their sovereign.

This Remonstrance was drawn up on 4th April, on which day the Houses stood adjourned until 13th April for the Easter recess.

The Commons did not allow the recess to weaken their determination to attack Buckingham. On 8th May their representatives, numbering eight managers, each of whom had two assistants, appeared before the Lords with thirteen charges of impeachment. The eight managers were Digges, Herbert, Selden, Glanville, Sherland, Pym, Wandesford, and Eliot ; and in that order they addressed the Lords. Sir Dudley Digges opened the proceedings by explaining the general nature of the impeachment charges ; and Sir John Eliot was entrusted with the concluding summary. Each of the other six was responsible for certain specific articles of impeachment. On 8th May the first four managers spoke on the first eight of the thirteen charges ; and on 10th May the process was completed.

It was on the latter day, therefore, that Pym delivered his speech —which occupies five full folio pages of Rushworth [1]—elaborating articles eleven and twelve which were his particular care. These articles related, respectively, to Buckingham's procuring of titles and pensions for his relatives, and his obtaining from the King large sums of money which were called secret-service money but which were really intended to enable Buckingham to maintain his " places, honours, and dignities ". Pym followed his usual practice of opening with an exposition of basic principles and then of elaborating and applying these principles to the particular

[1] I, 335-40.

subject under debate. With reference to the procuring of titles for members of Buckingham's family, Pym declared :

As this honour lifts them [that receive it] above others, so should they have virtue beyond others. And as it is also perpetual, not ending with their persons, but depending upon their posterity,—so there ought to be, in the first root of this honour, some such active merit to the commonwealth as may transmit a vigorous example to their successors, to raise them to an imitation of the like.

He then claimed the grievance of misplaced honours to be prejudicial " first, to the noble barons ; secondly, to the king, by disabling him from rewarding extraordinary virtue ; thirdly, to the kingdom, which comprehends all ". Each of these three contentions having been elaborated in turn, Pym proceeded to deal with article twelve which virtually charged Buckingham with embezzlement. Details were produced of lands which had irregularly fallen into the Duke's possession.

Divers parcels of land were sold and contracted for by his own agents, and the money received to his own use ; and yet tallies struck as if the monies had come into the exchequer. This is to be proved by his own officers, by the officers of the exchequer, and by the tallies themselves, which tallies amount to £44,090. 5s.

He then continued :

This is a great sum in itself, but much greater by many circumstances. If you look upon the time past, never so much came into any one private man's hands out of the public purse. If you respect the time present, the king had never so much want, never so many occasions, foreign, important, and expensive. The subjects have never given greater supplies ; and yet those supplies are unable to furnish those expenses. But as such circumstances make that sum the greater, so there are other circumstances which make the sum little, if it be compared with the inestimable gain the duke hath made by the sale of honours and offices, and projects hurtful to the states both of England and Ireland ; and if it be compared with his own profuseness. Witness, notwithstanding this gift, his confession before both houses of parliament to be indebted £100,000 and above. If this be true, how can we hope to satisfy his immense prodigality ? if false, how can we hope to satisfy his covetousness? And, therefore, no wonder the commons so earnestly desire to be delivered from such a grievance.

Such was the tenor of Pym's speech. Regarded calmly from this distance of time, and in the light of facts not then available, we may doubt whether it was entirely fair to Buckingham. In the first place, there is no evidence that Buckingham ever asked the King, either directly or by implication, for the rewards and honours which were so lavishly showered upon him. From the day in August 1614, when James was first captivated by the natural grace of the stripling, James' affection for his favourite sought exaggerated expression in gifts that bore no relationship to the value of the services rendered. Indeed, the gifts which Buckingham received from James had no properly political significance : they were rather personal gifts from one man to his intimate friend. Thus the persons who really deserved Pym's charges were not Buckingham but James who had chosen him and Charles who had continued and endorsed his father's choice. Further, a study of Buckingham fails to show that there was any deliberate duplicity, or even self-seeking in his make-up. That he was rash, and lacking in all the qualities necessary to a statesman, may be conceded at once. But it is equally true that he was passionately moved by a genuine patriotism, that he believed his own schemes would promote the nation's welfare, and, not least, that he gave himself and his possessions unstintingly to the promotion of that end. Not once, but repeatedly, he gave large sums out of his own private purse to supplement grants from the national exchequer for campaigns and expeditions. Here again, the real blame lay not with the favourite but with the King whose folly had promoted an utterly untrained and unsuitable individual to the position of supreme influence in the State. There had been a time when the King's will in such a matter would have gone unquestioned. That time had passed for ever. No individual had, in recent days, done more to ensure its passing than had Buckingham himself when, heedless of the warnings of James, he and Prince Charles had insisted on the impeachment of Middlesex. Digges, in his prologue to Buckingham's impeachment, had struck the fundamental note by declaring : [1]

The Laws of England teach us, That Kings cannot command ill or unlawful things, whenever they speak, though by their Letters Patents, or their Seals. If the things be evil, these Letters Patents are void, and whatsoever ill event succeeds, the execution of such commands must ever answer for them.

The immediate effect of this doctrine was to cut at the root of Charles' repeated statements that Buckingham had done nothing inconsistent with the King's commands ; and, for the future, it was the foundation of the constitutional theory, and practice, of the responsibility of ministers to Parliament.

Pym could not be expected either to judge dispassionately all the facts of Buckingham's career or to understand all the implications even of his own statements. He saw the King's government as thoroughly unsound at home and disgraced abroad, and he knew that in all matters connected with government Buckingham was the King's adviser. He saw the King's exchequer continually impoverished no matter what grants the Commons might put into it, and he knew that at the same time Buckingham and his relatives were growing fabulously richer at the King's hand. From these premises Pym built up a case that was logical in itself and moderate in its form of expression.

It is doubtful whether the same can be claimed for Eliot who, in summing up, seems to have been carried away by the heat of his own oratory. Eliot, as we have seen, had been Buckingham's companion when, as youths, they had passed a long stay in France. Later, Buckingham, as Lord High Admiral, had appointed Eliot to be Vice-Admiral of Devon, and Eliot had then served his friend gladly. Now, Eliot had become passionately Buckingham's enemy. In Devon, Eliot had observed the rotten ships and the rotten stores that had gone to make up Buckingham's naval expeditions ; and his fervent patriotism had convinced him that Buckingham was a danger to the welfare of the State. It was much to Eliot's credit that he allowed neither personal friendship

[1] Rushworth, I, 306.

nor personal indebtedness to interfere with what he believed to be the performance of a public duty. The pity was that, in performing that duty, he allowed himself to be carried away into exaggerations which detracted from the strength which his arguments naturally had for his contemporaries. Referring to Buckingham's character, he declaimed : [1] " I can express it no better than by the beast called by the ancients *stellionatus* ; a beast so blurred, so spotted, so full of foul lines, that they knew not what to make of it." Eliot's peroration included the following : [2] " I can hardly find a match or parallel in all precedents ; none so like him as Sejanus, who is thus described by Tacitus, *Audax : sui obtegens, in alios criminator ; juxta adulator et superbus.*" And much more in the same strain. These passages from Eliot's speech have often been quoted : they are worth quoting again here because, even when allowance is made to them as rhetorical hyperbole, they contrast unfavourably with the dignified but no less moving style of Pym.

There is small wonder that, according to contemporary report, when Charles heard of the speech, he exclaimed angrily : " If the Duke is Sejanus, I must be Tiberius." The effect was not long in showing itself. The next day Charles addressed the Lords on behalf of Buckingham, informing them that he would himself give evidence that would clear his minister. He added significantly : [3] " I have thought fit to take order for the punishing some insolent speeches lately spoken. I have been too remiss heretofore in punishing such speeches as concern myself." While this speech was being delivered to the Lords, the Commons were assembling in their own House. Suddenly it was noticed that Eliot and Digges were not in their places ; and the news quickly spread that they had been removed to the Tower. The Members rose in their seats, and the sitting broke up in commotion. Pym did his best to restore order, but to no purpose.[4] The imprisonment of the two Members produced yet further friction between King and Commons. Finally, the Lords examined Digges and found no

[1] Ibid., p. 353.   [2] Ibid., p. 357.   [3] Ibid., p. 357.
[4] Gardiner, VI, 109, quoting from Harl. MSS. 390, f. 57.

crime in his words, so that he was released on 16th May. Eliot, too, was examined and released three days later.

It was not until 8th June that Buckingham addressed the Lords on his own behalf. The speech displayed considerable ability; but by this time no one was in a condition to judge Buckingham's case on its merits alone. The decision which the Lords had given in the cases of Digges and Eliot was sufficient proof that even Buckingham's peers were not to be relied upon to favour either the King or his minister. The Commons, unaffected by the speech, continued to debate the best means of preventing further attacks upon their privileges. On 13th June the Commons submitted to Charles a formal Protest,[1] in which they justified their attack upon Buckingham and concluded with a demand that he be removed from the King's councils.

The result was deadlock. The Commons would not grant supply until Buckingham was removed : the King would not remove Buckingham. The next step was with the King ; and he, having completely exhausted his patience, determined to be rid of his parliament which, on 15th June, he accordingly dissolved.

This second parliament of Charles I had done much to strengthen the position of Pym not only as a debater but as a statesman. His speech at Buckingham's impeachment had shown his political thinking to be based upon positive, constructive principles which, both then and later, saved him from being carried away either by personal antipathies or by mere fanaticism. Even the King's party respected him : Carleton, when trying to calm the Commons on the day following the arrest of Digges and Eliot, had contrasted the violence of Eliot with the moderation of Pym.[2] These qualities of statesmanship would become increasingly evident in the crises of succeeding parliaments.

---

[1] Rushworth, I, 400–6.   [2] *Commons' Journals*, I, 859, ii.

CHAPTER V

THE PETITION OF RIGHT

Third Parliament of Charles I, March 1628–March 1629

THE King's ability to rule without a parliament would once more depend upon his ability to finance his government. Since he had no parliamentary grants, either of subsidies or of tunnage and poundage, all his sources of income would have to be non-parliamentary. His first problem, therefore, was to devise a variety of money-making expedients. Tunnage and poundage he continued to levy as though it had been granted by Parliament. A loan of £100,000 was demanded from the City of London : the demand was refused but, under heavy pressure, the city aldermen agreed to make to the King a personal loan of £20,000. Recusancy fines (for non-attendance at Church of England services), which formerly had been collected with great laxity, were now imposed vigorously. Charles sold large quantities of his plate. Dues were levied from the coast towns and coast shires to provide ships : for this there were precedents and, though there was much grumbling about the number of ships demanded (fifty-six altogether), most of them were ultimately provided. These piecemeal levies having proved inadequate as sources of supply for the war, the King adopted the further suggestion of a forced loan : the total amount to be collected by loan was five subsidies (£350,000), which was to be exacted from those individuals whose names were on the subsidy roll. In the immediate neighbourhood of London the loan was mostly paid ; but in the more distant counties there was much resistance. Even the King's judges refused to recognize the loan as legal ; and though in November the Chief Justice, Sir Randal Crew, was dismissed from his office, the remainder of the Bench refused to be intimidated. This stand by the judges encouraged the malcontents and, what was even more serious, damaged Charles' prestige in the eyes of the people at large. Poor folk who refused the loan were pressed into the army; gentry who refused were sent to prison. Among the latter class were Eliot, Hampden, and Wentworth. Strangely enough, there is no mention of Pym as refusing the loan. Evidently he judged it wiser not to struggle when at a hopeless disadvantage, that is, when a parliament was not in session. Instead, he reserved his strength until the next parliament should be called so that, taking advantage of parliamentary privileges, and in co-operation with other Members, he might more effectively renew the struggle for political freedom.

Five gentlemen who were imprisoned for refusing the loan demanded from the Court of King's Bench a writ of *habeas corpus* in order that they might receive proper trial. The legal arguments in what is always known as "The Five Knights' Case" were heard on 22nd November 1627. The counsel for the defence claimed that "no man can be justly imprisoned without a cause of the commitment expressed in the return". Lord Chief Justice Hyde, in giving judgment, countered this claim by stating "That if no cause of the commitment be expressed, it is to be presumed for a matter of state, which he cannot take notice of". Consequently he remanded the prisoners. This may have been good judgment in Law, but it failed to carry conviction among the mass of the English people, and the total sum collected fell short of the amount aimed at by more than £100,000. In any case, the King's efforts to raise revenue could be only palliatives, for Buckingham's policy abroad was draining the Exchequer much faster than the financial expedients were filling it.

The chief cause of expense was a war which had broken out between England and France. Several events had combined to reverse the policy of the Anglo-French alliance which had been based upon the marriage of King Charles with Henrietta Maria. Fundamentally, an alliance between Protestant England and Roman Catholic France was unnatural, and could not be expected

to endure beyond the particular circumstances which had evoked
it. The marriage itself, in its early stages, proved unexpectedly
irksome to Charles, for the Queen, notwithstanding her youth,
was wayward and obstinate. Charles believed that the Queen's
wilfulness was due to the encouragement it received from her
ladies and servants ; and as early as August 1626 he had had them
expelled from England. Louis of France resented this action as
being both a breach of the marriage treaty and as an insult to his
sister and to France. Another cause of friction was constant
conflicts between ships of the two countries. A climax was
reached when, in November 1626, the Governor of Guienne seized
a fleet of some two hundred English ships laden with wine from
Bordeaux. This action led to reprisals, and in March 1627 English
commanders were authorized to seize any French ships wherever
they were to be found. Such an order constituted a virtual state
of war. Buckingham, filled with enthusiasm for action, began
to plan a great expedition for the relief of La Rochelle. His hope
was that this would be followed by the rising of the Huguenots of
southern France and by the release of the English ships from
Bordeaux.

The expedition, commanded by Buckingham himself, set sail
on 27th June 1627 and reached the Island of Rhé, off La Rochelle,
on 10th July. It included about a hundred ships carrying some
six thousand soldiers and a hundred horsemen. Like the earlier
expedition to Cadiz, it proved a complete fiasco, but the cause of
failure was very different. At Cadiz the cause had been incompetent leadership ; at Rhé it was lack of support from England.
Buckingham proved himself to be brave, energetic, and resource-
ful ; but, when reinforcements and fresh supplies became necessary,
the officials at home remained apathetic to all his demands. Repeatedly he sent representations and representatives to explain his
desperate needs, but all in vain. Further, the King himself gave
repeated commands to Marlborough, the Treasurer, and to Weston,
the Chancellor of the Exchequer, that men and stores should be
sent forthwith, but still nothing happened. Thus the French had
time to throw reinforcements, munitions, and stores into the

island so that Buckingham, left stranded, was presented with an impossible task. By the middle of November the defeated remnants of the expedition were back in England. Though the failure at Rhé may not have been Buckingham's fault, the people of the time naturally saw it as yet another disgrace which his incompetence and his influence over the King had brought upon England. In one sense at least this judgment was sound, namely, that the root cause of the failure was the foolhardy policy of Buckingham whose unteachable optimism could never envisage defeat and who therefore made no adequate preparations for victory. The only event that might have made the English people lenient towards the man responsible for the Forced Loan and the other illegal taxation would have been his use of the proceeds in order to win a great naval victory. Defeat was the one thing certain to unite the country against him.

Nor was defeat limited to the war in France. In Germany a similarly dismal story had to be told. The promises of support made by Charles to the Protestant leaders were never fulfilled ; and what troops were sent from England were untrained and were left without reinforcements or supplies. In May 1626, the Protestant leader, Count Mansfield, was defeated by the Imperialists under Wallenstein ; and in August, Christian of Denmark was routed by Tilley at Lutter. The boasted English championship of an English princess and her husband had ended in disaster as complete as the English championship of the French Huguenots.

Buckingham and the King recognized that they could not leave the Rochellois to the mercy of Richelieu. A new expedition must be fitted out, and a new expedition would need new money. Experience had shown that adequate money for exceptional expenditure could not be raised without parliamentary grants. Thus, King and minister must face the inevitable. On 30th January 1628, writs were ordered for a parliament to meet on 17th March.

The elections reflected accurately enough the concensus of opinion against the King. Almost everywhere the opposition candidates were elected, especially those that had refused the loan.

Of about seventy-five individuals who had been imprisoned for refusing to pay the Forced Loan and were released at the time of the elections, at least one-third, including Wentworth, were returned as Members. That a House elected in such an atmosphere should prove to be extremist, or even revolutionary, in character, is not surprising.

John Forster, in his biography of Sir John Eliot, wrote that : [1]

Four days before the King went down to open the session some leaders of the commons met at Sir Robert Cotton's house. The numbers cannot now be stated ; but from a memorandum among Eliot's papers it is certain they comprised himself, Sir Thomas Wentworth and his now brother-in-law Mr. Denzil Holles, Sir Robert Philips, Mr. Pym, Mr. Edward Kyrton, Mr. Seldon, and Sir Edward Coke ; and that their conference turned mainly on the question whether the impeachment of Buckingham should be revived.

Gardiner also mentioned this meeting,[2] but offered no other authority for it than Forster's statement just quoted. Recent examination of the Eliot papers at Port Eliot fails to reveal any such memorandum as Forster refers to.[3] Incidentally, Forster, in his earlier life of Pym, stated that a similar meeting had taken place just previous to the 1621 Parliament,[4] though the lists of Members whom he mentions as present in 1621 and 1628 respectively are not identical. In this "preparation for the session" of 1621, Forster sees "the first formation of the system of parliamentary government which has brought such great results, for good and ill, in England". Strangely enough, for this momentous gathering he offers not the slightest historical evidence. Moreover, even if such a meeting did take place in 1621, Pym's attendance is extremely unlikely : Pym had never previously been a Member of Parliament—Forster wrongly thought that he had sat in the 1614 House—nor, so far as we know, had he distinguished himself in the country

[1] Forster : *Sir John Eliot*, Book IX, Section i.
[2] Gardiner : *History of England*, VI, 230–1.
[3] For this information the author is indebted to Mr. Harold Hulme of Larchmont, U.S.A.
[4] Forster : *Eminent British Statesmen*, III, 6–7.

at large. There is the further curious fact that, in his life of Pym, Forster makes no reference to the meeting of 1628 which he mentions in his life of Eliot. Forster's apparent confusion between these two meetings of 1621 and 1628, taken in conjunction with the frequent inconsistencies to be found elsewhere in his writings,[1] compels us, in the absence of other confirmatory evidence, to regard his account of both meetings as at best not proven.

Yet, though there may not have been any previously organized opposition to the Court, the session had hardly opened when opposition began to show itself. Indeed, the absence of previous organization makes the outburst of feeling the more significant.

If the King had deliberately planned to rouse the hostility of Parliament he could hardly have chosen phrases better suited to the purpose than some of those contained in his speech on the opening day. After informing the Members that they had been summoned in order that they might grant supply to meet the common danger, he warned them that if they failed to grant such supply " I must, in discharge of my conscience, use those other means which God hath put into my hands, to save that that the follies of particular men may otherwise hazard to lose ". Yet, said he, " take not this as a threatening (for I scorn to threaten any but my equals), but an admonition ".[2]

Sir John Finch was chosen as the Speaker of the Commons. His motto was that it was not " fit for private men, much less for me, to search into the counsels or actions of Kings ". He was to find that the House would make short shrift of such temporizing sentiments.

During this parliament, as during earlier ones, Pym served on an astonishingly large number of committees. Thus, on 20th March (which was the day following the election of the Speaker) he was appointed to no less than three committees : the Committee of Privileges, a Committee to consider the Cornwall election,

---

[1] For example, at the beginning of his life of Pym (p. 6) he states that Pym's elder son was named John ; yet towards the end (p. 303) he implies that the elder son was Alexander.

[2] *Lords' Journals*, III, 687 ; Rushworth, I, 477.

and a Committee to draw up a Petition to the King about a general fast. It was as a committee-man, rather than as a speaker in the House, that once again Pym's activity seems to have been expended. Though frequently he made weighty contributions to debate, the real leaders in the House were Eliot and Wentworth, whose outspoken oratory, at a time of heated feeling, was more to the liking of the Members than was Pym's balanced restraint.

The Commons, continuing the practice of recent parliaments, were soon discussing grievances as a preliminary to granting supplies. Most of the discussion hung round the grievance of illegal imprisonment. The practical difficulty was how to solve the dual problem of supplies and grievances without producing a new deadlock. There was a proposal before the House for granting five subsidies. Eliot opposed the grant as being too large in itself and too dangerous unless security were first obtained for redress of grievances. Pym, however, with his usual moderation, argued (on 4th April) in favour of the grant : [1]

That in business of weight, dispatch is better than discourse. We came not hither without all motives that can be towards his Majesty, had he never sent in this message ; we know the danger of our enemies, we must give expedition to expedition ; let us forbear particulars. A man in a journey is hindered by asking too many questions : I do believe our peril is as great as may be, every man complains of it, that doth encourage the enemy : our way is to take that that took away our estates, that is, the enemy ; to give speedily is that that the King calls for : a word spoken in season, is like an apple of silver ; and actions are more precious than words. Let us hasten our resolutions to supply his Majesty.

After this speech, Rushworth immediately records : " And after some debate, they came to this unanimous resolve, That five subsides be given to his Majesty ; and Mr. Secretary Cook was appointed to acquaint his Majesty with the resolution of the House."

So at last the five subsidies were granted. It was Wentworth who produced the solution to the problem of safeguards : he proposed that the five subsidies should not be reported—so that the

[1] Rushworth, I, 525.

King would not be able to levy them—but that they should be conditional upon Charles' giving consent to a Bill recognizing specific liberties as already belonging to his subjects. The House adopted Wentworth's suggestion, and, on 28th April, appointed a Committee—which included Pym, Eliot, Wentworth, and Sir Edward Coke—to draw up a Bill to this effect. Next day the Bill was introduced by Coke. After quoting Magna Carta and other medieval statutes of liberty, the Bill concluded:[1] "Be it enacted that no tax, tallage, or loan shall be levied etc., by the King or any minister without Act of Parliament, and that none be compelled to receive any soldiers into his house against his will." The King's only reply was to demand a vote on the question of whether Parliament would rest on his royal word. This occasioned further debates, and, following a speech by Wentworth, the Commons resolved to draw up a Remonstrance asserting that the laws had been broken by the King's ministers and that Parliament, in re-affirming these laws, was but carrying out its duty to the nation. On 5th May, Charles let it be known that he would not accept the Remonstrance, and next day the Commons went into committee to consider the King's answer and to decide upon their next action. In the midst of the heated debate Pym intervened:[2]

Our assurance in the King's word were sufficient if we knew what the King's sense and meaning is. We have not his word only, but his oath also at his coronation. We complain of unjust imprisonment upon loans, I hear not that any say we shall be no more, or that matter of State shall be no more pretended when there is none. . . . We all rest on the King's royal word. But let us agree in a rule to give us satisfaction.

Sir Edward Coke supported Pym's demand for a definition of "the King's word" and declared that the King could signify his word not by a verbal message but only "by a record and in particulars". Hence, he concluded,[3] "Let us have a conference with the Lords, and join in a Petition of Right to the King for our particular

[1] Gardiner : *Constitutional Documents of the Puritan Revolution*, pp. 65 and 66, quoting Harl. MSS. 1771, f. 123.
[2] Quoted, Gardiner : *History of England*, VI, 273.   [3] Ibid., p. 274.

grievances. Not that I distrust the King, but because we cannot take his trust but in a Parliamentary way."

The method of Petition of Right was thereupon adopted by the House, and the former committee was instructed to frame the Petition. On 8th May, Selden brought in the text which the committee had agreed upon. The Commons acted in conjunction with the Lords ; and there were lengthy debates in each House, and conferences between committees of both of them. On 17th May, the Lords, in order to facilitate the King's acceptance of the Petition, proposed to add the clause : [1]

We humbly present this petition to your Majesty, not only with a care of preserving our own liberties, but with due regard to leave entire that sovereign power wherewith your Majesty is trusted for the protection, safety, and happiness of your people.

This question of the sovereign power provoked a warm debate in the Commons. Pym summarized both his own view and the correct constitutional position with his usual clearness and moderation : [2]

I am not able to speak to this question, I know not what it is : All our Petition is for the laws of England, and this power seems to be another distinct power from the power of the law : I know how to add sovereign to his [the King's] person, but not to his power : and we cannot leave to him a sovereign power : also we were never possessed of it.

At last the Lords agreed to drop their additional clause and to accept the Petition as it stood. In this form, therefore, it was presented to the King on 28th May. The King's answer was vague and meaningless, avoiding both a clear rejection of the Petition and a clear promise to observe it. Further debates resulted in Eliot's proposing that a Remonstrance should be drawn up to recapitulate the Commons' grievances. Charles did his utmost to quash the Remonstrance by ordering the Commons to proceed with the business of a Subsidy Bill and by forbidding them to " lay any scandal or aspersion upon the State-Government, or ministers thereof ". [3]

[1] *Lords' Journals*, III, 801, ii.   [2] Rushworth, I, 562.
[3] Ibid., p. 605.

The Commons, during these debates, realizing that a breach with the King seemed inevitable, were deeply moved, and the Members gave way to tears and sobs which made speech difficult. It was Sir Edward Coke who at last expressed what all were thinking. Boldly defying the royal injunction, the veteran lawyer and parliamentarian—he was now seventy-seven years of age—declared : [1]

Let us palliate no longer ; if we do, God will not prosper us. I think the Duke of Buckingham is the cause of all our miseries ; and till the King is informed thereof, we shall never go out with honour, or sit with honour here ; that man is the grievance of grievances : let us set down the causes of all our disasters, and all will reflect upon him.

At this, the pent-up feelings of the Commons were released as the Members shouted, amid cheers: "'Tis he ! 'tis he !'" Even Charles had to recognize the deep conviction of the Commons ; and on 7th June he signified his approval of the Petition in the traditional form of words : " *Soit droit fait comme est desiré.*" [2]

While these political events were moving to their climax, the parallel question of religion was raising itself in an acute form, and once again it was to Pym that the Commons turned as their leader in a religious issue. That issue had been provoked by a Dr. Roger Manwaring who, in July 1627, had preached before the King two sermons which maintained that resistance to a king incurred eternal damnation as a penalty, and therefore that the King could levy taxes without Parliament's consent. Charles signified his pleasure that the sermons should be licensed for printing. Even Laud, foreseeing the antagonism which such sentiments would arouse, protested to Charles against the licensing of the sermons ; but his protest was in vain. The Commons were not likely to ignore such a public attack upon their privileges, and its Committee on Religion soon got to work to collect evidence on the subject. On the strength of this evidence, the Commons decided to impeach Manwaring, and on 9th June 1628 Pym appeared before the Lords with the charges against him. Pym's

---

[1] Rushworth, I, p. 607. [2] *Lords' Journals*, III, 844.

speech on this occasion was something more than merely an expression of the Commons' anger against an individual. As was his wont, he began with an exposition of basic principles and then proceeded to deal with the case in point as being an illustration of the violation of those principles. Pym's speech was, indeed, a summary of the political creed of the opposition elements in the Commons. The speech as reported by Rushworth occupies more than ten pages.[1] In the course of it Pym declared :

First, that the form of government, in any State, could not be altered without apparent danger of ruin to that State.

Second, that the law of England, whereby the subject was exempted from taxes and loans, not granted by common consent of Parliament, was not introduced by any statute, or by any charter or sanction of princes, but was the ancient and fundamental law issuing from the first frame and constitution of the kingdom.

Third, that the liberty of the subject is not only most convenient and profitable for the people, but most honourable, most necessary for the king.

Each of these three contentions was then elaborated and illustrated. A quotation from the elaboration of the first two will convey some idea of the tenor of the whole. As for the first question :

The form of government is that which doth actuate and dispose every part and member of a state to the common good ; and as those parts give strength and ornament to the whole, so they receive from it again strength and protection in their several stations and degrees. If this mutual relation and intercourse be broken, the whole frame will quickly be dissolved, and fall in pieces, and instead of this concord and interchange of support, whilst one part seeks to uphold the old form of government, and the other part to introduce a new, they will miserably consume and devour one another. Histories are full of the calamities of whole States and nations in such cases. It is true, that time must needs bring some alterations, and every alteration is a step and degree towards a dissolution ; those things only are eternal which are constant and uniform : Therefore it is observed by the best writers on this subject, that those commonwealths have been most durable and perpetual, which have often reformed and recomposed themselves according to their first institution and

---

[1] Rushworth, I, 595–604.

ordinance ; for by this means they repair the breaches and counter-work the ordinary and natural effects of time.

The second question is as manifest, there are plain footsteps of those laws in the government of the Saxons, they were of that vigour and force as to over-live the Conquest, nay, to give bounds and limits to the Conqueror. . . . It is true they have often been broken, they have been often confirmed by charters of kings, by acts of parliaments ; but the petitions of the subjects, upon which those charters and acts were founded, were ever Petitions of Right, demanding their ancient and due liberties, not suing for any new.

It is hardly possible to read the speech without being reminded of Edmund Burke. Both in their political principles and in their methods of exposition, the two men had much in common. Just as Pym, in attacking Buckingham and Manwaring and, later, Strafford, found the justification for his attitude in what he believed to be the fundamental principles of the English Constitution, so Burke, a century and a half later, treated the American and French Revolutions as exemplifying his own Whig philosophy of government. Indeed, the essence of Burke's *Reflections on the French Revolutions* is little more than an echo of Pym's insistence, in his Manwaring speech, upon the permanent character of the English constitution which has known reformation but never revolution. In his *Reflections*, Burke wrote :

The Revolution [of 1688] was made to preserve our *ancient* indisputable laws and liberties, and that *ancient* constitution of government which is our only security for law and liberty. . . . We wished at the period of the Revolution, and do now wish, to derive all we possess as *an inheritance from our forefathers*. Upon that body and stock of inheritance we have taken care not to inoculate any scion alien to the nature of the original plant. All reformations we have hitherto made have proceeded upon the principle of reverence to antiquity ; and I hope, nay I am persuaded, that all those which possibly may be made hereafter, will be carefully formed upon analogical precedent, authority, and example.

John Pym and Edmund Burke were philosopher statesmen in the same class. All that we shall see of Pym in our subsequent study will confirm this estimate of him.

Incidentally, it is difficult to believe that Pym, holding as he did these views of the unbroken continuity of the English constitution, could ever have consented, had he lived until the overthrow of Charles I in 1645, to the execution of the King or to the replacing of the monarchy by a form of government without precedent in the nation's history. We can do little more than guess what Pym's solution of the political problem might then have been ; but we can be reasonably certain that he would never have been a regicide and that his prestige in the nation would have enabled the Parliamentarians to carry through their solution—that is, Pym's solution—of the problem as against the Army. To this point we shall have to return later.

The chief interest which Manwaring's case has for us lies less in the fate of Manwaring than in the opportunity which the trial provided for the exposition of these views of Pym. Nevertheless, we must complete the story. Manwaring was condemned by the Lords to be imprisoned during the House's pleasure, to pay a fine of £1,000, to be suspended from any preaching for three years and from preaching at court for the rest of his life. Charles, however, saw to it that the prisoner did not suffer. Early in July, Manwaring received a royal pardon and was appointed to the rectory of Stamford Rivers, from which Montague had just passed to the bishopric of Chichester ; and in 1636 Manwaring was further promoted to be Bishop of St. Davids.

Charles could not so easily dispose of all his difficulties. While Manwaring's case was proceeding, the Commons had been continuing their preparation of the Remonstrance which Eliot had proposed during the debates on the Petition of Right. Charles had hoped that his acceptance of the Petition would induce the Commons to drop the Remonstrance, but he miscalculated the Commons' determination. The Commons agreed to the terms of the Remonstrance on 11th June.[1] It contained three main complaints : first, that the penal laws against Roman Catholics had not been carried out ; second, that the Arminians—of whom Laud was the leader—were unduly favoured ; and, third, that the Duke of Buckingham was the cause of all the ills under which

---

[1] Rushworth, I, 619.

the kingdom suffered. Under this third heading, the Remonstrance could not have been more explicit : [1]

Our humble desire is further, that your excellent Majesty will be pleased to take into your most princely consideration, whether, in respect the said Duke hath so abused his power, it be safe for your Majesty and for your Kingdom, to continue him either in his great offices, or in his place of nearness and counsel about your sacred person.

When, on 17th June, the Remonstrance was presented to Charles, his only answer was that " he would consider of [the grievances] as they should deserve ". The fact was, of course, that he would not accept any remonstrance that included an attack on Buckingham.

The Commons, baulked of satisfaction in this direction, prepared another Remonstrance against the levying of tunnage and poundage without Parliament's consent. On 23rd June, the King announced that Parliament would be prorogued on the 26th. The Commons therefore hurried their Remonstrance which was voted on the 25th.[2]

The receiving of tunnage and poundage and other impositions, not granted by Parliament, is a breach of the fundamental liberties of this kingdom, and contrary to your Majesty's royal answer to our late Petition of Right : and therefore they do most humbly beseech your Majesty to forbear any further receiving of the same ; and not to take it in ill part from those of your Majesty's loving subjects who shall refuse to make payment of any such charges without warrant of law demanded.

In proroguing Parliament next day the King addressed to the Commons a sharp reprimand which included the declaration that, in the Petition of Right, " I have granted no new, but only confirmed the ancient liberties of my subjects ". He therefore contended that " as for tunnage and poundage, it is a thing I cannot want, and was never intended by you to ask—never meant, I am sure by me to grant ".[3] Parliament that day stood adjourned till 20th October.

During the recess, events of critical importance were to take

---

[1] Rushworth, I, 626.   [2] *Parliamentary History*, II, 431-4.
[3] *Lords' Journals*, III, 879 ; Rushworth, I, 631 ; *Parliamentary History*, II, 434.

place. The first was related to the renewed attempt to relieve La Rochelle. We have seen that such an attempt had been determined upon when Buckingham had sailed to the Isle of Rhé, June–November 1627. In May 1628 an expedition of more than fifty vessels had been sent out under Buckingham's brother-in-law, the Earl of Denbigh, carrying foodstuffs sufficient to revictual the town for six months. But the mere sight of the defences erected by Richelieu was enough to daunt Denbigh who, without making the slightest effort either to storm or to evade the fortifications, promptly returned to England. As soon, therefore, as Parliament was prorogued, Buckingham began preparations for yet another expedition ; and for this purpose he went to Portsmouth. There, on 23rd August, he was stabbed to death by Felton, who harboured a grudge against the Duke and had walked from London of set purpose to commit the crime.

The removal of Buckingham seemed to offer some hope of easier relations between King and Commons during the forthcoming session. Events were to prove that his removal had the reverse effect. For this there were two reasons. First, Charles never forgave the outburst of delirious joy with which everywhere the people greeted the news of the murder : from that moment there was a barrier between the King and his subjects. Second, whereas formerly it had been the Duke whom Parliament had persisted in regarding as the person responsible for the ill-advised actions of Charles, henceforward Charles must himself bear the whole blame for unconstitutional conduct.

No one ever replaced Buckingham in the King's affections or in the intimacy of his political confidence. Nevertheless, the second significant event of the recess was that the King found another counsellor. This was none other than Sir Thomas Wentworth. The reasons for Wentworth's defection to the Court party are aside from our main purpose. There always has been, and probably always will be, diversity of opinion about his motives. As a summary of those motives, we may accept the balanced judgment of one of his biographers : [1]

[1] C. V. Wedgwood : *Strafford*, pp. 72, 73.

Wentworth had never been a political theorist : the only argument he recognized was practical necessity. . . . He had never belonged wholly either to the Court or to the Country party, instead he had tried to steer between the two in hopes of an accommodation between King and Parliament : . . . all that had ever mattered to him and all that mattered to him now was the good government of the Commonwealth of England.

He seems to have believed that the Petition of Right had tipped the balance of government too heavily on the side of Parliament, and thenceforward he preferred to throw himself on to the side of the King [1] On 22nd July he was created Lord Wentworth. What his attitude might have been had Buckingham continued to dominate the Court it is impossible to say. Certainly it had been Buckingham rather than Charles that Wentworth, like most of his fellows, had opposed ; and Buckingham's murder, only a month after Wentworth had become a peer, disposed of any hesitation that Wentworth might still feel to unreserved support of Charles.

A further effect of Buckingham's death was that La Rochelle was not likely to receive any further effective help from England. Though in September a relieving expedition was sent, under the command of the Earl of Lindsay, nothing decisive was accomplished, and by mid-October La Rochelle surrendered to Richelieu.

A few days after Lindsay's fleet had sailed, Parliament, which was to have reassembled on 20th October, was further prorogued till 20th January 1629 ; and on that day it at last met.

The Members assembled in no happy mood. During the recess the King had committed a number of acts of arbitrary government. The Petition of Right, as it was circulated, included not the King's final and formal acceptance of its terms but his original and vague answer—" The King willeth that right be done according to the laws and customs of the realm "—which Parliament had refused to accept. This action naturally encouraged the suspicion that Charles was not to be trusted, a suspicion that

[1] For other " Theories of Wentworth's Apostasy " see Traill : *Strafford*, pp. 32–42.

was substantiated by other actions whereby Charles had infringed the terms of the Petition itself. He had continued to raise money by means not granted by Parliament, including the levying of tunnage and poundage ; and some individuals who had refused to pay the taxes had had to submit to the confiscation of their goods. Worse still, from the immediate viewpoint of the Commons, was the fact that one of the sufferers from confiscation was a Member of their House, a merchant named John Rolles. No sooner was Parliament in session than these irregularities were the subject of heated discussion.

Thursday the 22nd of January. One Mr. Rolles, a merchant and a member of the House, informed the House that his goods were seized by the customers for refusing to pay the custom by them demanded, although he told them, what was adjudged to be due by law he would pay.[1]

Phelips and Eliot took up the cudgels in defence of the privileges of the House. But, in spite of all their arguments, it could not be proved beyond dispute that the privileges of the House had been infringed. A Member's right to freedom from arrest while a parliament was sitting was a well-established privilege. But Rolles had not been arrested ; and there was no clear precedent to prove that the exemption applied to his goods as well as to his person. Moreover, his goods had been seized in October when Parliament was not in session. On 24th January, Charles tried to placate the Houses by a speech which declared that if men :[2]

imagined that I have taken these duties as appertaining to my hereditary prerogative . . . they are much deceived ; for it ever was and still is my meaning, by the gift of my people to enjoy it ; and my intention in my speech at the ending of the last Session

---

[1] *True Relation*, p. 7.   [2] Ibid., p. 11.

NOTE.—For the remainder of this chapter, the references to :

1. *A True Relation of every day's proceedings in Parliament since the beginning thereof being the 20th of January 1628 ;*

2. *The Notes of Sir Edward Nicholas for the session of the Commons in 1629.*

are to *Commons' Debates for 1629* critically edited by Notestein and Relf (University of Minnesota, 1921).

concerning this point was not to challenge Tonnage and Poundage as of right, but *de bene esse* ; showing you the necessity, not the right, by which I was to take it, until you had granted it to me ; assuring myself according to your general professions, that you wanted time not will to give it to me.

This renunciation of a prerogative right to tunnage and poundage made a favourable impression. Nevertheless, the Commons refused to be cajoled thereby into granting the customs until the question of irregular impositions had been satisfactorily dealt with. Meanwhile, for several days, religion chiefly occupied the House.

Tunnage and poundage was again brought to the notice of the Commons by the continued action of the Court of Star Chamber against recalcitrant merchants, and in particular by its summoning of Rolles to appear before it during the session of Parliament.

(Tuesday, 10th February) *Mr. Rolles* complaineth that since his last complaint of the breach of the liberties of this House, his warehouse hath been locked up by one Massey a pursuivant ; and that yesterday he was called forth from the Committee in the Exchequer Chamber, and served with a subpœna to appear in the Star Chamber ; but that since he received a letter from Mr. Attorney that it was a mistake.[1]

Such a clear violation of a Member's privilege was certain to inflame the temper of the House which the Attorney-General's admission of error did little to cool. The champions of the Commons' liberties, with Eliot leading, were soon again in full cry. On 19th February the customs officers were summoned to the bar of the House to answer for their action in seizing Rolles' goods.

Mr. Dawes, a customer, was called to the Bar and was asked by what authority he took Mr. Rolles his goods. He said by virtue of a warrant sent from his Majesty, and being asked if Mr. Rolles demanded privilege, he said he knew Mr. Rolles was a Parliament man, and had privilege for his person, but not for his goods as he conceived.[2]

Another customs official named Carmarthen gave similar evidence, whereupon Eliot rose : [3] " We are to consider first whether these

[1] *True Relation*, p. 55.　　　　　　　　[2] Ibid., p. 84.
[3] Nicholas' *Notes*, pp. 156–7.

parties Dawes and Carmarthen be delinquents both or one for having violated the priviledges of this house ; and desires that this may be here debated of them severally."

In the first instance, Charles' seizure of tunnage and poundage, and his other resulting actions, had raised two issues : one, the rights of his subjects generally ; two, the privileges of Parliament in particular. As the debates in the Commons had proceeded, the Commons became obsessed by the second, and narrower, of the issues, to the almost entire exclusion of the first and greater of them. The speech just quoted shows that Eliot himself was blind to the real significance of the King's arbitrary actions. All the more remarkable, therefore, is it to find Pym speaking after Eliot and presenting exactly the opposite point of view : [1]

That it is noe diversion for a member of this house to wishe to forbeare a debate question att this tyme : the liberties of this house are inferior to the liberties of the Kingdome, to determyne the previledge of this house is but a meane matter, and the mayne end is to establishe possession of the Subjects, and to take of[f] the Commissions and Records and orders which are now against us, this is the mayne business and the way to sweeten the busines with the King and to rectify ourselves is first to settle these things and then we may in good tyme proceede to vindicat our owne priviledges.

Here, once again, is the voice of wise statesmanship : Pym was anxious lest the determination of the Commons to establish a minor privilege should so provoke the King as to jeopardize the establishment of a liberty fundamental to the whole nation. No incident could illustrate more perfectly the contrast between the political qualities of Eliot and of Pym. At the moment, it was the former who was more in tune with the high-pitched mood of the Commons, and we need not be surprised to read : [2]

Resolved that this House shal now take into their consideracion the violacion of the previledge of this House by Mr. Dawes and Carmarthen.

Resolved that this busines of Dawes Carmarthen shalbe debated now of att a grand Comittee : Mr. Herbert in Chayre.

[1] Ibid.   [2] Ibid., p. 158.

The House thus followed Eliot and not Pym. The time would come when the Commons would better appreciate the statesmanship which they now rejected.

Tunnage and poundage was not the only subject to occupy the attention of the Commons during their second session. Intermingled with debates on supplies, and often taking precedence of them, were debates on religion. An illustration of this fact was provided on the very first debating day after the recess. The King's Speech at the opening of the session had been delivered on Saturday, 24th January. On the following Monday, so the *True Relation* pithily informs us,[1]

> *Mr. Secretary Coke* then moved that the bill of Tonnage and Poundage might be read, and after some debate it was diverted, and then they fell upon points of Religion.
> *Mr. Rouse* concerning Religion.

Then follows a long account of Rouse's speech in which he emphasizes that the preservation of true religion is of even greater moment than freedom from illegal taxation. He therefore desires :

> that there may be a deep and serious consideration of the violations of it. I desire first that it may be considered what new paintings are laid upon the old face of the whore of Babylon to make her seem more lovely, and to draw so many suitors to her. . . . I desire that we may consider the increase of Arminianism, an error that maketh the grace of God lackey it after the will of man, that maketh the sheep to keep the shepherd.

Nothing could have been more exactly to the mind of the House. Several other speeches followed on the same theme.

Next day,

> The King sent a message by Secretary Coke . . . hoping that you proceed with the Bill of Tonnage and Poundage and give precedency to that business, to give an end to further dispute between him and some of his subjects.[2]

In spite of this message, Coryton interposed :[3]

> Let us not do God's work negligently. We receive his Majesties messages with all duty ; for our proceedings, let us so proceed,

---

[1] Nicholas' *Notes*, pp. 12–14.   [2] *True Relation*, p. 18.
[3] Ibid., pp. 19–20.

as may soonest conduce to his Majesties desires. Religion concerneth the King as well as us. . . . Let us be resolved into a committee, and presently debate thereof.

To this resolve the House agreed. The committee on religion forthwith sat, with Pym in the Chair. Pym's speech was framed on his usual orderly plan. He recognized : " Two diseases, the one old, the other new. The old Popery, the new Arminianism." Under each of these " two diseases ", he set out " three things to be enquired after ". The new disease of Arminianism he declared to be condemned by the orthodox standards of the Church, namely,[1]

by the Articles set forth 1552, and by the Catechism set forth in King Edward VI his days, and by the writings of Peter Martyr and Martin Bucer, Wycliffe, and others, and by the constant profession sealed by the blood of so many martyrs as Cranmer, Ridley, and others ; and by the 39 Articles set forth in Queen Elizabeths time ; and by the Articles set forth at Lambeth as the doctrine of the Church of England, which King James sent to Dort and Ireland as the truth professed here.

If we may assume that this speech reflects not only the decisions of the committee but also Pym's personal religious conviction— and no other assumption appears tenable—it affords further proof of the fact to which reference has already been made, namely, that he was not an advocate of further change in Church practices but was a staunch upholder of the doctrines of the established Church as set forth in the Thirty-Nine Articles of Elizabeth. It seems, indeed, impossible to endorse the view that Pym was a Puritan except in the sense that he was opposed to such changes in doctrines and in practices as would move, or had already moved, the Church from its orthodox Elizabethan position. From his attitude of a supporter of the Church, as it had been under Elizabeth and James I, Pym never wavered right down to his death in 1643.

Immediately after Pym's speech, the *True Relation* notes :[2] " It was then ordered that Religion should have the precedency." And so, throughout the remainder of the session, it had. The

---

[1] Ibid., pp. 20–1.   [2] P. 21.

sub-committee on religion continued to sit, and it was the *Heads and Articles* [1] which this Committee prepared, and to which the House agreed on 23rd February, that led indirectly to the violent close of the session. In great detail the *Heads and Articles* gives evidence of the alarming growth of "Popish, Arminian, and superstitious opinions and practices", one of the practices complained of was : "That those persons who have published and maintained such Popish, Arminian, and superstitious opinions and practices, and who are known to be unsound in Religion, are countenanced, favoured, and preferred," whilst the orthodox were "discountenanced and hindered". The names of Arminians thus advanced were quoted as evidence of this contention, among them being the Bishops of Winchester and London, that is, Neile and Laud. To these complaints was added a list of ten "remedies" which were so stringent that the King, alarmed at the determined attitude of the Commons, ordered (on 25th February) that the House should adjourn for a week, his hope apparently being that the interval might cool the factiousness of the opposition leaders.

The adjournment had, if anything, the reverse effect. On Monday, 2nd March, when the Members reassembled, their discontent was increased by rumours of a dissolution. The Speaker, Sir John Finch, announced an immediate adjournment till 10th March. At once Sir John Eliot vehemently protested that the House could be adjourned only by its own vote. It was at this point that the Speaker was forcibly held in his Chair by Holles and Valentine, and the door was locked, while Eliot spoke in justification of his protest. This speech was followed by the passing of the famous resolutions against innovations in religion and against the illegal levying and paying of tunnage and poundage. The House then voted its own adjournment, which was at once followed by a royal proclamation of the dissolution of Parliament.

Immediately after the close of the Parliament, nine Members, including Eliot, Holles, Valentine, Selden, and Strode—but not Pym—were imprisoned. Most of the prisoners sooner or later made their submission to the King and were released. Three

[1] *True Relation*, pp. 95–101.

remained obdurate : Eliot continued to be a prisoner until his death in 1632 ; Valentine and Strode were still in prison when their election to the new parliament of 1640 at last released them.

What is of particular interest for our purpose is that Pym had no share, either by word or by action, in the scene of violence on 2nd March. Here is yet further evidence of his moderation and of his lack of sympathy with the extremist opponents of the King. From the facts available, it seems fair to deduce that after 19th February, when the Commons followed Eliot and rejected Pym's plea to safeguard the liberties of the nation rather than merely the privileges of Parliament, Pym had ceased to co-operate with the Eliot section in the House. To this fact must be attributed his immunity from arrest at the close of the Parliament. The whole Parliament had shown once more the statesmanship which was to win increasing recognition as the years passed and which was to be the most valuable asset of the Parliamentary party. Only after Eliot had passed from the scene, and Wentworth had transferred himself to the King's side, did Pym's wisdom have the opportunity to display itself to full advantage. It was in the Short Parliament (April–May 1640) that this parliamentary supremacy of Pym first had a chance to show itself. In view of the contrast which has here been drawn between Pym and Eliot as champions of the popular cause, there is peculiar significance in a comment of Gardiner on a great speech which Pym delivered to the Short Parliament : [1]

It may possibly have occurred to Pym's hearers—it will certainly occur to his readers—that the cause which Pym and Eliot had alike at heart had gained not a little by the sad fate which had condemned the stainless martyr to an early grave.

A more just summary of the relative influence of Pym and Eliot would be difficult to frame.

The dissolution of the third parliament of the reign marked the end of Charles' chance of governing through Parliament. During the following eleven years he tried to rule without a parliament——the longest non-parliamentary period in English history. Such

[1] *History of England*, IX, 102 ; also see below, pp. 146–8.

was the pass to which the country had been brought by bankrupt statesmanship, for which the ultimate responsibility must rest with the King. Though the Commons had been guilty of occasional factiousness, the root cause of it had been not their own unreasonableness but their lack of confidence in the King who could be induced to attend to Parliament's petitions about grievances only when the Commons exercised their " power of the purse " : even then he would almost certainly violate his promises as soon as Parliament was dissolved. At no point within the parliamentary experience of Pym had either James or Charles met the complaints of the Commons by a clear and comprehensive policy based upon facts. The unchanging moderation of Pym in leading the Commons, and the defection of Wentworth from the popular to the royal side as soon as the demands of the former seemed to be growing excessive, show that a policy of even moderate reforms, granted by the King and genuinely carried out, would have won the grateful loyalty of the mass of the nation. Moreover, Charles seemed incapable of learning any lesson from past failures. Both his first and his second parliaments had been called to supply the King with money, and dissolved because the Commons would not grant money before the redress of grievances. Each time this took place, the relationship between King and Parliament became more strained ; and, if the process were continued, the day would come when their relationship would reach breaking-point. Yet the third parliament had been called for the same reason as the previous two, and once more the King had no policy to lay before the Members. This time the breaking-point had been reached.

Years afterwards, Clarendon, who could not be accused of prejudice against the King, thus summarized the position at the close of the 1629 Parliament : [1]

No man can show me a source from whence these waters of bitterness we now taste have more probably flowed, than from this unseasonable, unskilful, and precipitate dissolution of Parliaments, in which, by an unjust survey of the passion, insolence, and ambition of particular persons, the Court measured the temper

[1] *Great Rebellion*, I, 6 and 7.

and affection of the country. . . . It is not to be denied that there were in all those Parliaments, especially in that of the fourth year, several passages, and distempered speeches of particular persons, not fit for the dignity and honour of those places, and unsuitable to the reverence due to his majesty and his councils. But I do not know any formed Act of either House . . . that was not agreeable to the wisdom and justice of great courts upon these extraordinary occasions. And whoever considers the acts of power and injustice in the intervals of Parliaments, will not be much scandalized at the warmth and vivacity of those meetings.

During the eleven years following the dissolution of 1629, Charles ruled without a parliament. When at the end of that period the expenses of a threatened war compelled him to summon another parliament, the supreme crisis of the reign would be upon him. In that day it would once more be John Pym who would lead the nation in demanding redress of grievances before the grant of supplies. We have now to try to trace the activities of Pym during the eleven years' interval.

CHAPTER VI

THE PROVIDENCE ADVENTURERS
1629–40

NO-one, in March 1629, could foresee that more than eleven years would elapse before the meeting of another parliament. Yet no-one could fail to see that relations between Charles and the nation—as represented in Parliament—had reached an acute crisis and that Charles would not summon another House of Commons until necessity left him no alternative. Until that day arrived, be it soon or late, Pym and his associates would be bereft of the centre of their interest and activity. Pym, however, was the last man to remain idle ; and, as events turned out, at the very moment when Parliament ceased to engross him, another sphere for the employment of his qualities of statesmanship was opening in a quite unlooked-for direction. This was none other than a scheme of colonization in the West Indies. Though Westminster and the Island of Providence—that is, of Old Providence which lies some hundred and twenty-five miles off the Mosquito Coast of Central America, and is not to be confused with New Providence of the Bahama group—were separated geographically by the Atlantic, they were, in several respects, to be very closely related. It is for this reason, as will appear later, that we have to turn our attention to the colonizing enterprise in which Pym played a decisive part.

The first contact, so far as can be ascertained, that Pym made with affairs overseas occurred in 1628. In 1612 a company had been formed to colonize the Somers Islands, that is, the Bermudas. During the early years of the plantation, its prospects had seemed bright ; but gradually disputes arose, and the colony deteriorated until in 1628 the colonists requested that their plight might be considered : [1]

Petition of the poor planters of the Somers Islands to the Privy Council. Have lived in the islands since the infancy of the plantation, and lately brought to England their small means in tobacco, which has been detained in the custom house four months, under an imposition of 9d. in the lb., more than the tobacco will yield.

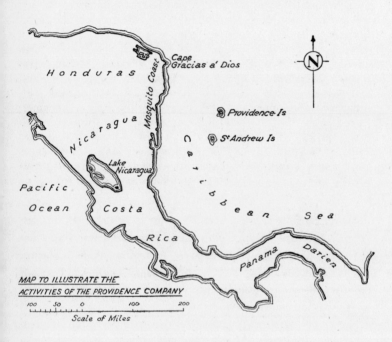

MAP TO ILLUSTRATE THE
ACTIVITIES OF THE PROVIDENCE COMPANY

Scale of Miles

Are driven to the greatest extremity, some of them having been arrested for payment of victuals, lodgings, and clothes, and anxious to return very soon. Pray for relief, and " to have their tobacco by bills of store for this present year ". Signed by Robert Staples, minister and 67 others. [This petition was presented to Parliament on 4 June 1628 ; and on the 16th June Mr. Pym reported from the Committee for the Somers Islands, and a petition to the King,

[1] C.S.P., Col. 1628, 4th June.

concerning this imposition, was ordered to be drawn by Sir Nath. Rich, Mr. Pym, Mr. Packer, and Mr. Rolles.]

On 19th June, this committee presented its report ; and a Petition, explaining the planters' case, was drawn up and agreed to by the Commons for presentation to the King.   Its terms were as follows : [1]

In discharge of the trust committed to them, [the Commons] beseech His Majesty to take into consideration the heavy pressures of the adventurers and planters of the Somers Islands, who, having about fifteen years since, first discovered the place, obtained a patent from King James, with divers privileges, to encourage them to attempt the plantation and fortifying thereof, which, with much labour and hazard, they have at length effected.   Above 2,000 people have been transported from hence ;   many houses and churches have been built, and forts and castles furnished with ordnance and ammunition.   For support of their annual expenses, those islands yield at present nothing of value but tobacco, which is so overcharged that great numbers of the planters are in danger " utterly to perish ". . .   The King is therefore prayed to grant the planters of the Somers Islands such relief as is agreeable to his princely justice, and may encourage them and others in the prosecution of similar designs.

Nothing of any consequence seems to have resulted from the Petition, perhaps because both King and Parliament were too engrossed with what to them were more immediate problems. The incident is of interest to us only because it connects Pym for the first time with colonial affairs.   His real, effective introduction to them occurred very shortly after.

In October 1629 an expedition was sent out to establish a colony on the Island of Old Providence.   The moving spirit behind the expedition was the Earl of Warwick, one of the leading Puritans of his day.   Information about the island and its neighbours had already been gathered by preliminary expeditions, and the settlement was started without serious difficulty.   In order to put it upon a sound foundation and to facilitate its development, Warwick invited subscriptions from friends.   The Colonial State Papers record the " Minutes of a Meeting of Adventurers to the Islands

[1] C.S.P., Col. 19th June.

of Providence and Henrietta" held at Brooke House on 19th November 1630. The minutes are as follows : [1]

To increase their former adventure from £200 to £500 ; amounts to be paid by each. The first voyage of discovery undertaken in 1629 by the Earl of Warwick, Sir Nath. Rich, and others, " which stood them in 2000 and odd pounds" to be discharged out of the first proceeds from those islands ; also the money already paid by those wishing to give up their shares. The Earl of Holland chosen Governor of the Company for the first year, John Dike, deputy, John Pym, treasurer, and Wil. Jessop, secretary.

On 4th December following, a patent formally incorporated those who had subscribed—eighteen in number—and who were named in the patent, into : [2]

. . . the Governor and Company of Adventurers for the Plantation of the Islands of Providence, Henrietta and the adjacent islands, between 10 and 20 degrees of North latitude and 290 and 310 degrees of longtitude.

Certain additions to the Company shortly afterwards brought the total number of members to twenty, each of whom was supposed to subscribe to shares to the value of £200—which subsequently was increased to £500—and was to receive profits on the venture in proportion to his paid-up shares. Among the members, in addition to Pym, were the Earl of Warwick (who, formerly Robert Rich, had succeeded his father to the Earldom in 1619), Lord Brooke, Sir Nathaniel Rich (a kinsman of Warwick), Sir Benjamin Rudyerd, and Sir Thomas Barrington (Pym's brother-in-law). All of these were leading Puritans, and the last three had already been closely associated with one another and with Pym in the parliamentary struggle against the arbitrary government of Charles I ; and they would be associated with him yet again in later parliaments. It was this relationship between the colonial and the political activities of the members of the Providence Adventurers which made the Company of paramount importance in the career of John Pym. To the political significance of the Company we shall return later. But, in order to see the activities of the Company

[1] C.S.P., Col.   [2] Ibid.

in their right perspective, we have first to try to understand why this group of parliamentary leaders became engrossed in the project of colonization.

The term "Adventurers" in their official title must, of course, be interpreted according to the meaning which it held in the seventeenth century and had held for centuries before that : they were men who ventured capital for the promotion of a commercial enterprise from which they hoped to derive profit, this profit being distributed among them in proportion to the sums they had respectively invested. The final outcome of the enterprise might be additional territory or prestige for the State ; but the immediate purpose of the adventure was commercial profit. Nor was the Providence Company either an exception to this rule or an isolated instance. Nevertheless, the element of colonization was becoming more prominent in the companies of the time. Whereas the closing years of Elizabeth's reign had seen the formation of numerous purely trading companies (such as the Turkey Company which was incorporated in 1587, and the East India Company of 1600), the opening years of the Stuarts were seeing companies which included among their activities not only trading but settlement. Thus, in 1606 the London and the Plymouth companies were incorporated for the foundation of Virginia where a permanent settlement was made in the following year ; in 1620 the Pilgrim Fathers founded the first New England Colony at New Plymouth ; and this was followed in 1628 and 1629 by the foundation of Massachusetts. In part, this expansion overseas was due to the maritime activity which characterized the Age of Elizabeth and after, but only in part. Latterly other motives had been having an increasing influence.

First, the period was one of economic derangement and of widespread poverty. The fall in the value of money, owing to the influx of the precious metals from Spanish and Portuguese America, caused the serious impoverishment of large numbers of English people, especially of those whose incomes were more or less fixed, not least of those whose wealth consisted of land. At the same time, landowners were being adversely affected by the general depression in the cloth trade. Crises in the cloth industry were no new phenomenon.[1] If we consider only the period covered by Pym's life, we may notice that at the beginning of that period the export of English cloth was being crippled by England's enemy, Philip II of Spain, who was using his influence in Europe to hamper the sale of English cloth. But the restoration of peace with Spain at the beginning of James I's reign did not restore the clothiers' prosperity, and by 1622 the widespread depression was so acute that a commission was appointed to investigate the problem. The resulting report referred to numerous contributory causes, such as bad workmanship, faulty materials, and dyes, and the like. One of the explanations offered was that :

The present state of the times by reason of the wars in Germany is conceived by many to be some present impediment to the vent of our cloth, partly by the interruption of passages, partly for want of money occasioned by foraging of the countries.

If the Thirty Years' War was a cause of the decline of the English wool trade—and hence indirectly of the impoverishment of the English landowners—as early as 1622, when that war had been raging for only three or four years, its crippling effect must have been an ever-increasing factor in the years that followed. The final outcome of the war was to lay the German countries waste and to turn them into a desert which would not fully flourish again for nearly two centuries. The process of devastation would not be complete until the end of the war in 1648 ; but by 1630 —when the Providence Company was incorporated—the impoverishment of the people of Germany was already so marked as to reduce considerably their ability to continue to buy English wool. The decline in the wool trade, added to the decline in the value of money, was a serious blow to the English landowners. They therefore had to seek some means of supplementing their incomes. It is surely more than mere coincidence that the leaders of the Providence Company—including John Pym himself—were not merchants or mariners but were landowners.

[1] See Lipson : *The Economic History of England*, III, 303–10.

A second motive undoubtedly was fear for the security of religious freedom, a motive exemplified notably by the expedition of the Pilgrim Fathers of 1620. But their expedition was as much a symbol and an example as it was a fact. The growing influence which Laud was exercising over the King—Laud was made Bishop of London in 1628, and Archbishop of Canterbury in 1633—and his growing activity in enforcing High Church practices, acted as a correspondingly growing incentive to the Puritans and to the hitherto orthodox Churchmen (like Pym) to establish settlements overseas where there might be freedom of conscience and of worship.

To these two motives of profit and religious freedom which inspired the Adventurers, there must be added a political motive, namely, that of providing a means of escape from the increasingly arbitrary government of Charles.

That all the twenty members of the Company were consciously inspired by all three of these motives equally would be an assumption unwarranted by the facts at our disposal. Doubtless some were moved more by one consideration than by the others. Even so, there cannot be any real doubt as to this three-fold explanation of the growing interest in the seventeenth-century settlements beyond the sea. To John Pym, all three motives would make their appeal : he was a considerable landowner, a staunch Elizabethan Churchman, and a champion of the rights of parliamentary government.

As the period of arbitrary rule continued after 1629, men's minds turned more and more to the lands overseas as providing a solution of their problems. Thus in March 1632, the Earl of Warwick, who was President of the New England Council, made a grant at Saybrook (Connecticut) to eleven individuals of whom five were already members of the Providence Company. These five were Lord Saye and Sele, Lord Brooke, Sir Nathaniel Rich, Richard Knightley, and John Pym, not to mention the Earl of Warwick himself. Another well-known name among the grantees is that of John Hampden. Nearly four years passed before a small settlement was made at Saybrook. Even then its progress was slow, and nothing very considerable had been accomplished by the time that the energies of the Saybrook patentees were once more absorbed by the political crisis of 1637-40 in England.

The first expedition to Providence set sail in February 1631 [1] in the *Seaflower* and reached Providence in May. The little vessel, of only two hundred tons burden, carried ninety emigrants of various classes. The influence of Pym is indicated by the appointment of William Rous as a member of the Council of the Island, he being a grandson of Pym's stepfather, Sir Anthony Rous. Also, in 1632, one of Sir Anthony's sons, Arthur, was sent out with two other ministers to care for the religious and moral welfare of the settlers. [2] " Arthur Rous is elected one of the ministers for that island, he being contented to transport himself and family thither ; a fit place and lands are assigned to him and further encouragement promised." Incidentally, Arthur Rous' career on the island proved to be brief : within a few months fever had carried him off. Nor was his career entirely commendable. In June 1634 an enquiry into the conduct of another minister— Ditloff by name—served to reveal certain facts about the conduct of Arthur Rous which were not regarded as consistent with his office. According to the minutes of a meeting held at Brooke House on 19th June 1634 : [3]

Mr. Ditloff adds that he was informed Mr. Rous was insufficient, not able to pray extempore, and would, soldierlike, beat his men ; that he wrote if those things were true Mr. Rous was fitter for a buff coat than a cassock, but afterwards found it otherwise. Mr. Rous taught him songs called catches, " the meaning of which word he understood not ", the matter of which was the motion of creatures as the nightingale and the like, and Messrs. Rous and Sherland sang with him, but never on the Sabbath day.

About the same time, councillor Lieutenant William Rous also was causing difficulties. He was reported to have attacked the person of Forman—who, as a smith, was of more than average value on the island—during an argument ; and a meeting of the Company, held at Brooke House on 1st July 1634, [4] " Ordered

---

[1] C.S.P., Col., 7th February 1631.   [2] Ibid., Col., 13th April 1632.
[3] Ibid., Col., under dates quoted.   [4] Ibid., Col., under dates quoted.

that Rous be suspended until he makes a public acknowledgment, according to the censure". According to the "Minutes of a Court of Providence Island", held at Brooke House on 30th July 1634, this situation was cleared up at the instance of Pym:[1] "Lieut. Rous, at the request of Mr. Treasurer, is pardoned with a caution." And again, under date 6th August: "his offence of striking Forman, is freely remitted at the entreaty of John Pym, Treasurer of the Company, without any public acknowledgment."

But Pym's influence is to be seen in more than the favours that he gained for his relatives. Just as, during the Long Parliament and during the opening stage of the Civil War, Pym was to be the pivot of the parliamentary resistance to the King, so he was the pivot of the enterprise in Providence. At every step in the history of the settlement, his strong directing purpose and his tireless attention to details are alike evident. Through his hands passed the entire business of the Company. This included what we should now regard as a treasurer's proper care, namely, the raising —partly by the subscriptions of members and partly by short-term loans from friends—of the capital necessary for the Company's various expeditions and activities and for the payment of accounts and wages. But it included also much that had no direct connection with finance. Thus, when, in March 1633, the Company decided to send out a trading expedition to Darien,[2] it was Pym who not only made the business arrangements for the voyage but who in addition drew up detailed instructions to the commander, Richard Lane, about the conduct of the expedition. The following instruction is typical:[3]

After having planted his madder, to take on board Roger Floud and other persons, not to exceed eight, as the Governor and Council of Providence think fit. To go to the Bay of Darien, with goods for trade. To provide against fear of discovery by the Spaniards, and foul weather. To use means to ingratiate himself and company with the Indians. Not to give cause to suspect the value of their gifts. To conceal the object of their coming, but to express a

[1] C.S.P., Col., under dates quoted.
[2] Ibid., Col., 26th March 1633.
[3] Ibid., Col., 15th April 1633.

desire of renewing friendship with them, " favourers of the English nation, and especially of Don Francisco Draco (whose name they seem to honour) ". To make advantage of them by trade for gold, etc. ; discover what things may be obtained from them, and their value ; labour to possess them with the natural goodness of the English nation ; and restrain any boisterous carriage to the women, and particularly " mocking, pointing, or laughing at their nakedness ".

—and so on, and so on. There seems no limit to the multiplicity of the tasks to which Pym gave his attention. What is of even greater interest than the instructions themselves is the reflection which they give of the man that lay behind them : that reflection is entirely in keeping with what we see of him elsewhere, consisting, as it does, of carefully thought-out instructions relieved by touches of naïve shrewdness—" Not to give cause to suspect the value of their gifts. To conceal the object of their coming, but to express a desire of renewing friendship with them." That the Darien project soon proved a failure was due not to any fault of Pym but to the fact that the Company's ship, the *Elizabeth*, found herself forestalled by three Dutch ships.

Hardly had the *Elizabeth* sailed for Darien when Pym devoted himself to a scheme for opening up trade with the Indians at Cape Gracias á Dios, that is, on the mainland almost immediately to the west of Providence. Once again there is abundant evidence of the meticulous care which he bestowed upon every detail of the Company's activity. During May and June 1633, he was busy with the preparations : these involved securing further contributions from the members of the Company in order to form a specific fund for the new adventure, the chartering of the ninety-ton *Golden Falcon*, the appointment of officers and crew, the purchase of supplies, and the drawing up of a policy and of instructions for trade and plantation. The treasurer's orders to Captain Sussex Camock include the following : [1]

Therefore we pray and require you to make it your first and principal care to carry God along with you in all places by the diligent performance of holy duties in your person by setting up

[1] *Colonial Entry Book*, IV, 56.

and presenting the true worship of God in the hearts and lives of all your company, so far as you shall be able. Also to restrain and prevent to your utmost power all sins and disorders, as swearing, drunkenness, uncleanness or the like, which will render the name of Christians odious to the very Heathen and be infinitely prejudicial to the business you take in hand by drawing the curse of God upon your endeavours.

This instruction, notwithstanding its mixed reference to good living and good business, is significant of the deep religious basis of the colonizing enterprise. The adventurers were not content merely to make an immediate commercial profit : they looked forward to permanent settlements where religion would be free ; and such settlements could succeed only on condition that the lives of the individual pioneers were soundly religious and that friendly relations were maintained with the natives. Pym was anticipating by half a century the principles of William Penn in Pennsylvania ; and subsequent events were to prove, in both instances alike, that success would be assured only while these two conditions were fulfilled.

What was true of Pym's influence in these early days of the Company's history remained equally true throughout the dozen years of its effective life ; it was his directive energy alone which made its enterprise possible. The value which the Company placed upon his services was indicated when, towards the close of 1633, Pym was sued by the Attorney-General for remaining in London. This was in pursuance of a royal Proclamation of June 1632 ordering country gentlemen to leave London and to return to their estates so that they might discharge their public duties as Justices of the Peace. Heavy fines were imposed upon offenders. A meeting of the Court for Providence Island " ordered that the Company petition the King for the Treasurer's stay in London as their affairs would be greatly prejudiced should he be forced to remove to the country ".[1] Probably it was the enormous and constant toll which the treasurership exacted from him which led him, more than once, to try to remove the burden. The minutes

[1] C.S.P., Col., 2nd December 1633.

of a court for Providence Island, held on 14th May 1632, include the note : [1] " Request of John Pym to be relieved from his place of treasurer, referred to the next meeting." In May 1635, the minutes of the Company show that Pym once again had raised the same question : [2] " Mr. Treasurer's Proposition to be discharged with credit and without loss, from the office he had held from the first incorporation of the Company, to be considered." His anxiety on this latter occasion to be released was very possibly connected with his desire to settle once more at Brymore. As we saw in our opening chapter, it was in March 1635 that he revoked the indenture which, twenty-one years earlier, had granted away the use of his estates. What arguments were brought to bear upon him is unknown : but three days later he consented to be re-elected as treasurer. From that point he seems to have placed himself unreservedly and unflaggingly at the disposal of the Company : only on such an assumption is it possible to explain the work that he managed to do in its service. It was Pym who directed the experimental planting and treating of various types of tobacco, cotton, madder, indigo, and flax ; and it was he who arranged for their marketing not only in England but also on the continent of Europe. For the work in the plantations white men proved unsuitable, and in 1633 negroes were introduced into the island. By 1635, the settlement included : [3] " About 500 able persons, and 30 or 40 women, who have as yet no commerce, but are endeavouring to trade with the Indians." In addition to the white men and women mentioned above, there were the Indians, perhaps bringing the total population to about six hundred and fifty.

The members of a settlement numbering more than five hundred men and women were not likely to preserve a uniform view of life or to be inspired by identical principles of conduct. That is to say, the mere size of the settlement was likely to foster divergences of opinion among its members. More than that, there were features in the character of the settlement which intensified such diver-

[1] Ibid., Col., 14th May 1632.   [2] Ibid., Col., 4th May 1635.
[3] Ibid., Col., 21st December 1635.

gences. Not the least of these features was the dominant religious motive of the promoters who had encouraged a religious type of settler and had sent out ministers to ensure a general decorum of conduct and, in particular, proper observance of the Sabbath. Such settlers were likely to be men of determined views. The effect of these conditions was the kind of controversy that we have already seen respecting the behaviour of ministers Ditloff and Arthur Rous. The ministers, in such a community, were almost certain to fall between two stools : if they mixed freely with the generality of their flock they would be charged by the " Godly " section with being false shepherds ; if they tried to carry out the stricter functions of their office and to restrain the more pleasure-loving members, the latter would regard them as straight-laced busy-bodies. Certain of the ministers, whose views about the relation between religion and politics were not very different in principle from the views of the Scottish Covenanting ministers, interfered unduly with the governors and their subordinates. The general effect of these conditions was twofold. First, the settle-ment lost its original religious character ; and, second, friction and division grew between the settlers. As the years passed, this two-fold effect became more and more marked, and not all the vigilance and skill of Pym in England could arrest it. Before long, Provi-dence ceased to be fitted for development into a peculiarly religious commonwealth and a home of freedom from arbitrary govern-ment. Instead, it had become a typical settlement of various sorts of people anxious only to secure a livelihood no matter by what means, not least by fortifying the island as a centre of piratical expeditions against Spanish settlements and ships in the neighbour-hood.

These years, during which Pym was absorbed by colonial diffi-culties, were years also of acute political difficulties in England. It was these latter difficulties which brought the Providence Adventurers back into the full flood of English politics. The ship-money question provides a perfect illustration of this process. In 1634, Charles I levied his first writ of ship money ; and in 1635 he extended his demands to inland towns. In 1636, three men refused to pay the ship money demanded by the King's writ, namely, the Earl of Warwick, Lord Saye, and John Hampden ; and of these the first two were members of the Providence Company, and all were members of the Saybrook Company. Warwick did his utmost to induce the Court to take proceedings against him, but without success ; Lord Saye was dealt with indirectly by being tried before the Star Chamber on another charge ; and only Hampden's refusal was made a test case by the Court. In March 1637 the writ was issued from the Chancery against Hampden. During February 1637 several meetings of members of the Providence Company had been held not in London but at Preston in Northamptonshire where was the house of Richard Knightley, a member of the Providence and Saybrook Companies.[1] In the light of the co-operation of these same individuals later against the King, and of the leadership which they provided for the Parliamentary party, it is difficult to resist the conclusion that at the Northampton meetings the plans were formulated for concerted action against ship money. Here was the nucleus of what was to become, in the Long Parliament, the great Parliamentary party in regular opposition to the Court. When that day came, it was Pym who provided the party's statesmanship ; and we may make a fairly confident guess, in view of all that we have seen of his activity as Treasurer of the Company, that it was he also who was the director of the plans made at the Company's meetings early in 1637.

One other connection there was between politics and the members of the Providence Company, namely, that, with the increase of political and religious opposition, certain members of the Company turned their eyes to their lands overseas as providing a way of escape. Reports of specific plans of emigration by Warwick and Saye, and even by Hampden and Pym, are conflicting and uncertain. Perhaps all that we are justified in deducing from the prevalence of the reports is that emigration was in the air and that, if affairs in England had taken a somewhat different course, the leading Adventurers might have transferred themselves to Provi-

[1] C.S.P., Col., 24th, 26th, 27th February 1637.

dence. What were the motives which kept them in England—
whether attachment to England and to their estates, or whether
the plans which they were maturing for a political campaign—
we can only guess at. What is certain is that, had they gone abroad,
the whole course of subsequent English history must have been
changed, and that it was their decision to remain which settled
the fate of the Stuarts.

Meanwhile, conditions in Providence were going from bad to
worse. When once the original, uniform character of the colonists
was broken down, so that the control of the Company's officials
at home grew less effective, deterioration was inevitable. Moreover, piracy against the Spaniards was at best a short-sighted policy
certain to provoke reprisals ; for, if the Spaniards determined upon
reprisals on a large scale, the colonists would be in a helpless plight.
Providence was a tiny, isolated island against which the neigh-
bouring Spanish settlements would be able to muster forces so
overwhelming as to be ultimately irresistible, no matter how
skilful and valiant the English defence might be. Such was, indeed,
exactly the course which events actually followed.

As early as July 1635, a fleet of Spanish vessels tried to rush the
island's defences and land parties of troops. The difficulty of
manœuvring in the treacherous shoals close in shore, and of landing
men in face of the settlers' fire, compelled the Spaniards to withdraw discomfited. News of the attack was brought home by the
Expectation in December 1635.

Letters have been received from the Governor, Council, and
other inhabitants there, which state that upon 24 July last a Spanish
fleet attacked the island, but unable to land amongst the rocks,
were, after five days, beaten off, being much torn and battered
by the ordnance from the forts.[1]

Though the Spaniards were repulsed for the moment, they would
certainly return more adequately prepared both in equipment and
in numbers. From the beginning of 1636, therefore, the policy
of Pym and his fellow-Adventurers changed. Instead of aiming
at establishing in Providence a settlement for the reception of

[1] C.S.P., Col., 21st December 1635.

colonists with lofty political and religious ideals, the Company became concerned chiefly with perfecting the island's defences and equipping the settlers to undertake reprisals. This policy would involve heavy expenditure ; and in January 1636 the Company decided to reorganize itself at home and to raise new stock to the extent of £10,000.

1636. January 29. Minutes of a Court for Providence Island. The Treasurer informs the Company that upon arrival of the Expectation, a declaration concerning the state of the island was addressed to the Earl of Holland, who having acquainted the King therewith, liberty was given to the Company to right themselves ; and that whatever they should take in the West Indies by way of reprisal, should be adjudged lawful. The Sec. is directed to send letters to the absent adventurers, to give notice of the ship's arrival, of the necessity of a speedy supply, and of the encouragement received from the State. The proportion of charge to pay off debts and to carry on the work is computed at £10,000. Several propositions are made as to whether the Company should carry on the plantation by themselves, deliver it over to the State, or otherwise.

Several meetings of the Company followed during February 1636.

February 13. Minutes of a Court for Providence Island. Lord Brooke undertakes to supply the money not underwritten for, short of £10,000 for sending 500 men and ammunition to Providence. After serious deliberation touching the present state of the plantations, it is ordered that the subscription of a new joint stock be offered to every adventurer who will enjoy certain privileges.

1st March, 1636. Agreement between the Company and Captain Robt. Hunt. Capt. Hunt to go by the next ship, and be Governor of Providence Island during the Company's pleasure.

The terms of the minute of 29th January show that piracy had become part of the official policy of the Company. From the very outset the new enterprise seemed ill-fated. The frequent piratical expeditions of the settlers met with only a small measure of success, and certainly failed to justify the hopes that the plunder obtained would more than compensate for the heavy cost of the preparations. Also, the period beginning 1637 saw the increasing preoccupation of the members of the Company in politics in England ; hence, when the Spaniards should renew their attack, the colonists were likely to have to rely largely upon their own resources. In May 1640 a Spanish attack once again failed to effect a landing. But the triumph of the settlers was to prove only a short breathing-space. In May 1641 the Spaniards sent from Cartagena an expedition of several large vessels carrying some two thousand men. Such a force was irresistible. We need not delay over the details of the fight. Before May 1641 was out, the whole Island of Providence was in Spanish hands. Of the settlers, some of the men managed to escape ; their less fortunate fellows remained prisoners to the Spaniards, while the women and children were allowed to return to England in an English ship.

So ended the colonizing enterprise on Providence. The Adventurers, instead of reaping a substantial profit, were left heavily in debt. On 8th February 1642, at a company meeting held at Brooke House, the facts were laid before the members present and the liability of each Adventurer was explained. " A note of the Company's debts was now presented by the Secretary and it is ordered that the same be distributed amongst the several members of the Company." [1] By this time the Civil War was in sight, and no final settlement of the Company's affairs was then possible. When the war was over, Pym was no longer alive to direct the Company's business. The last known meeting of the Company took place on 5th February 1650,[2] after which, so far as can be traced, the Company ceased to exist.

Perhaps the only measure that could have saved the settlement would have been that, early in its history and before deterioration set in, some at least of the leading Adventurers should have carried out their half-formed idea of themselves going out as settlers. Just as the emigration of the Pilgrim Fathers to New England in 1620 ensured to their venture a success such as would have been impossible had they tried merely to direct affairs from this side of the Atlantic, so only could the original character and purpose of the Providence settlement have been preserved.

[1] *Colonial Entry Book*, III, 393.   [2] C.S.P., Col.

For our purpose, the failure of Providence is of minor importance. What was of far greater consequence was that the experiment had given to Pym yet further opportunities to display and improve his capacity for leadership, and, even more, that it had brought into constant and active co-operation the men who were to champion the rights of Parliament and of the nation against the arbitrary rule of Charles I.

Part III

KING CHARLES *VERSUS* JOHN PYM

CHAPTER VII

THE SHORT PARLIAMENT

THE eleven years during which the activities of Pym and his friends had been engaged in colonizing were the years also when the struggle between the King and the majority of the nation was working to a climax. Pym was not directly concerned in any of the conflicts with the King during the period : for example, his name does not appear in the lists of those who refused to pay ship-money. Of this apparent acquiescence in the " Eleven Years' Tyranny "—constitutional, legal, and religious—there are two explanations. First, and obvious, Pym's absorption in the Providence Adventure left him but little opportunity for political activities : his return to political life in 1640 coincided with the virtual end of the adventure. Second, and more important, this politically passive attitude was consistent with Pym's practice throughout his career, namely, that he never challenged the King's government except in and through Parliament. He had adopted a similar attitude between Charles' second and third parliaments when he had contributed to the Forced Loan, or so we must suppose in the absence of evidence to the contrary. In this respect, as in others, consistency was one of Pym's outstanding characteristics. Always he seems to have avoided any action which would have given the Court an excuse to proceed against him when Parliament was not in session, that is to say when he could not claim freedom from arrest. Pym had no intention of engaging in a duel in which his opponent would have, for the moment, the monopoly both of weapons and of seconds : he preferred to reserve his resources for a contest in which the chances would be more even.

Though Pym took no personal share in national affairs between 1629 and 1640, those affairs would shape the stage on which, for the brief remainder of his life, he was to play the leading part. As before, it was over finance that the sharpest and most immediate clash took place. Charles' first care was to curtail his extraordinary expenses, particularly those due to war. Parliament had been dissolved on 10th March 1629. On 14th April, peace was signed at Susa between England and France ; and in November 1630 a treaty was signed with Spain, this being followed by the Spanish king's promise to try to secure the restoration of the Palatinate to the Elector—which evidently marked a return to the inept foreign policy of James I. The death of Gustavus Adolphus in the hour of victory at Lützen on 6th November 1632 ended the last chance that the Elector Frederick would have of recovering the Palatinate. Within a fortnight of Lützen, Frederick himself was carried off by fever. Frederick's death removed one of the more serious encumbrances of both James and Charles ; for, though his claims descended to his eldest son, Charles Louis, the cause of the Palatinate ceased to agitate the people or the policy of England. Incidentally, King Charles' neglect of Charles Louis was reciprocated ; for Charles Louis, unlike his brother Rupert, favoured the Parliamentary cause in England—a fact to which we shall refer again.

At the same time as Charles was reducing his expenditure by making peace abroad, he was trying to raise non-parliamentary revenue at home. This he did mainly by reviving obsolete statutes. In January 1630 a statute of Edward I was invoked to compel the owners of land worth more than forty shillings to take up knighthood ; those who refused were fined, and within two years well over £100,000 had thus accrued to the King. Fines were imposed also for encroachments on forests ; and, once again, it was a survey carried out under Edward I which was taken as the basis of the forest boundaries. Though these, and other similar, fines could be justified by ancient statutes, they were more, rather than less, irksome on that account. Other financial expedients lacked even that much legal pretence : tunnage and poundage continued to be levied without parliamentary authority ; forced loans and benevolences were exacted ; monopolies were revived—the

1624 law against them being evaded by granting monopolistic rights to companies instead of to individuals—which brought in handsome profits to their holders who had paid large sums to the royal exchequer for the privilege ; and, as we have already seen, ship-money was levied. The question of ship-money was not easy to pronounce clear judgment upon. No one denied that there were precedents for the levy upon seaports in time of war (that is, in national danger) or that the decision as to what constituted national danger rested with the King. The contention of the opponents of ship-money was that the country was not at war and that there existed no emergency so urgent as to preclude the summoning of a parliament in time to deal with it. This was, in effect, the contention of Hampden's counsel, Oliver St. John, at the great trial of 1637. That trial was a test case in more ways than the King had originally intended : the intensity of the public interest which it aroused, and the fact that the defendant was condemned by the smallest possible majority (seven out of twelve) of the King's judges of the Exchequer Court, showed how narrow was the margin of safety which Charles was allowing himself. Moreover, the small majority was hailed by the nation as tantamount to a victory for political freedom, and the supporters of parliamentary government were thereby encouraged to press their advantage.

In fairness to Charles it must be stated that the suspicion which formerly rested upon him of using the revenue brought in by ship-money for purposes other than the building of ships is now recognized as groundless. " It is now known that ship-money was really used to build a fleet of great ships which was to serve as the nucleus of the naval power of the Commonwealth in the first Dutch War." [1] This appears to have been typical of Charles' financial system. Charles' idea was that he was responsible for the conduct of the State, and if Parliament would not grant him the necessary resources he must find other means of raising the funds necessary for the purpose. Not only were the taxes and loans applied to the purpose for which they were raised, but

[1] Tanner : *English Constitutional Conflicts*, p. 77.

finances as a whole were efficiently administered. Indeed, it was this efficiency which, from Parliament's point of view, constituted its greatest danger. Towards the end of the Eleven Years' Tyranny, the King's revenue from unparliamentary taxation was sufficient to meet his needs. Unless some exceptionally heavy national expenditure had become necessary, Charles might apparently have continued without a parliament indefinitely.

It was in 1637, the very year of Hampden's case, that events elsewhere—namely, in Scotland—were shaping themselves as though to suit the purposes of the parliamentary party. In order to pick up the threads of these events, we have to retrace our steps over a few years. If finance was the cause of outward clashes between King and people, the underlying motive was still religion. The religious issue centred around William Laud. About Laud's personal piety, ecclesiastical sincerity, and organizing efficiency there never has been any doubt. His strongest passion was to ensure the supremacy of Episcopacy, as the divinely appointed system of church government, and to use that system in order to enforce uniformity of belief and ritual. As Bishop of London (1628), and later as Archbishop of Canterbury (1633), Laud accomplished much commendable work in removing irregularities from the lives of the clergy and from church services, and in restoring church fabrics. But along with these reforms, he introduced such changes as removing the communion table from the centre of the church to the east end where it was railed off and reserved for the priest, and insisting on the use of the surplice and on bowing at the name of Jesus. Further, he suppressed Puritan preachers— most of whom were still clergy in the Established Church—and Puritan books ; and in October 1633 James I's *Declaration of Sports* was reissued to encourage games on Sundays after afternoon services, a practice which the Puritans regarded as a desecration of the Sabbath. Laud's High Church innovations thus offended both the orthodox Elizabethan churchmen, like Pym, and the Puritans.

Individuals who ventured to oppose the Laudian régime were dealt with by the arbitrary courts of Star Chamber and High

Commission. For example, in February 1634 the lawyer Prynne was brought before the Star Chamber. In his book *Histrio-mastix* (that is, Actor's Scourge) he had written against stage plays and particularly against female actors. This was interpreted as an attack on the Court, since the King loved to watch plays and the Queen loved to act in them ; also it was one of the Archbishop's functions to licence stage plays. Prynne was sentenced to a fine of £5,000, life imprisonment, expulsion from his profession, and to have both ears cut off in the pillory. The ears were duly shorn and Prynne was imprisoned, but he remained undaunted. He spent his time in prison in writing attacks on the bishops. In 1637 he was accordingly brought a second time before the Star Chamber. Along with him, and charged with similar offences, were Henry Burton, a clergyman, and John Bastwick, a physician. *The Litany of John Bastwick* had included the prayer : " From plague, pestilence, and famine ; from bishops, priests and deacons, good Lord deliver us " ; and Bastwick had further declared the Church to be " as full of ceremonies as a dog is full of fleas ". On 30th June the three were set in the pillory in Palace Yard where the remaining stumps of Prynne's ears were severed, and his companions suffered similarly. Thence they were despatched to their respective prisons at Carnarvon, Lancaster, and Launceston, the roads being lined with sympathizers who supplied the prisoners with refreshment for the journey. Such brutalities became associated in the people's minds with Laud's system. In July 1637 the hands of Laud were further strengthened against Puritan writings by a Star Chamber decree forbidding the printing or reprinting of any unlicensed book or pamphlet and ordering that any printer who set up an un-authorized press should be sent to the pillory.

In order to ensure the success of his aims, Laud strengthened the traditional co-operation between Church and Crown. He became one of the foremost champions of Divine Right, so that, in the eyes of the nation, Laud's Arminianism became identified with Charles' Absolutism. Opposition to the one therefore implied opposition to the other. And Laud possessed a superb talent for provoking opposition. His methods of carrying out his reforms, no less than the reforms themselves, aroused widespread antagonism. He was tactless in dealing with individuals, had no conception of compromising temporarily on details in order finally to achieve his main objective, and regarded inflexibility of will as identical with strength of character. In a word, he lacked the touch of genius necessary to transform administrative efficiency into statesmanship. Of Archbishop Laud, as of no one else, except perhaps of Buckingham, the King might have prayed : " Save me from my friend " : within a short time of his elevation to the Primacy, Laud had combined so many elements of the nation in bitter opposition to himself and his ecclesiastical system that his fall was inevitable ; and of necessity his fall involved that of the King.

The details of Laud's career are beyond our province. The climax came not in England but in Scotland. In 1633 Charles visited his northern kingdom, and in June he was crowned at Holyrood. Laud did not become Primate until August, but, as Bishop of London, he accompanied the King to Scotland. The future Archbishop's interest in the condition of the Church in Scotland was natural and even commendable, Episcopacy having been already established in Scotland by Acts of 1584 and 1612. It was during this visit that the decision was taken to introduce an English Prayer Book to Scotland, though the introduction was postponed. In 1636 Charles issued new Canons for Scotland. These enjoined numerous practices and principles utterly repugnant to the Presbyterian mind : the removal of the communion table to the upper end of the church, the confession of offences to the presbyter, the acceptance of the whole Prayer Book when it should be published, and the recognition of the King as the head of the Church. What was as objectionable as the contents of the Canons was their being issued on the authority of the King alone without the approval of either Parliament or Assembly. Not until the middle of 1637 were all the preparations for the new Prayer Book regarded as complete ; and on 23rd July the book came into use in St. Giles' Cathedral in Edinburgh. The result was uproar in the cathedral, followed, during several months, by a series of riots against the Town Council and against the Lord Treasurer Traquair who was regarded as the representative in Scotland of the King and his archbishop.

In February 1638 the popular opposition to the new religious order expressed itself by the formation of an organization known as The Tables, consisting of four committees representative of the chief sections of the nation : the first of nobles, and the others of four gentlemen, four ministers, and four burgesses respectively. The Tables might meet either separately or together. Before February was out, the Covenant of 1581—provoked by the Roman Catholic crisis of that period—was renewed, and copies were being distributed through Scotland for signatures. The response was immediate and all but universal : clergy and laymen, nobles and peasants flocked to sign. So menacing was the prospect that in May 1638 Charles sent his cousin the Marquis of Hamilton as special Commissioner to negotiate with the Covenanting leaders. The latter demanded the abolition of the Prayer Book and of the Court of High Commission, and the calling of a free parliament and a General Assembly of the Scottish Church. From these demands the leaders refused to budge. After long negotiations, and three visits by Hamilton to Scotland, Charles granted the Covenanters' demands (August 1638). His real object was to gain time in which to gather forces to suppress the Covenant. But Charles was dealing with a depth of religious conviction and fervour beyond his nature to plumb. The General Assembly met on 21st November, and began by debating the conduct of the bishops. Hamilton tried to check the enquiry, but his efforts were useless. In little more than a week Hamilton declared the Assembly dissolved. The only result was that the Assembly continued its work without him. Before the year was ended, the Assembly had abolished episcopacy and the service book, and had restored the Presbyterian form of church government.

This challenge to royal authority was in essence an act of rebellion and could have only one issue—war. The early months of 1639 were therefore filled with warlike preparations. In Scotland were large numbers of soldiers—both officers and men—returned from service in the Thirty Years' War, who would be immensely superior to any hastily collected levies that the English Court could put into the field. Moreover, whereas the Scottish people were solid behind the National Covenant, Charles could rely upon the whole-hearted support of only a section of the English ; indeed, the opponents of Laud's Arminianism in England were much more likely to co-operate with the Scots than to oppose them. Proof of this likelihood was forthcoming in April when Lords Brooke and Saye refused to take the oath to fight for the King—thus incidentally providing yet further evidence of the connection between the Providence Adventure and politics at home. Alexander Leslie, who had seen honourable service under the great Gustavus Adolphus, was chosen as the Scottish commander. Leslie led his men southward to a point within ten miles of the border whence he could command the roads through Berwick. Charles marched north as far as Berwick but, having no army fit to challenge the Covenanters (nor, in the absence of a parliament, the means of raising one), was compelled to negotiate ; and in June 1639 terms were arranged. The Treaty of Berwick stipulated that both the Scottish and the English armies should be disbanded, that the Covenanters should restore the royal castles which they had already seized, and that a Scottish parliament should meet to decide civil matters and a General Assembly to decide ecclesiastical matters.

The General Assembly duly met at Edinburgh on 12th August. Any chance of success that the meeting might have had was already prejudiced by Charles' action in summoning the bishops to be members of it. The Assembly took up the challenge and once more abolished Episcopacy, an action to which Traquair, its president, assented in the King's name. With the Parliament, Charles fared no better than with the Assembly. Since neither side was willing to compromise, a renewal of war was almost inevitable and war would necessitate supplies which, in adequate quantities, only a parliament could provide. Accordingly, writs for a new English Parliament were issued. The elections were held in March 1640. On 13th April, the Eleven Years' Tyranny came to an end with the opening of what was to be known as the Short Parliament.

The summoning of this parliament had been in accordance with the advice of Wentworth, and from the moment of its meeting Wentworth became more and more the pivot of the political situation. We have seen how in 1628, after the passage of the Petition of Right and before the murder of Buckingham, Wentworth had offered his services to the King and had become Lord Wentworth. In December 1628 he became President of the Council in the North (which had been established—or, according to modern historians, re-established—by Henry VIII in 1537 to restore and maintain order in the northern shires after the Pilgrimage of Grace) and was further created Viscount Wentworth. The vigour of his rule in the north led to his being transferred, in January 1632, to Ireland where he was appointed Lord Deputy. Ireland was then in a desperate condition, torn with strife, both political and religious, and seemed on the verge of complete anarchy. Hopeless as the situation seemed, Wentworth's appearance wrought a transformation. An army with Protestant officers was raised; Laud's High Church system was rigorously enforced; and the Protestants of Ulster were encouraged by the introduction of the linen industry. Efficiency, with its motto of "Thorough", was the hall-mark of Wentworth's administration. As never before in its history, Ireland had peace and security. A man who could thus produce order for disorder, soundness for rottenness, in Ireland, was evidently of a calibre exactly suited to solve the even greater problems of the King in England and Scotland; and by September 1639 Wentworth had become Charles' most valued counsellor. He was not slow to take in the essentials of the situation. He had no patience with the Scots or with those Englishmen who truckled to them instead of supporting their king, and he was at Charles' side during the fruitless negotiations with the Scots in the latter part of 1639. Nevertheless, he realized that adequate resistance to the Scots could be made only with parliamentary support: hence his advice that the King should summon another parliament. As a mark of royal confidence, in

January 1640 Wentworth was raised to be Earl of Strafford. To the Members of the Short Parliament, therefore, it was clear that, in any struggle against the King, their real and most formidable enemy would be Strafford. Hence, the parliamentary leaders set themselves to pursue him to his fall. From that purpose they refused to be deflected ; and their pursuit was further embittered by what the opposition regarded as Strafford's apostasy from their ranks and by certain personal animosities. A month before Parliament met, Strafford had crossed over to Ireland for the meeting of the Dublin Parliament. So great was his prestige that the four subsidies for which he asked were granted amid wild enthusiasm. Within ten days of the opening of the English Parliament, Strafford, in spite of a violent attack of gout, was back at the King's side.

In certain respects the new parliament was very different from the first three parliaments of the reign. First, the elections had gone badly for the King's party, so that the opposition was appreciably strengthened. Second, the passing of eleven years since the previous parliament had caused a change of personnel : Clarendon's comment is that " much the greatest part [had] never before sat in Parliament ".[1] (It was in this parliament that Clarendon himself, as Edward Hyde, first became a Member.) Among the leaders, the effects of time were as marked as among the rank and file, death having removed Sir John Eliot (in prison), Sir Edward Coke, and Sir Robert Phelips. Pym alone remained equipped both by personal qualities and by experience as the champion of parliamentary government and national liberty. Clarendon writes of him as " a man of good reputation, but much better known afterwards, who had been as long in those assemblies as any man then living ".[2] The only other Member who had already made a national reputation for opposition to the Court, and who was not new to Parliament, was John Hampden. From the opening of the Short Parliament until Pym's death, Hampden and Pym worked in close co-operation. For several years Pym had had his lodgings in Gray's Inn Lane (it was there that the Providence Company

[1] *Great Rebellion*, Book II, Section 68.   [2] Ibid.

had held numerous meetings), and to a near-by house, in the same lane, Hampden now took his family ; [1] and when, early in the Long Parliament, Pym moved to Westminster, Hampden moved to the same district. Among other Members who were to distinguish themselves sooner or later was Oliver St. John, the defender of Hampden and now in his first parliament as Member for Totnes, and Oliver Cromwell who in the previous parliament had sat for Huntingdon and now was sitting for Cambridge town.

The attitude of Charles at the beginning of the new parliament was not encouraging. In January 1640 he had raised Sir John Finch to the Peerage as Lord Finch and had appointed him to be Lord Keeper. It was Finch who, as Speaker of the Commons, had been held down in his chair in 1629, and who, as Chief Justice of the Common Pleas, had zealously supported ship-money. Now, as Lord Keeper, at the opening of Parliament he expatiated on the King's policy. Referring to the invasion by the Scots, Finch urged the voting of subsidies for an army to repel the invaders, and promised that grievances could then be considered. On 16th April, the first day of general debate, the common resentment of this demand was expressed by Grimston, the Member for Colchester, who plainly intimated that danger from a Scottish invasion was less menacing than the danger from arbitrary government at home. Said he : [2]

There hath now a great and weighty business been presented to this House, and a Letter hath been read, importing . . . a defection of the King's natural subjects. This is a great cause, and very worthy of the consideration and advisement of this great Council. But I am very much mistaken, if there be not a case here at home of as great danger as that which is already put. . . . The danger that hath now been presented to the House, it standeth at a distance ; and we heartily wish it were further off : yet as it stands at a distance, it is so much the less dangerous. But the case that I shall put, is a case of great danger here at home.

The following day the debate became at once broader and deeper. The lead was given by Pym. In a speech of the then

[1] Nugent : *Memorials of Hampden*, I, 296.
[2] Rushworth, III, 1128–9.

exceptional length of two hours, Pym expounded the fundamental principles of government, both political and religious, which his party regarded as in jeopardy through royal encroachments.[1] He divided his speech into three parts, each dealing with a type of grievance :

The First, are those Grievances, which during these eleven years interval of Parliaments, are against the Liberties and Privileges of Parliament.
The Second, are innovations in matters of Religion.
The Third, Grievances against the propriety of our goods.

In characteristic fashion, having recited certain acts to which he objected, he related them to fundamental principles. Under the first heading, for example, he declared :

A Parliament is that to the Commonwealth, which the soul is to the body, which is only able to apprehend and understand the symptoms of all such diseases which threaten the body politic. It behoves us therefore, to keep the faculty of that soul from distemper.

Thence he proceeded to elaborate the restraints which were imposed upon Members at the close of the previous parliament :

First, In that the Speaker the last Parliament, (the last day of it) being commanded to put the question, the House was commanded they should not speak. . . .
Secondly, In that the Parliament was then dissolved, before our grievances had redress, or before we could make our Wills known, which is the privilege of dying men, and to be heard before condemned is not denied to private persons.
Thirdly, that the Judges presume to question the proceedings of this House : it is against nature and order, that inferior courts should undertake to regulate superior. . . .
Fourthly, The several imprisonments of divers gentlemen for speaking freely in Parliament.
Fifthly, That . . . divers Members of the House were so kept in prison, till they had put in security for their good behaviour ; and some of them died in prison, others not released until writs came for this Parliament.

[1] Rushworth, III, pp. 1131–6 : another version, more elaborate, and possibly revised by Pym, is in the British Museum.

On the subject of religion he declared :

I will first observe, the great encouragement that is given to them of the Popish Religion, by an universal suspension of all Laws that are against them, and some of them admitted into public places of trust and power.

I desire not to have any new laws made against them . . . nor a strict execution of the old ones, but only so far forth, as tends to the safety of his Majesty, and such a practice of them, that the Religion that can brook no co-rival may not be the destruction of ours, by being concurrent with it.

From this point Pym went on to complain both of the encouragement which was being given to Popery in England and of the Popish innovations in the established Church, together with " the countenancing and preferring those men who were most forward in setting up such innovations " and " the discouragement of those who were known to be most conscionable and faithful followers of the truth ". In particular he complained :

We are not now contented with the old ceremonies, I mean such as the constitution of the Reformed Religion hath continued unto us. But we must introduce again many of those superstitious and infirm ceremonies, which accompanied the most decrepit age of Popery, bowing to the Altar and the like.

I shall observe the daily discouraging of all godly men, who truly profess the Protestant Religion, as though men could be too religious. . . .

The Parliament ever since Queen Elizabeth's time, desired the Bishops to deal moderately ; but how they have answered those desires we all know, and these good men for the most part feel.

Once again Pym had displayed the staunchness of his own religious convictions combined with a desire to accord freedom to others so far as the safety of the realm allowed, which provides yet another example of his typically Elizabethan attitude both to politics and to religion.

Under the third heading of the interruption in the justice of the realm, he enumerated the grievances we have already seen, including impositions, compounding for knighthood, monopolies, " that great unparalleled grievance of the ship-money ", enlargements of the forests, the misuse of the Court of Star Chamber, the making of edicts and proclamations, and the long intermission of parliaments. His opposition to these practices he bases upon historical precedent, and his conclusion contained the following ominous words :

The not observing of laws, but countenancing of monopolies and such like, breed jealousies in the minds of many, and may prepare a way for distempers, though (thanks be to God) as yet there have been none ; our Religion having preserved us. But if anything but well should happen, one summer's distempers would breed great change, and more than all unlawful courses would recompense.

We know how unfortunate Henry III and other princes have been, by the occasion of such breaking of their laws. I pray God we may never see such times. . . .

I hope the wisdom of this House will prepare such a remedy, as will make the King a great King, and the people happy.

From beginning to end, even the summary of Pym's speech which we possess shows the firm grasp of principles and the ability to shape present means to great ends, which are the marks of the highest statesmanship. The speech was a landmark both in the career of Pym and in the progress of the parliamentary struggle against the King. Gardiner's comment on the speech is not only sound judgment on the speech itself, but might well stand as a summary of the quality of Pym's statesmanship throughout his career : " That which marked Pym from henceforth as a leader of men was the moderation combined with the firmness with which every sentence was stamped." [1]

The practical effects of Pym's speech were soon evident. On 18th April, the day following its delivery, the Commons ordered that the records of Eliot's case and of the ship-money case should be produced for its consideration. The King seems to have realized the need for placating Parliament, and on 21st April both Lords and Commons were summoned to Whitehall where Finch, the Lord Keeper, informed them that the King was prepared to consider any means that Parliament could suggest as an alternative

[1] *History of England*, IX, 102.

to ship-money. Next day, Convocation voted six subsidies from the clergy (£120,000). This grant, instead of spurring on the Commons to similar generosity, had rather the opposite effect ; and when, on 24th April, the Lords, following a personal appeal by Charles, voted that supply ought to precede the redress of grievances,[1] the Commons were infuriated. The King's appeal to the Lords was due to the advice of Strafford who had only just returned from Ireland and did not appreciate either the difference between England and Ireland or the change that had taken place in the temper of Parliament since he had left the popular side : the opposition was no longer swayed by the wild oratory of Eliot but was led by the statesmanship of Pym who was quick to see that the King, through the Lords, had taken a constitutionally false step infringing the unquestionable right of the Commons over the Lords in matters of finance. The Commons, when the question was considered on 27th April,[2] drew up an address of protest which Pym was deputed to carry to the Lords. The protest which he delivered is thus recorded :[3]

Their lordships meddled with, and advised concerning, both the matter of Supply and the time when, and that before such time as the same was moved to them by the Commons. . . . The course the Committee doth offer, for repair of this breach of Privilege, is, That their Lordships be desired in their Wisdom to find out some way of Reparation of their Privileges for the present, and of prevention of the like infringement for the future. . . . They desire their Lordships to take no notice of any things that shall be debated by the Commons until they shall themselves declare the same to their Lordships, which the Commons will always observe towards the proceedings of their Lordships.

This prompt and pointed reply to the King's attempt to detach the Lords from the Commons led Strafford to advise Charles to make some concession in the matter of ship-money. Accordingly, on 4th May, the elder Sir Henry Vane, Treasurer of the Household and Secretary of State, informed the Commons that his master

[1] *Lords' Journals*, IV, 67.   [2] *Commons' Journals*, II, 13, ii.
[3] Rushworth, III, 1146.

this day hath thought fit to let you know, that of his grace and favour he is pleased, upon your granting twelve subsidies to be presently passed and to be paid in three years, . . . his Majesty will not only for the present forbear the levying of any *Ship Money*, but will give way to the utter abolishing of it, by any course that yourselves shall like best.

And for your Grievances, his Majesty will (according to his Royal Promise) give you as much time as may be now, and the next *Michaelmas* ; and he expects a present and positive answer upon which he may rely, his affairs being in such a condition as can endure no longer delay.[1]

There ensued a fierce debate both upon the principle of granting supply before the redress of grievances and upon the huge amount of the supply which the King was demanding in compensation. Vane's final refusal to make the slightest concession in that amount brought the debate to an end. Matters had evidently reached a crucial pass. At the early hour of six o'clock next morning the Privy Council met ; whereupon a dissolution was decided upon and forthwith carried out. This first parliament of 1640 had sat for only three weeks.

There can be no doubt that the immediate responsibility for the dissolution must rest upon Vane whose declaration that the King would accept nothing less than twelve subsidies had been made without fresh consultation with the King. Whitelock's comment is :[2]

Sir Henry Vane escaped not without his censures, that his commission from the King was but to demand six subsidies ; and that his mistake in requiring twelve subsidies was industrious, and on purpose to rouse the house to animosity : which took effect, but whether intended or not is hard to judge.

No satisfactory explanation of Vane's action has ever been adduced ; the only one that seems to fit the facts is that suggested by Clarendon :[3]

What followed in the next Parliament, within less than a year, made it believed that Sir H. Vane acted that part maliciously and

[1] Rushworth, III, p. 1154.
[2] Whitelock : *Memorials of English Affairs, 1625–60* (edition, 1853), I, 94.
[3] *Great Rebellion*, Book II, Section 76.

to bring all to confusion ; he being known to have an implacable hatred against the Earl of Strafford, Lieutenant of Ireland, whose destruction was then upon the anvil.

The circumstances of Strafford's impeachment, in which Pym played a decisive part, were certainly to demonstrate beyond doubt Vane's hatred of Strafford.[1]

Whatever effect Vane's action may have had in precipitating a dissolution, another factor which convinced the King of the uncompromising temper of the Commons, and of the impossibility of their making grants to enable him to suppress the Scots, was the news that some of the parliamentary leaders—including Pym —were ready with a petition that the King should make an agreement with the Scots.

Indeed, the relationship between Pym's party and the Scots was closer even than this. Whitelock, in a note which has reference to events as early as January 1640, says that :[2]

> The Scots Covenanters sent new commissioners to the king ; the Earl of Dunfermling, the Lord Loudon, Sir William Douglas, and Mr. Berkley ; the two last not mentioned in the commission. . . .
> They had great resort to them, and many secret counsels held with them by the discontented English, chiefly by those who favoured presbytery, and were no friends to bishops, or had suffered in the last censures in the star chamber, exchequer, high commission, and other judicatures.
> The Earls of Essex, Bedford, Holland, the Lord Say, Hampden, Pym, and divers other lords and gentle men of great interest and quality were deep in with them.

Among the "other lords and gentlemen" were Lord Brooke, Lord Saye's second son Nathaniel Fiennes, the younger Vane, and Oliver St. John. After the dissolution of the Short Parliament there were joint meetings at the home of Lord Saye at Broughton in Oxfordshire, and at the home of Hampden's son-in-law, Sir Richard Fawsley, at Fawsley in Northamptonshire, and also on occasion at Pym's house in Gray's Inn Lane.[3] Incidentally, this

---

[1] See below, pp. 166–70. [2] Whitelock : *Memorials*, I, 98.
[3] Nugent : *Memorials of John Hampden.*

list of names emphasizes once more that the personnel of the leaders of the parliamentary opposition was almost identical with that of the Providence Company.

Meanwhile, the dissolution of the Parliament had made the King's position worse rather than better. With every day that passed, his financial problems became more acute. The Scots still remained in arms, and if the King was unable to raise adequate supplies before summoning Parliament he would have still greater difficulty after dissolving it. All that the opposition had to do was to play a waiting game : another parliament would soon become inevitable, and that parliament, when it met, would be exasperated against the King, determined not to disperse as quickly as its predecessor, and, above all, would know that the necessities of the King placed him in their power. Nor were some of Charles' actions likely to mollify sore tempers, as the following extract illustrates :

1640. May 12 : News letter (from Edmund Rossingham).
Last Wednesday the Earl of Warwick, Lord Saye, Lord Brooke, Sir Walter Earl, John Pym, and John Hampden, all Parliament men, all had their papers taken from them.[1]

The King doubtless hoped to find incriminating evidence of the Scottish negotiations in which these men had been involved, for such negotiations with the King's enemies were undoubtedly treason. If this was his object, he was disappointed, and no further action was taken.

The best immediate policy for the King to follow was not easy to determine. His counsellors were divided in their advice. Strafford was for applying against the Scots similar offensive measures to those which had proved so successful in Ireland :

Go on with a vigorous war, as you first designed : loose and absolved from all rules of government, being reduced to extreme necessity, everything is to be done that power might admit, and that you are to do. . . . You have an army in Ireland you may employ here to reduce this kingdom. Confident as anything under heaven Scotland shall not hold out five months.

[1] C.S.P., Col.

Such, at least, was the version of Strafford's advice to the King as recorded in Vane's notes.[1]

The dissolution of the Parliament had provoked an ugly temper among the masses of the people. In and around London particularly there was an outbreak of riots. Though these outward expressions of discontent were suppressed, the discontent remained and deepened underground. In order to raise money, the government resorted to the old expedients of ship-money and forced loans. Such methods could not suffice to carry on war against the Scots for long, especially as large numbers of English people regarded the Scots as fighting the people's battle. From the companies of pressed men and from the trained bands there were numerous desertions ; and soon it became clear that neither the quality of the English army nor the desperate financial expedients for keeping it together could stand the strain for long.

The details of the outbreak and of the events of the " Second Bishops' War " are not our present concern. Suffice it to say that, on 23rd August, Charles himself reached York, having journeyed from London in an effort to restore order and confidence in his armies ; but his efforts were in vain. Three days previously, Leslie, at the head of the Scottish army, had crossed the Tweed, and in less than a week had crossed the Tyne also and occupied Newcastle. Within a short time the Scots were in possession of all Northumberland and Durham.

While the King was meeting these disasters in the north, his opponents were busy in London. A letter from Lord Savile to Lady Temple [2] makes reference to " the petition which we delivered at York, and was drawn, as you know, by Mr. Pym himself and Mr. Solicitor ". This petition which Pym and St. John drew up recited the grievances of people and parliament, and asked for a new parliament and for peace with the Scots. It bore the signatures of twelve peers—including those of Bedford, Warwick, Brooke, and Saye—and was dated the 28th August. The King, in

[1] *H.M.C. Report*, III, 3.
[2] *Camden Miscellany*, Vol. VIII. " Papers relating to the Delinquency of Lord Savile ", p. 2.

an effort to put off the evil of a parliament, adopted the alternative suggestion made by his council, namely, that all the peers of the realm should meet at York. This famous gathering assembled on 24th September. Two days previously the King had received a petition signed by 10,000 Londoners reinforcing that of the twelve peers. So impressed was the King by the unanimity of the demand for a parliament—and also, doubtless, by his inability to continue to find supplies without one—that when the peers met at York he informed them that writs would be issued for a parliament to meet on 3rd November.

In order to negotiate with the Scots, the peers deputed sixteen of their number. The Scots were in a politically impregnable position, and the severity of their demands showed their determination to press their advantage to the full. Long debates between the sixteen peers and the Scots failed to produce a settlement of the fundamental points at issue. Consequently, by the Treaty of Ripon, signed on 21st October, both sides agreed that a final treaty should be hammered out in London and that, meanwhile, the Scots should remain in possession of Northumberland and Durham and should receive from Charles £850 a day to maintain their armies. A more perfect instrument for compelling the King to call a parliament could scarcely have been devised; the only source of money to keep up the payments to the Scots was a parliament.

In such circumstances the Parliament—which was to be famous through succeeding centuries as the Long Parliament—met on 3rd November 1640. It is fair to say that no individual had been more influential in bringing about this result than John Pym. He had been a party to the negotiations with the Scottish Commissioners which helped to induce Charles to call the Short Parliament; he had drawn up, along with St. John, the terms of the Peers' Petition which asked for a new parliament; and he had helped to influence the Londoners whose Petition, presented to Charles at York, finally led to the promise to summon the Long Parliament. And when that parliament met, it would be Pym's statesmanship that would use it to shape the political destiny of the nation.

CHAPTER VIII

THE IMPEACHMENT OF STRAFFORD

Long Parliament, 3rd November 1640–Adjournment, 9th September 1641

THE interval between the two parliaments of 1640 was so short that the two were almost continuous : the leaders of the first were returned to, and were at once recognized as the leaders of, the second ; and the subjects of debate in the one continued to engage the attention of the other. In a word, the Short Parliament had been the gambit whereby already the opposition had the King in check. Whether the advantage thus secured would degenerate into yet another stalemate, or whether the King would this time be forced into a final checkmate, would depend upon the skill with which the opposition leaders used their opening.

The hasty dissolution of the Short Parliament had increased the popular distrust of, and had hardened the opposition to, both the King and his ministers. The ensuing election showed that this distrust and opposition existed not only among the Members of Parliament but also in the nation at large. Whether or not it is true that Pym had deliberately " forced the dissolution of the Short Parliament in order to inflame public opinion, and ensure the recall of a more organized Parliament on its own, not Strafford's, terms ", the effect of the dissolution was indeed " to give Charles time to put himself more completely at the mercy of his subjects ".[1] Public opinion was reflected in the composition of the new House. Since organized political parties did not then exist, exact numbers cannot be assigned to " government " and " opposition " sup-

[1] See *English Historical Review*, Vol. XXXVIII (October 1923), article by R. N. Kershaw : " The Elections for the Long Parliament."

porters. It is known, however, that the Court's nominees fared badly at the polls except in Wales and in the extreme north and west of England.[1] Even within these latter royalist areas, the number of the Court's nominees that were elected was not, for the most part, greatly in excess of the number of its opponents returned in those same areas. In securing this popular majority, Pym had displayed his usual energy. Anthony à Wood wrote that Pym " rode about the country to promote elections of the Puritanical brethren to serve in Parliament, wasted his body much in carrying on the cause, and was himself elected a burgess twice in 1640 ".[2]

A curious commentary on ·Pym's efforts is the fact that one of the few districts to return a large majority of Members favourable to the Court was his own county of Somerset which had thirteen royalist Members as against only five " parliamentarians ". Even Cornwall returned only two more royalists than parliamentarians (23 against 21) ; while in the adjoining county of Devon the royalists were in a minority (10 against 16). Incidentally, Pym himself was one of these sixteen Devonian " parliamentarians ", his constituency being once again the borough of Tavistock. The comment in the *English Historical Review* [3] that " the richest and most populous part of the country (with the exception of Somerset) thus declared against the King " is amply borne out by the subsequent proceedings of Parliament.

Yet this popular majority in the House was far from being a homogeneous body. Before the end even of the first session of the Parliament (9th September 1641), an unmistakable rift had appeared ; and because Pym was to figure prominently both in the formation of the rift and in its results, we shall do well at the outset to get some idea of its nature. Both sections of the opposition alike were upholders of the rights of the Commons, and both were opposed to the King's arbitrary methods of government. The differences between them were not political but

[1] I. D. Jones : *The English Revolution*, p. 33.
[2] *Athenae Oxonienses*, edited Bliss, Vol. III, 73.
[3] *E.H.R.*, XXXVIII, 508.

religious. On the one hand, the strong Puritans regarded Charles' arbitrary government and Laud's Arminianism as identical : hence they were sternly and, as time went on, even bitterly opposed to Laud and his régime both in itself and as the bulwark of despotism. From this position there was but a step to antagonism towards the Church itself and to Episcopacy which was the Church's characteristic feature. On the other hand were the non-Puritans, the staunch Churchmen who, if they mistrusted Laudianism, misliked extreme Puritanism yet more.

Each of these two sections had its own spokesmen. The representative leader of the latter group was Lord Falkland, Member for Newport in the Isle of Wight (his Viscounty being Scottish), who combined a love of liberty with devotion to Anglicanism and who, when the two seemed no longer mutually compatible, chose to support the Church.

Of the stricter Puritan section the most prominent leaders were Oliver St. John, Oliver Cromwell, and the younger Sir Henry Vane. Few would at that time have predicted that Vane would be the successor to Pym—in so far as he had a successor—as the leader of the House of Commons. In many respects the two men were strangely dissimilar. Clarendon describes Vane [1] as

a man of great natural parts and of very profound dissimulation, of a quick conception and very ready, sharp and weighty expression. He had an unusual aspect, which . . . made men think there was somewhat in him of extraordinary ; and his whole life made good that imagination.

His religious views were unorthodox even among the Puritans. He was a mystic, and he believed in complete toleration for all creeds and in the separation of Church and State. After travelling in Europe, young Henry went to America where for twelve months (1636–7) he was Governor of Massachusetts. He then returned to England, and in 1639 was made Joint Treasurer of the Navy with Sir William Russell. In the Short Parliament, and again in the Long Parliament, he sat for Hull. Up to this point, notwithstanding his Puritanism, he had been in favour at Court :

[1] *Great Rebellion*, Book III, Section 34.

in February 1640 the elder Sir Henry became Secretary of State, and in June (that is, during the interval between the two parliaments of that year) the younger Henry was knighted. It was the impeachment of Strafford which was the occasion of the breach between the two Vanes and the King. To this aspect of the subject we shall return later in the present chapter.

Between these two sections of the Members opposed to the Court, Pym held the balance : he was neither an extreme Puritan nor an Arminian ; and he was supremely a statesman. Clarendon's description [1] is in keeping with all that we know of him :

> Mr. Pimm was looked upon as the man of greatest experience in Parliaments, where he had served very long, and was always a man of business, being an officer in the Exchequer, and of a good reputation generally, though known to be inclined to the Puritan party ; yet not of those furious resolutions against the Church as the other leading men were, and wholly devoted to the earl of Bedford, who had nothing of that spirit.

The respect commonly felt for Pym must not be interpreted to mean that he was able at once and always to impose his will upon the Commons. On the contrary, there were several occasions—particularly during the early part of the session—when he failed to carry the House with him. Gradually, the House learned by experience to recognize both the wisdom of his views and the skill of his tactics. Pym's firmest ally, as we have seen, was Hampden who, though far less impressive than Pym as a debater, had a profound influence over his fellow-Members and, indeed, over the country at large. " He was that rare combination, an idealist with an acute judgment of ways and means, perhaps at the moment the wisest head in England." [2]

The Long Parliament met, as we have seen, on 3rd November 1640. Two days later Charles accepted a lawyer, William Lenthall, as the new Speaker. On the 6th, Strafford left his home at Woodhouse in Yorkshire to go to London to stand by the King in the hour of crisis. In so doing, Strafford realized well enough the

---

[1] *Great Rebellion*, Book III, Section 30.
[2] Buchan : *Oliver Cromwell*, p. 101.

personal danger into which he was walking, though, according to Whitelock, Charles had personally assured him that " as he was King of England he was able to secure him from any danger, and that the Parliament should not touch a hair of his head ". That very day, on Pym's proposition, the Commons resolved that a committee should be established to enquire into Irish grievances.[1] Though Strafford was not mentioned by name, the resolution was of ill omen for him inasmuch as the grievances referred to were obviously those of his administration.

On the evening of 9th November Strafford arrived in London. News of his arrival reached Pym next day. Thenceforward events moved with dramatic rapidity. Pym knew Strafford well enough to realize that his arrival presaged swift, decisive action : in all probability he would pursue his plan of accusing the parliamentary leaders of treason and conspiracy with the King's enemies the Scots. The opposition's tactics evidently must be to forestall him and so to frustrate his designs. Their hands were strengthened by the flood of petitions which had been pouring in from all over the country : in particular, on the very morning of the 10th, a petition against the Scottish war and the expense it was entailing had been received from the gentry of Strafford's own county of York.

On 11th November, Pym struck and struck hard. He first moved that the doors of the House should be locked ; and then in the tense atmosphere which such an unusual secret session naturally fostered, Pym proceeded to open his charge against Strafford. Clarendon's account is that : [2]

Mr. Pimm, in a long, formed discourse, lamented the miserable state and condition of the kingdom. . . . He believed there was one more signal in that administration than the rest, being a man of great parts and contrivance, and of great industry to bring what he designed to pass ; a man who in the memory of many present had sat in that house an earnest vindicator of the laws and a most zealous assertor and champion for the liberties of the people ; but that it was long since he turned apostate from

[1] *Commons' Journals*, II, 21, i.   [2] *Great Rebellion*, Book III, Section 3.

those good affections and, according to the custom and nature of apostates, was become the greatest enemy to the liberties of his country, and the greatest promoter of tyranny, that any age had produced.

Here lay the explanation of the bitterness with which Pym and his supporters attacked Strafford. They were too close to him to gain a true perspective of his greatness, which only the calm investigation of subsequent centuries could establish. What impressed them was Strafford's apostasy which coloured all their views of him and inevitably warped their interpretation of his actions.

As soon as Pym resumed his seat, Sir John Clotworthy, an Irish landowner who resented Strafford's régime in Ireland, gave a somewhat incoherent account of Strafford's oppressions. After a general debate, a committee—consisting of Pym, Strode, St. John, Holles, Digby, and Clotworthy [1]—was appointed to prepare charges against Strafford in readiness for a conference with the Lords. The Committee immediately set to work ; and that same afternoon Pym carried up to the Lords the charges of Strafford's impeachment. He then withdrew while the Lords considered the charges.

News of the turn of events was hurried to Strafford who forthwith repaired to the Lords to meet his accusers. While the Lords were in the act of debating his impeachment, he entered the House and was striding towards his place when he was greeted with cries of : " Withdraw, withdraw." After he had spent a few minutes of suspense in the Lobby, he was recalled to the bar where he was compelled to kneel while listening to the charge against him. Then, without being allowed to speak in self-defence, he was bidden to withdraw from the House and to deliver up his sword to the Usher of the Black Rod who conveyed him to safe custody.

Such a rapidly dramatic fall scarcely has its parallel in English history. Even the fall of Wolsey is not its equal. In large measure,

[1] *Commons' Journals*, II, 26.

the turn of events had been due to Strafford's own misreading of
the situation. He had suffered from the

fatal delusion that the English Parliament could still be used as
the tool of monarchy. . . . He must be condemned for failing
to see that the King had no resources left but the goodwill of
his subjects, and that such goodwill could only be gained by a
sacrifice of the men and methods of "Thorough". . . . Pym
beat him in tactics at every point.[1]

On 25th November, Pym carried to the Lords the formal
charge of impeachment, drawn up in seven articles.[2] The fundamental charge was the first, which the other six articles elaborated
and illustrated. It declared that :

Thomas, Earl of Strafford, hath traitorously endeavoured to
subvert the Fundamental Laws and Government of the Realms
of England and Ireland, and instead thereof, to introduce an
arbitrary and tyrannical Government, against Law, which he
hath declared by traitorous Words, Counsels, and Actions, and
by giving His Majesty Advice, by Force of Arms, to compel
His loyal Subjects to submit thereunto.

As soon as this charge was received, the Lords ordered that Strafford,
as an accused traitor, should be committed to the Tower.

Pym and his supporters, now feeling safe from Strafford's
machinations, set to work collecting evidence in support of his
impeachment and debating other urgent measures. To these
latter we shall return after we have watched the completion of
Pym's pursuit of Strafford. Meantime, one matter of personal
injustice was redressed, namely, that the men who had been
pilloried and imprisoned for opposition to the bishops were released : Prynne and Burton returned to London in triumph at
the end of November, and Bastwick early in December. This
action soon had its logical conclusion : on 11th December a
monster petition against episcopacy, signed, it was said, by 15,000
Londoners, was presented to the Commons.[3] The preamble to
the Petition was couched in the following phrases :

[1] I. D. Jones : *The English Revolution*, p. 33.
[2] *Lords' Journals*, IV, 97.   [3] Rushworth, III, 93.

That whereas the Government of Arch-Bishops and Lord Bishops, Deans and Arch-Deacons, &c., with their Courts and Ministrations in them, have proved prejudicial and very dangerous both to the Church and Commonwealth. . . . We therefore most humbly pray, and beseech this Honourable Assembly, the premises considered, That the said Government, with all its Dependencies, Roots and Branches, may be abolished, and all Laws in their behalf, made void, and the Government according to God's Word may be rightly placed amongst us. And We your humble Suppliants, as in Duty we are bound, will daily pray for your Majesty's Long and Happy Reign over us, and for the prosperous Success of this High and Honourable Court of Parliament.

On 18th December, on the motion of Pym, Archbishop Laud also was impeached of high treason and committed to the Tower.

During the interval between Strafford's arrest and the opening of his trial, there was mooted—according to the accounts of certain contemporaries—a project of first-rate importance. This was none other than that the parliamentary leaders should be given high offices under the Crown. Whitelocke's statement of the scheme is as follows : [1]

There was a proposal (the subject of much discourse) to prevent all this trouble, and to restore the earl of Strafford to his former favour and honour, if the King would prefer some of the grandees to offices at court, whereby Strafford's enemies should become his friends, and the King's desires be promoted.

It was, that   should be made lord chancellor, the lord Say master of the wards, Mr. Pym chancellor of the exchequer, Mr. Hollis secretary of state, Mr. Hampden tutor to the prince, others to have other places.

In order whereunto the bishop of London resigned up his treasurer's staff, the lord Cottington his place of master of the wards, and the rest were easily to be voided. But whether upon the King's alteration of his mind, or by what other means it came to pass, is uncertain, these things were not effected ; and the great men baffled thereby became the more incensed and violent against the earl, joining with the Scots commissioners, who were implacable against him.

[1] *Memorials*, p. 41.

Clarendon [1] confirms the main features of Whitelocke's account, but he offers a much more satisfactory explanation of the reason both for the initiation of the scheme and for its failure. (Incidentally, also, he states that the Earl of Bedford was to have been Treasurer.) On the purpose of the scheme, Clarendon writes :

From the time that there was no more fear of the archbishop of Canterbury nor the Lord Lieutenant of Ireland, nor of any particular men who were like to succeed them in favour, . . . the Great Patriots thought they might be able to do their country better service if they got the places and preferments in the Court, and so prevented the evil counsels which had used to spring from thence.

After giving the list of proposed offices and officials, Clarendon continues :

Thus far the intrigue for preferments was entirely complied with, and it is a great pity that it was not fully executed, that the King might have had some able men to have advised him or assisted ; which probably these very men would have done, after they had been so thoroughly engaged : whereas the King had none left about him in any immediate trust in business, . . . who either did not betray or sink under the weight or reproach of it.

The only item of the proposal that was carried out was that Oliver St. John became Solicitor-General. That the scheme finally miscarried was due—according to Clarendon—partly to the " Great Patriots " and partly to the King. Of the former he writes :

The Earl of Bedford was resolved that he would not enter the Treasury till the revenue was in some degree settled, and at least the bill for tonnage and poundage passed, with all decent circumstances and for life ; which both he and Mr. Pimm did very heartily labour to effect, and had in their thoughts many good expedients by which they intended to raise the revenue of the Crown. And none of them were very solicitous to take their promotions before some other accommodations were provided for some of the rest of their chief companions, who would be neither well pleased with their so hasty advancement before them, nor so submissive in the future to follow their dictates.

[1] *Great Rebellion*, Book III, Sections 83–9.

Of the King's point of view, Clarendon's account is :

The King's great end was, by these compliances, to save the life of the earl of Strafford. . . . And there were few of the persons mentioned before who thought their preferments would do them much good if the earl were suffered to live. . . . And so the continued and renewed violence in the prosecution of the earl of Strafford made the King well contented (as the other reasons prevailed with the other persons) that the execution of the promotions should be for a time suspended.

The extent to which Clarendon's details are to be relied upon is uncertain. In this, as in all else that he wrote, even if for the moment we ignore any question of partisanship, we have to remember that many years had elapsed between the events themselves and Clarendon's committing them to paper, and in the interval many details may have become dim or confused in his mind. Nevertheless, there is nothing improbable either in the proposal to give offices to the parliamentary leaders or in the reasons that Clarendon adduces for the failure of the proposal. Whatever the truth about it, we may share Clarendon's view that "it is a great pity that it was not fully executed". Later he added : [1]

If Mr. Pym, Mr. Hambden, and Mr. Hollis had been . . . preferred with Mr. St. John, before they were desperately embarked in their desperate designs, and had innocence enough about them to trust the King and be trusted by him, having yet contracted no personal animosities against him, it is very possible that they might either have been made instruments to have done good service, or at least have been restrained from endeavouring to subvert the royal building, for supporting whereof they were placed as principal pillars.

What the outcome might have been cannot now, of course, be determined with any degree of detail. Certain things may be concluded with some confidence : with such counsellors Charles would have been saved from the follies of his later career so that the clash between King and Parliament would never have become one of armed force, and hence there would have been no execu-

---

[1] *Great Rebellion*, Book IV, Section 76.

tion of Charles and no Cromwellian Commonwealth. It is even possible that some form of responsible government—government, that is, in which the ministers are responsible to Parliament—might have been evolved without either the Civil War of 1642-9 or the Revolution of 1688. Whether this be so or no, the whole subsequent history of England would certainly have been deflected into a different channel ; but it was not to be. Instead, the prosecution of Strafford was continued.

Not until 28th January 1641 did Pym present to the Lords the detailed charges against Strafford—nine general and twenty-eight particular charges—as drawn up by the committee appointed for the purpose. Two days later Strafford was brought from the Tower by water to listen to the articles of his accusation. They were put to the vote of the House and passed, and Strafford was given a week in which to prepare his reply. Various causes, including Strafford's continued illness, lengthened this period. Three weeks elapsed before his written answer was in the hands of the Lords ; and the trial did not actually begin in Westminster Hall until 22nd March. The full details of the trial—the fashionable concourse, the day-to-day thrust of arguments on both sides, the unfaltering courage of the prisoner—all have been related at length many times. In any case, they are not an essential part of our story. Our primary concern must be with the part played by Pym.

It was Pym who opened the process of accusation. His speech on 23rd March, which was the opening day of the trial proper, was a summary of the charges and a series of comments on the answers which Strafford had submitted to them. The articles showed that there were two matters on which the Commons placed the emphasis in their accusation, namely, Strafford's arbitrary Irish administration (occupying sixteen of the twenty-eight particular charges), and his advice and actions to undermine the just power of the English Parliament. Pym's opening words were intended to discredit the whole basis of the prisoner's position : [1]

[1] Rushworth : *Trial of Strafford*, p. 103.

The unhappy Earl, now the Object of your Lordships' Justice, hath taken as much care, hath used as much cunning to set a face and countenance of Honesty and Justice upon his Actions, as He hath been negligent to observe the rules of Honesty in the Performance of all these Actions. My Lords, it is the greatest baseness of wickedness, that it dares not look in his own Colours, nor be seen in its natural Countenance.

Next day Pym spoke again, elaborating somewhat the charges and supporting them with reference to specific actions by the Earl.

Day by day thereafter the Court listened to the prosecution lawyers, John Glyn and John Maynard, as they pursued clause by clause of the accusation, and to the prisoner's replies. The prosecutors' case suffered from one fatal weakness. An impeachment was a trial by law, the Commons being the accusers and the Lords being the judges : consequently, the prosecution must prove, as in an ordinary law-court, that the accused had infringed a particular clause of a particular statute. Strafford, therefore, must be proved to have violated the law of treason for which the penalty was execution. And treason was conspiracy against the King. That the King's most stalwart adviser had conspired against the King was, on the face of it, absurd. Conspiracy against the King had, therefore, to be interpreted as including conspiracy against the State. Even with this extension of meaning, treason was not easy to prove. Strafford was able to give a good account of himself. Point by point the Commons' case was shown to rest upon shaky evidence. The item which, if it could be proved, came nearest to positive treason was Article 23 which charged Strafford with intending to bring over Irish troops to subdue England. The elder Vane, when interrogated by Whitelocke as to whether Strafford had urged upon the King that he had in Ireland an army that could be used " *here* to reduce *this* Kingdom ", replied categorically : " Yes." The next stumbling-block was that no means could be found to prove that " this Kingdom " was England and not Scotland, the latter being the country which, at the moment the phrase was uttered, was needing subjugation. Other members of the Council, who had been present at the time, had only a vague recollection of the phrase, and they seemed to have interpreted it as referring to Scotland. In any event, Vane's evidence against Strafford was suspect, for, as we saw in connection with the Short Parliament,[1] Vane bitterly hated the prisoner. The feud between them appears to have had its origin in the fact that Wentworth, when receiving his Earldom in January 1640, had adopted also the title of Baron Raby, the barony of Raby having formerly been in Wentworth's family but forfeited by attainder in Elizabeth's reign. Since that date, Raby Castle (in Durham) had become the property of Sir Henry Vane who, hoping that a peerage might be conferred upon him, had intended to take Raby as his title. Thus, if there was nothing unnatural in Wentworth's desire to revive the former barony in his own family, there was equally nothing unnatural in Vane's regarding his so doing as a personal affront. Circumstances now placed in Vane's hands the opportunity for sweet revenge.

There was yet a further difficulty about the validity of the evidence concerning Strafford's advice to bring an army from Ireland to subdue " this Kingdom ", namely, that two witnesses were necessary in order to establish a conviction of high treason. And no amount of ingenuity by the prosecuting lawyers had been able to find a witness to support Vane's evidence ; yet the point in question was the crux of the prosecutor's case, so that if it were not established the whole case must collapse. As a last resort, Pym produced a secret paper which had been in his hands since September 1640. The elder Vane had given his evidence at the trial on 5th April 1641. On 8th April Pym and his fellow-managers resolved to play their trump-card. That day, however, Strafford was again too unwell to appear ; and on the following day no opportunity presented itself either. Accordingly it was on 10th April that the facts, which hitherto he had kept secret, were revealed to the Commons :[2]

Ordered, That the Doors be shut, and the Key brought up ; and that none go forth without Leave. . . . Sir *H. Vane* the younger, and Mr. *Pimme*, are enjoined, by this House, to declare

[1] See above, p. 151.   [2] *Commons' Journals*, II, 118.

their whole Knowledge concerning the Matters, contained in the Three-and-twentieth Article, against the Earl of *Strafford* ; and how, and by what means, they came to the Knowledge thereof : Which when they had done, a Paper was produced by Mr. *Pimme*, and so much of it read by him as concerned the Earl of *Strafford* : And then it was ordered, upon the Question, that That Paper, whereof Mr. *Pimme* had now read part, shall be all of it read. So it was. And, Notice being given of a Message from the Lords, it was ordered, that all the Members keep their Seats.

The facts, thus related by Pym and Vane, were that in the previous autumn the younger Vane had been searching among his father's papers and had come across notes of the meeting at which Strafford had given the incriminating advice about bringing over the Irish army. As an invasion from Ireland was, in September 1640, believed to be impending, he had thought that his duty was to place in Pym's hands this confirmatory evidence of the danger. He therefore had taken a copy of the original notes—which he had then replaced—and passed it to Pym. Pym then made his own copy and destroyed the one in young Vane's handwriting.

Pym had scarcely resumed his seat after this recital when the elder Vane, hotly indignant, rose in his place. He publicly lamented that he had such " an unhappy son ", and declared that his original notes of the council meeting had been destroyed at the King's express command ; but, when further questioned, he allowed that the notes produced by Pym were an accurate copy of the original. This evidence seemed a complete corroboration of that given by the elder Vane at the trial five days earlier, unless, of course, the whole matter of the notes was a forgery. Such a forgery might have been of either of two kinds, and, in either case, must have involved at least four persons. On the one hand, the incriminating notes might never have existed. In that case, the two Vanes and Pym were brazen liars : the elder Vane had never written the supposed original notes, his son had never discovered them nor carried a copy of them to Pym, and Pym had concocted the document with the connivance of the other two. On the other hand, the original notes might have existed but have been a deliberate misrepresentation by the elder Vane as an instrument whereby, at a convenient season, to destroy his enemy. In that case the guilt of forgery rested upon him, and only to a much less degree, if at all, upon either his son or Pym. But neither of these theories takes account of a fourth person whose evidence would have been most valuable of all. This person was the King himself. The elder Vane agreed that the copy produced by Pym tallied with his original notes and that those notes had been destroyed at the King's express command. If either of those statements, particularly the second, had been untrue, Charles—either personally or through another—could not have failed to repudiate it immediately, especially as the life of Strafford, and hence the security of the King himself, was at stake. Even when, on 1st May, Charles went to the Lords and summoned both Houses to appear before him in order to listen to his final plea for Strafford, he made no specific reference to Vane's notes but contented himself with a general statement denying that he had ever been advised to bring an Irish army to England or to alter the laws of England. Said he : [1]

I must tell you Three great Truths, which I am sure no body can know so well as my self. 1. That I never had any intention of bringing over the Irish Army into England nor ever was advised by any body so to do. 2. There never was any debate before me, neither in publique Council, nor at private Committee, of the Disloyalty, and Disaffection of my English Subjects, nor ever had I any suspition of them. 3. I was never Counselled by any, to alter the least of any of the Laws of England, much less to alter all the Laws.

The elder Vane may have been using a despicable means to work off a personal spite, but the King's failure to vindicate Strafford more specifically was conclusive proof that Vane's statement of fact was a true one. In these circumstances, to blame Pym for using such evidence is absurd. If he believed Strafford to be a danger to the State, he had no alternative to using the strongest evidence that he could lay his hands upon.[2]

[1] Rushworth : *Trial of Strafford*, p. 734 ; another version in C.S.P. (Dom.), 1640–1, p. 567.
[2] See Gardiner : *History of England*, IX, 124–5 (note), and IX, 329.

Yet, though the new evidence might carry conviction to any reasonable mind, there was much doubt as to whether it altered the legal position. All that it did was to vindicate the witness of the elder Vane; but the second witness demanded by the law was still missing. Pym seems to have taken the view that the other witness need not be a person, but that Vane's notes might be regarded as constituting a second witness within the meaning of the Act. Such a view, however, was hardly likely to carry in a court of law. Yet to allow Strafford to slip out of their hands would be fatal not only to the parliamentary opposition but to all that they understood by liberty, both religious and political. The truth was that Pym and his supporters had started the impeachment without any clear idea of what it would involve or of the legal problems that would need to be solved. Convinced that Strafford was a danger to the State, they seem never to have foreseen that the law would hinder rather than help his removal. As difficulty after difficulty appeared in the process of impeachment, the minds of some of the prosecutors began to turn to an alternative process, namely, a Bill of Attainder which, consisting of a mere declaration that the Earl of Strafford was guilty of high treason, would not need to be supported by legal proof of his guilt. Even this would have a drawback from the point of view of its promoters, for, in order to become an Act, it would need not only to pass Commons and Lords but also to receive the royal assent. That Charles would ever sign away the life of his most able and devoted servant was improbable to the verge of impossibility; and that any party, knowing this, should drop the impeachment in favour of an attainder showed that they recognized how completely their legal case had broken down.

On 10th April, the very day on which Pym disclosed to the Commons his possession of Vane's notes, a Bill of Attainder was brought in and read a second time, though the impeachment process still went on. From the outset Pym, followed by Hampden, had opposed the method of attainder, and for two reasons: first, by implying the Commons' distrust of the Lords, it would cause a rift between the two Houses; and second, Pym still believed that the impeachment could be carried. Thus d'Ewes notes that on 12th April : [1]

Mr. Hotham moved to have the bill of the Earle of Strafford's attainder read.

Mr. Pymme would not have the bill read, but to goe the other way : because this is the safer to show that wee & the Lords are reconciled & not sundred : and soe wee shall proceed the moore speedilie by demanding iudgment.

To that policy in spite of the originally unsuspected difficulties which its adoption involved, Pym continued to adhere. But after 10th April, more and more of the members of his party turned against it. The utmost concession that Pym and Hampden could gain from the more extreme of their associates was that the impeachment should continue alongside the stages of the Bill of Attainder.

The last day of the impeachment trial at Westminster was 13th April, on which day Pym delivered one of the most eloquent speeches of his career. Robert Baillie (a member of the Glasgow General Assembly, and afterwards Professor of Divinity at, and Principal of, Glasgow University, who had been sent to London as the agent of the Covenanting Lords) wrote that Pym " to the confession of all, in half an hour, made one of the most eloquent, wise, free speeches, that ever we heard, or I think shall ever hear ".[2] Even the written accounts of the speech that remain to us amply confirm this judgment.[3] Pym's object was to summarize the argument that Strafford had violated the laws which were the foundation of the State and thereby had committed an offence which was essentially treason. It was a theme exactly suited to Pym's mind and oratorical style.

My lords, many days have been spent, in maintenance of the impeachment of the earl of Strafford, by the House of Commons, whereby he stands charged with high treason ; and your lordships have heard his defence with patience and with as much favour as justice would allow. We have passed through our evidence, and

---

[1] *Journal* : Harl. MSS. 164, f. 165a. [2] *Letters and Journal*, I, 348.
[3] Rushworth : *Trial of Strafford*, pp. 661–70.

the result of all this is, that it remains clearly proved, That the earl of Strafford hath endeavoured by his words, actions, and counsels, to subvert the fundamental laws of England and Ireland, and to introduce an arbitrary and tyrannical government. . . .

The law is that which puts a difference betwixt good and evil, betwixt just and unjust ; if you take away the law, all things will fall into a confusion, every man will become a law to himself, which in the depraved condition of human nature, must needs produce many great enormities. Lust will become a law, and envy will become a law, covetousness and ambition will become laws ; and what dictates, what decisions such laws will produce, may easily be discovered in the late government of Ireland. . . .

The law is the boundary, the measure, betwixt the King's prerogative and the people's liberty ; whilst these move in their own orbs, they are a support and a security to one another ; the prerogative a cover and defence to the liberty of the people, and the people by their liberty are enabled to be a foundation to the prerogative ; but if these bounds be so removed, that they enter into contestation and conflict, one of these mischiefs must ensue : If the prerogative of the King overwhelm the liberty of the people, it will be turned to tyranny ; if liberty undermine the prerogative, it will grow into anarchy.

It would be difficult to express the principles of the Parliamentarians, in their struggle against the tyranny of the Stuarts, more succinctly or more justly than this. Pym's statement affords yet further evidence of his basic political views. Once more, we may note in passing, it is difficult to believe that anyone holding this view that the King's prerogative was an integral part of the constitution would ever have consented to the execution of Charles or to the overthrow of the monarchy.

So far as the impeachment of Strafford is concerned, Pym's speech shows why he was not troubled overmuch in his own mind whether Strafford had or had not infringed particular laws of treason. Pym was convinced that, whether the laws declared Strafford to be technically innocent or not, morally he was guilty. To Pym, the Law was greater than any number of laws ; and, no matter what opinion a law-court might take, to have broken the spirit of Law was to be guilty of treason to a far higher degree than to have contravened particular statutes. This view is expressed repeatedly in the later, and more detailed, sections of the speech.

Shall it be treason to embase the King's coin, though but a piece of twelvepence or sixpence ? and must it not needs be the effect of a greater treason, to embase the spirits of his subjects, and to set up a stamp and character of servitude upon them, whereby they shall be disabled to do anything for the service of the King and Commonwealth ?

And again :

If this be treason, in the nature of it, it doth exceed all other treasons in this, That in the design and endeavour of the author, it was to be a constant and permanent treason ; other treasons are transient, as being confined within those particular actions and proportions wherein they did consist ; and those being past, the treason ceaseth. . . . But this treason, if it had taken effect, was to be a standing, perpetual treason, which would have been in continual act, not determined within one time or age, but transmitted to posterity, even from one generation to another.

Thus Pym worked to his peroration :

The forfeitures inflicted for treason, by our law, are of life, honour and estate, even all that can be forfeited ; and, this prisoner having committed so many treasons, although he should pay all these forfeitures, will still be a debtor to the commonwealth : Nothing can be more equal than that he should perish by the justice of that law which he would have subverted ; neither will this be a new way of blood, There are marks enough to trace this law to the very original of this kingdom : and if it hath not been put in execution, as he allegeth, these two hundred and forty years, it was not for want of law, but that all that time hath not bred a man bold enough to commit such crimes as these.

At this point, the eyewitness Baillie records a curious incident : [1] " To humble the man, God let his memory fail him a little before the end. His papers he looked on ; but they could not help him to a point or two, so he behoved to pass on." What we may perhaps be inclined to regard as a more natural explanation than the one suggested by Baillie, of Pym's sudden loss of the thread of the argument, was sheer mental weariness. For a

[1] *Journal*, I, 348.

number of years without intermission he had borne heavy burdens of responsibility, first in the Providence Company, and latterly in the Short and Long Parliaments. In particular, the conduct of Strafford's trial had very largely rested upon Pym. The mental strain must have been enormous, and was surely increased by the knowledge that the end would be the death of one with whom formerly he had lived and worked on terms of intimacy. We do well to remember that within two and a half years of this time Pym was dead, worn out by cares of the State. The lapse of memory was almost certainly a forewarning of physical and mental decline.

Notwithstanding Pym's efforts, and the effect which his speech produced, it is doubtful whether the impeachment action would have secured a verdict against the prisoner. In order to make sure that he did not after all elude their grasp, the parliamentary leaders pushed the Bill of Attainder through its remaining stages. On 14th April it was read a second time, and a third time on the 23rd when the voting was 204 for the Bill and 59 against it. The majority was a substantial one ; but what was at least equally significant was that in a House of 493 there were nearly 140 abstentions. Though some of these may have been genuinely neutral or undecided, many others must have favoured Strafford yet have shrunk from declaring convictions which were contrary to those of the majority of the House ; while 59 were staunch enough to brave unpopularity. Here we may detect the beginnings of the division within the ranks of the opposition-Members which was to be widened by the subsequent debates on the subject of religion.

Two days later Charles wrote to Strafford a reassuring letter which, while recognizing that he could not again be employed in the royal service, gave a pledge " that, upon the word of a king, you shall not suffer in life, honour or fortune ". In keeping with this recognition of the end of Strafford's ministerial career was the revival of the project to give places to some of the popular leaders. In particular, Pym was to become Chancellor of the Exchequer.[1]

[1] C.S.P. (Dom.), 1640–1 (26th April), p. 560.

Mr. Pym . . . has been with the King twice of late, and since the Lord Cottington laid his offices at the King's feet, is designed by the voice of the people to be his successor in the Chancellorship of the Exchequer.

Nothing is known of the details of the interviews nor of the reasons why Pym did not accept office. The obvious explanation seems to be that, as before, the King's object was to save Strafford and that Pym would never accept office on those terms. Even if a compromise were arrived at, and that life imprisonment were substituted for the death penalty, while the King gave an assurance of banishment from Court and of permanent exclusion from office, there was no security that the promise would be observed longer than immediate circumstances necessitated. In any case, Pym was not a Strafford, anxious for office and royal favours. Once again the possibility of responsible government faded away.

On 24th April the parliamentary precincts were invaded by 2,000 Londoners, carrying a petition with 20,000 signatures, demanding Strafford's life. As the days passed, the clamour in the city rose continually. Nor was excitement limited to the mob. Sober traders put up their shutters and crowded round the Houses, especially demanding that the Lords should grant them justice. In the Lords on 8th May, when the final vote was taken, only forty-eight peers dared to press their way through the mob into their House. Of these, thirty-seven voted for the Bill of Attainder and eleven against it.

Henceforward, the responsibility for Strafford's fate must rest solely with the King. We need not linger over Charles' agonizing indecision while he sought in vain some way out of the death-trap for the erection of which no one was so responsible as himself. But no avenue of escape existed. On 10th May the Bill of Attainder received the royal assent. Efforts by the King and the Prince of Wales to save the condemned minister were unavailing, and on 12th May the execution took place on Tower Hill in the presence, according to contemporary estimates, of 20,000 spectators.

The death of Strafford did more than merely demonstrate the

supremacy of Parliament over the King's ministers and remove a dangerous upholder of royal prerogative. We saw that when Charles lost his first great adviser, the Duke of Buckingham, by assassination in 1628, the effect was that henceforward no one but Charles himself could be blamed for the follies and mistakes of government. In principle, the removal of Strafford had a similar effect ; but the circumstances of 1641 made that effect more critically significant than it had been a dozen years earlier. Hitherto Pym and Hampden, and at least their more moderate followers, had persisted in regarding Strafford not as strengthening but as undermining the true prerogative of the Crown. In his speech on 13th April, at the conclusion of the impeachment trial, Pym had declared : [1]

Arbitrary power is dangerous to the King's person, and dangerous to his crown : it is apt to cherish ambition, usurpation, and oppression, in great men, and to beget sedition and discontent in the people ; and both these have been, and in reason must ever be, causes of great trouble and alteration to princes and states. . . . If any man shall look into our own stories, in the times when the laws were most neglected, he shall find them full of commotions, of civil distempers ; whereby the kings that then reigned were always kept in want and distress ; the people consumed with civil wars ; and by such wicked counsels as these some of our princes have been brought to such miserable ends as no honest heart can remember, without horror and earnest prayer, that it may never be so again.

Not only does this declaration itself bear the stamp of sincerity, but the whole of Pym's career, both before and after Strafford's death, witnesses to his desire to support and not overthrow what he recognized as the King's just prerogative.[2] It was the expression of the Elizabethan conception of government which, as we have seen, had prevailed in his youth and which continued to guide him for the remainder of his life. In a word, Pym still believed that the maladies of the State were due not to the King's ill-will towards his subjects but to his "evil counsellors". The removal of Strafford therefore was essential for the cure of those

---

[1] Rushworth : *Trial of Strafford*, p. 663.   [2] See above, pp. 28, 101.

maladies. But when, after Strafford's execution, weeks and months passed without the hoped-for improvement in the King's government, the conviction was forced even upon Pym that the responsibility for misgovernment must rest upon Charles and upon no one else and that the safety of the State, and the liberty of the people, could be secured only by radical, and not by merely superficial, changes in constitutional practice. In this sense, the execution of Strafford was a crisis in Pym's career.

Meanwhile another impeachment case had been occupying the attention of the Commons, and particularly of Pym, namely, that of Archbishop Laud. It was on 24th February 1641 that Pym presented to the Lords the fourteen articles of the Archbishop's impeachment. Parts of the speech, in which Pym expounded the several articles, belong, both in modes of thought and in language, to the period in which it was delivered. In certain particulars we know Pym's view to have been wrong, as, for example, when he declared that Laud was hankering after "Popery". Even in this respect Laud's actions—both in his own ecclesiastical changes and in the freedom which he allowed to Roman Catholics—gave some support to such a view.

The accusation [of being Papists] was rightly directed against two bishops—Goodman and Montague ; and though its absurdity in Laud's case seems manifest today, it must be remembered that the Pope fell into the same confusion as the Puritans when in 1633 he offered Laud a Cardinal's hat. Only Henrietta knew the full extent of his obstinate Protestantism.[1]

In the main, Pym's opposition to Laud, as expressed in his impeachment speech, had two motives. First, he regarded Laud's changes as contrary to the essential character of the English Church : hence his antagonism to them as tending to Romanism. Second, he distrusted the political implications of Laudianism. It was this latter motive which occupied the greater part of Pym's speech :[2]

In the second article, your lordships may observe absolute and unlimited power defended, by preaching, by sermons, and

---

[1] I. D. Jones : *The English Revolution*, p. 50.
[2] Rushworth, III, 199–202.

other discourses, printed and published upon that subject. And truly, my lords, it seems to be a prodigious crime, that the truth of God and his holy law, should be perverted to defend the lawlessness of man. . . .

In the third article my lords, you have the judges, who under his majesty are the dispensers and distributors of justice, frequented by fear and solicitation. . . .

In the sixth article, you have the King robbed of his supremacy . . . And herein your lordships may observe that those who labour, in civil matters, to set up the king above the laws of the kingdom, do yet, in ecclesiastical matters, endeavour to set up themselves above the king.

In both these respects, Pym's opposition to Laud, like his opposition to Strafford, was based upon the principles which he had inherited from Elizabethan times. The result of the impeachment proceedings was that, on 1st March, Laud was imprisoned in the Tower, though his case was not brought to a final issue for nearly another four years.

While Strafford's case had been proceeding, the Commons had also been taking steps to prevent a repetition of the Eleven Years' Tyranny and to ensure that they should not be suddenly dissolved, as previous Houses had been, at the convenience of the King or his ministers. The first of these two objects was secured, after other methods had been discussed, by a Triennial Bill which, having passed through all its stages in the Commons and Lords, was finally presented to the King for signature on 15th February 1641. It made provision whereby, at the end of any period of three years during which the King had failed to summon a parliament, elections should be held ; and it stipulated that the resulting assembly should be a legal parliament and should not be dissolved within fifty days of its first meeting. The second object was secured by what came to be called the " Own Consent Act " which enacted

that this present Parliament now assembled shall not be dissolved unless it be by Act of Parliament to be passed for that purpose ; nor shall be, at any time or times, during the continuance thereof, prorogued or adjourned, unless it be by Act of Parliament to be likewise passed for that purpose.

Such an Act, flatly contrary to previous constitutional practice and principle, shows how deep was the distrust which Parliament was feeling for the King. It is not without significance that the Bill was presented for the royal assent on 10th May—the same day as was the Bill for Strafford's attainder. This was followed by an Act (22nd June) declaring that tunnage and poundage were not to be levied " without common consent in Parliament ", by Acts (5th July) abolishing the prerogative Courts (including those of the Star Chamber, Council in the North, and High Commission), and by an Act (7th August) " for the declaring unlawful and void the late proceedings touching ship-money, and for the vacating of all records and process concerning the same ".

The subject which, in this parliament as in earlier ones, provoked the bitterest controversy was religion. It was this subject which, as the opening paragraphs of the present chapter anticipated, provoked the fateful rift in the ranks of the parliamentary opposition. All but a small minority were opposed to Laudianism, but beyond that point unanimity ceased. This was clearly revealed when the London Petition of December 1640 against Episcopacy came before the Commons for consideration on 8th February 1641. The question before the House was whether the Petition should be sent to a committee for report. Falkland, Hyde, and Culpepper were among those who voted against committing the Petition, while St. John, the younger Vane, and Nathaniel Fiennes favoured its committal, as did also Pym and his ally Hampden. This division within the parliamentary opposition was of the highest significance for the future. Hitherto the group had been unanimous, or nearly so, in vindicating what they believed to be national liberty : thus all the Members just mentioned had voted for Strafford's impeachment. Henceforward their unanimity was at an end, and the line of division concerning the religious issue became, in the main, a permanent one. By the time the Civil War broke out, Falkland, Hyde, and Culpepper had gone over to the side of the King. Indeed, but for these men it is difficult to see that there could have been a royalist party at all. Pym's attitude, at the outset at least, was more moderate than that of the opponents of the bishops. Thus, Edward Bagshaw, M.P. for Southwark, writing to prove that he had not supported the Petition for " the total extirpation of Episcopacy, Root and Branch ", declared that when the Petition was introduced into the Commons : [1]

> Mr. *John Pym* (a Gentleman with whom I had familiar acquaintance, and knew his mind on that point) spake to this purpose, *That he thought it was not the intention of the House to abolish either Episcopacy or the Book of Common Prayer, but to reform both*, wherein *offence was given to the people.* And that if that could be effected, and assented to by them with the concurrence of the King and Lords, they should do a very acceptable work to the people, and such as had not been since the Reformation, which was then about eighty years.

This is further borne out by Clarendon : [2]

> In the House of Commons, though, of its chief leaders, Nathaniel Fynes and young sir H. Vane, and shortly after Mr. Hambden (who had not before owned it), were believed to be for " root and branch " (which grew shortly after a common expression, and discovery of the several tempers,) yet Mr. Pimm was not of that mind, nor Mr. Hollis, nor any of the Northern men, or those lawyers who drove on most furiously with them : all who were pleased with the government itself of the Church.

Finally the House agreed, without a division, that the question of Episcopacy should not be sent to a committee but should be considered at a later date by the House itself.

On 10th March, the Commons again had the subject before them and finally resolved [3]

> That the legislative and judicial Power of Bishops, in the House of Peers in Parliament, is a great Hindrance to the Discharge of their Spiritual Function, prejudicial to the Commonwealth, and fit to be taken away, by Bill : And that a Bill be drawn to that Purpose.

[1] *A Just Vindication of the Questioned Part of the Reading of Edward Bagshaw, Esq.* London, 1660 (pp. 3 and 4).
[2] *Great Rebellion*, Book III, Section 147.
[3] *Commons' Journals*, II, 101, i.

Next day they passed another resolution debarring the clergy from exercising any judicial function.[1] The first of these resolutions was implemented by a Bill introduced into the Commons on 30th March to exclude the bishops from the Lords. The Commons were on dangerous ground, for the Lords might well resent this interference with the composition of their House. The upshot was that, though the Bill passed the Commons, the Peers, on 27th May, resolved that the clergy should be incapable of discharging civil functions but that an exception should be made to allow the bishops to retain their seats in the Lords.[2] On 8th June, after a fruitless conference with the Commons on the subject, the Lords finally rejected the Exclusion Bill.[3]

By coincidence, on the morning of 27th May, a Bill providing for the abolition of episcopacy was introduced into the Commons. For this Bill, the younger Vane and Oliver Cromwell were responsible. The Commons evidently regarded the measure as highly urgent, for they accorded it two readings on the same day. On the second reading the voting was 139 for the Bill and 108 against.[4] Included in the minority were again Falkland and Hyde, and in the majority were Pym, Hampden, St. John, Vane, and Fiennes. When the Bill went to committee, of which Hyde was chairman, it was the subject of fierce debates, so that it had not completed its stages by the close of the session, and was then dropped, though the project was revived in a new Bill early in the following session.

An interesting problem is presented by Pym's change of attitude on this question of episcopacy. There can be little doubt that in the first instance his policy was that implied by Bagshaw not " to abolish either Episcopacy or the Book of Common Prayer, but to reform both, wherein offence was given to the people ", yet within a short time he was supporting first the exclusion of bishops from the Lords and then the abolition of the episcopal system of Church government. The absence of any explicit statement on the subject by Pym himself leaves us to deduce an explanation from what we know of his general principles and

[1] Ibid., p. 102, ii. [2] *Lords' Journals*, IV, 159, i.
[3] Ibid., p. 169, i. [4] *Commons' Journals*, II, 259, i.

methods. We are on safe ground in assuming that his great aim, in matters of religion, was the restoration of what to him was a thoroughly orthodox Protestant Church. This would involve such reforms in the Laudian Church as would restore the powers of the bishops and the use of the Prayer Book and ceremonies as they had been before Laud. To the achievement of these aims the bishops naturally offered a stiff resistance. It would therefore seem that Pym took the view that if a soundly Protestant Church was unattainable with bishops, it must be attained without bishops. Faced with a choice of evils, he chose the less : that is, he sacrificed what after all was a matter of ecclesiastical administration in order to secure the fulfilment of fundamental religious principles. It was the decision of a statesman shaping means to ends, and conceding—however reluctantly—a practical point in order to realize a principle to which all his life he had inflexibly adhered.

In the midst of the debates on the bishops, it became known that Charles was contemplating a visit to Scotland. The news caused the parliamentary leaders some apprehension. Of late there had been a growing coldness between the Parliament and the Scottish commissioners, partly because the money grants for the Scottish armies were slower and less generous than the commissioners had hoped, and partly because, though the Puritans were increasingly opposed to the Laudian Church, they showed little desire to set up a Presbyterian system in its place. The parliamentary opposition therefore feared lest the proposed royal visit should presage a reconciliation between Charles and the Scots, for such a reconciliation would break the Parliament's most powerful lever for obtaining religious and political concessions from the King. Apart from this, the mere removal of the King four hundred miles from London to Scotland would give him a much larger measure of independence from parliamentary pressure. The King's real purpose was to be found in the fact that the Scottish Covenanters had quarrelled among themselves, and Montrose was making overtures to the King. At the moment, Montrose was the prisoner of his rival Argyle ; but if Charles by persistent negotiations could unite the followers of Montrose to the other elements among the Scots who were discontented with the English Parliament, he might transform the situation not only in Scotland but in England. Added to this was information received by Pym of a plot to cause disaffection against Parliament in the English army.

To counteract these dangers, Pym drew up " Ten Propositions " which were passed by the Commons and which, on 24th June, Pym carried up to the Lords.[1] Among other matters, the Propositions provided for the disbanding of the English armies, besought " that His Majesty will be pleased to allow a convenient time before his journey into Scotland ", made

suit to His Majesty, to remove from him all such counsellors as . . . have been active for the time past in furthering those courses, contrary to religion, liberty, good government of the Kingdom, and as have lately interested themselves in those Counsels, to stir up Division between him and his people

and for the appointment of " such officers and counsellors as his people and Parliament may have just cause to confide in ", and proposed the appointment of a joint committee of the two Houses " to consider of such particular courses as shall be most effectual for the reducing of these propositions to effect the public good ". The significance of the Propositions lay not only in their terms but also in the fact that they passed both Lords and Commons with almost complete unanimity. For the moment, at least, both parties in the Commons and both Houses were united on a common policy. Some concessions to these demands Charles made, for example on the following day he agreed to the disbanding of the armies ; but he refused to alter his plans for his journey to Scotland. Nor could subsequent, repeated requests by Parliament change his purpose ; and on 10th August he set out from London for the north. Parliament countered his move by appointing six commissioners whose ostensible business was to negotiate with the Scottish Parliament but whose real purpose was to watch the movements of Charles. The Lords' nominees to

[1] Rushworth, III, 298–300 ; also *Lords' Journals*, IV, 285–7.

the Commission were the Earl of Bedford (who had succeeded to the Earldom as recently as May 1641 on the death from small-pox of his father the patron of Pym) and Lord Howard of Escrick ; and the Commons were represented by Fiennes, Armyn, Stapleton, and Hampden. As the resolution appointing the Commissioners was passed in the absence of the King, it could not become an Act, and was therefore known as an Ordinance—the first of many Ordinances to be passed by the Long Parliament.

The sense of insecurity which overshadowed Parliament was revealed also by its orders to the Lord General, the Earl of Holland, to make secure both Hull and the store of munitions therein, and to the Constable of the Tower that he should reside in the Tower and should strengthen its guard.

On 9th September both Houses stood adjourned for six weeks, each appointing a committee to keep in touch with current affairs and with the joint committee that had gone to Scotland. Of the Commons' Committee, Pym was chosen to be chairman.[1]

The first stage of the Long Parliament had closed in circum-stances that were full of evil omens for its future sessions.

[1] *Commons' Journals*, II, 288, ii.

CHAPTER IX

THE FIVE MEMBERS

DURING the interval between the adjournment of Parliament on 9th September and its reassembly on 20th October events, both in Scotland and in England, had changed the political situation.

In Scotland Charles set himself by every means in his power to win the goodwill of his subjects. He assented to every Bill which the Edinburgh Parliament presented to him, even though the 1640 Parliament, which had passed them, had continued in session after being formally prorogued. In his personal dealings with individual Scottish leaders he used all his royal charm, and distributed titles and honours, in order to win popularity. But neither his public nor his private efforts achieved the purpose for which he had made the long journey north. The Scots, with native shrewdness, refused to become the tools of the King's schemes. They even disbanded their armies, of which Charles had fondly hoped to secure control, as a weapon against Parliament. Whatever chance of success Charles' visit might have had was wrecked by the bitter mutual jealousies of the Scottish leaders. Montrose, still in prison, repeatedly wrote to the King denouncing Argyle and Hamilton as being traitors. The outcome of these jealousies was the plot known as the Incident, many of the details of which are still obscure. In the middle of October, information reached Argyle and Hamilton of plans made by certain Roman Catholic lords to seize, and possibly murder, both of them. The arch-plotter appears to have been either the Earl of Crawford or the Earl of Montrose, or perhaps both of them. Very probably some hint of the scheme was communicated to Charles, but to what extent he had a complete or accurate version of the plot, or whether in any way he was himself implicated, has never been certainly established. The leakage of information meant that the Incident came to nothing. Its larger effect was that Charles' visit, instead of uniting the Scottish nobility, had further fomented strife and incidentally had raised at least a suspicion of his own not very creditable partisanship. Scarcely less important was the effect which Charles' Scottish visit had upon the situation in England. Every move in Edinburgh was being watched by Hampden and the other English commissioners, who thus both gained an insight into the King's shiftiness and also became assured that Scotland was a weakness rather than a strength to his cause.

On 20th October the English Parliament reassembled. The recess had done nothing to ease the sense of crisis and suspicion, and the old questions were at once reopened.

During the opening day of the new session two items of business came before the Commons, in both of which Pym was concerned. First, " Mr. *Pym* reports and gives an Account of what the Committee appointed to sit during the Recess had done in pursuance of the Order of the House given to that Committee ".[1] Second, Pym reported the result of a conference with the Lords on the safety of the Kingdom. This had been due to a widespread fear that the Scottish Incident might have its counterpart in London. Pym's report of the conference was as follows : [2]

1. That when there was a Design, somewhat of the same Nature, in this Kingdom, to seduce the King's Army, to interrupt the Parliament here, that there was the like design at that time in *Scotland*.

Next, the principal Party named in that Design in *Scotland*, is a person suspected to be popishly affected ; and therefore may have Correspondency with the like Party here.

That it hath been published here lately, that some Things were to be done there in *Scotland* before it broke out there. Therefore we may suspect some Correspondency here.

So, upon these grounds, to propound, That a strong Guard be kept in the City of *Westminster* and *London* : Then, 2, that Care be taken for the future for the Defence of the whole Kingdom.

[1] *Commons' Journals*, II, 289, i.   [2] Ibid., p. 190, ii.

This resolution was agreed to, and henceforward a guard of a hundred men from the trained bands of Westminster kept watch both night and day in Palace Yard. The unwonted presence of armed men in the neighbourhood of Parliament was an object-lesson to Londoners, and encouraged among them a sense of vague apprehension.

Gardiner, summarizing at this point in the story the trend of events, delivered a sharp stricture on Pym's leadership : [1]

> Everything that [the Long Parliament] had done up to this point, with the single exception of the compulsory clauses of the Triennial Act, was accepted at the Restoration and passed into the permanent constitution of the country. Everything that it attempted to do after this was rejected at the Restoration. The first was the work of the whole Parliament, the second was the work of the majority. Failure, and it must be confessed deserved failure, was the result of Pym's leadership.

Any judgment delivered by such an unrivalled authority on seventeenth-century history must obviously be received with the deepest respect. And this judgment, as far as it goes, is incontestable ; but it is a judgment that seems to neglect at least three important factors. First, the situation—as subsequent events were to show—was rapidly becoming revolutionary in character. For this development, though neither side can be held solely blameworthy, the responsibility must rest primarily, as we have seen, not upon any extreme demands of the Parliament but upon the complete failure of both James I and Charles I, either to produce any plan of their own or to accept sincerely the successive moderate suggestions of Parliament. Hence Parliament found itself compelled, reluctantly and gradually, to bring pressure to bear upon the King. As soon as this pressure became continuous, Parliament had virtually assumed the initiative in the government of the State. This in itself was a revolutionary proceeding in which Pym played a leading part. And revolutions notoriously and necessarily are destructive rather than constructive. In so far, therefore, as the work of the latter part of the Long Parliament

---

[1] *History of England*, X, 34.

proved not to be permanent, the failure was due not to Pym's leadership as such but to the political circumstances which were not of his creation. Second, if it be the function of a revolutionary to destroy what is evil as a means to the construction of what is better, even the later sessions of the Long Parliament can hardly be labelled as unsuccessful; for the monarchy that was restored in 1660, and still more explicitly the monarchy of 1689, was one that recognized most of the principles upon which the Long Parliament had insisted, including the responsibility of ministers to Parliament and the supremacy of the Commons in matters of finance. Third, it can hardly be too often insisted upon that Pym's early death removed the one man with supreme powers of statesmanship that could both control the existing situation and find a permanent solution for the future. In so far, therefore, as the Long Parliament, under Pym's leadership, failed to evolve a permanent cure of the nation's ills, the failure was superficial rather than real, and was due to the lack of statesmanship of the King rather than of Pym.

On the second day of the session, a new Bill was introduced to exclude the bishops from the House of Lords and to prevent the clergy in general from exercising temporal powers. The Root and Branch Bill for the abolition of episcopacy had evidently been abandoned. On 23rd October, only two days after its introduction, the second Exclusion Bill received its third reading in the Commons and was sent to the Lords. There can be no doubt that the Commons' motive in hurrying the measure through was political rather than religious: that is to say, they saw that the twenty-six bishops would use their votes in the Lords in defence of the Court. In the Lords, the Bill met a mixed reception. This also was political as much as religious, for, whatever individual peers might think about episcopacy as a system, the Lords as a body resented the Commons' interference with the constitution of the Upper House. Hence, proceedings there were slow; and a protest by the London citizens was necessary on 12th November, as well as a women's petition against Popery on 4th February 1642, to induce the Lords at last to pass the Bill on 5th February. On 13th February it received the royal assent.

In order to complete the account of the Bishops' Exclusion Bill, we have anticipated by several months the chronological order of events. To that order we must now return. On 25th October 1641 Pym had been the subject of a mysterious personal attack in the House.

> Master *Pym* declares, that he received a letter from a porter at the doore, and opening it dropped a plaister, which came from a wound full of corrupt matter, and the letter full of rayling against Master *Pym* ; the Porter being examined, said a gentleman on horse back in a gray Coat, gave him twelve pence for the speedy delivery of it.[1]

The purport of the letter, and the action taken to discover its author, are thus described in a contemporary pamphlet :[2]

A Damnable Treason by a Contagious Plaster of a Plague Sore ; Wrapt up in a Letter and sent to Mr. Pym

To my honoured friend John Pym, Esq. ;

> Mr. Pym, Doe not thinke that a Guard of men can protect you, if you persist in your Traytorous courses, and wicked Designes. I have sent a Paper-Messenger to you, and if this doe not touch your heart, a Dagger shall, so soon as I am recovered of my Plaguesore : In the mean time you may be forborne, because no better man may bee indangered for you. Repent Traytor.

The true Relation how he was Descryed

Search being made (by Command from the House) for the finding out of this wretched fellow, who delivered the Letter to the porter. They came to the Inne where it was supposed he lay, as he was described by the Porter, and a Boy : who also casually looked upon him when he sent the Porter. This boy comming to the Inne puts on a Tapsters Apron, and ranne up the Staires into his Chamber, with a good spirit (as he was directed) that so he might see whether it was the man, or not, Anon, anon, anon Sir, saith he, what lacke ye : who being in Bed ; said, he did not call, but being to goe out early that morning, before it was day : he therefore called for a Candle, which was brought him. Then the boy looked upon his nose, and saw a Wart, of which

---

[1] *The Diurnall Occurrences or Dayly Proceedings of Both Houses in this Great and Happy Parliament.*

[2] B.M. *Thomason Tracts*, E 173 (23).

before he took notice, as also a red Ribond about his arme ; of which he gave information to the Constables, he were there ready and to apprehend him presently, who denied it. But the Porter and the Boy accused him : he being asked if he had taken the Oath of Allegeance ; he said, he never knew what it meant.

But in *fine* he is committed to the Gate-house, & when it shall please the Honourable Assembly to bring him to his tryall : I pray God that his providence may so rule the matter ; that what mischiefe, plots, Innovations, or popish Treacheries, lye hid under his knowledge, may, by him be discovered, and all other whatsoever, in Gods good time ; which God grant, for his Christ, his sake, Amen.

That this prayer apparently went unanswered is suggested by an entry in the *Commons' Journals* for the next day : [1]

Sir *Robert Pye* reports the Examination of Mr. *Mordant* and the Witnesses, touching the threatening Letter, sent Yesterday to Mr. *Pym* : And they find, upon strict Examination of his Attorney at Common Law, and some others, that this Mr. *Geo. Mordant* was not the Man that delivered the Porter the said Letter ; And that therefore he ought to be discharged.

Ordered that *Geo. Mordant* shall be discharged from any further Restraint touching the Matter informed of against him.

The outrage shows clearly that it was Pym who was regarded as the leader of the parliamentary opposition to the Court. The *Diurnall Occurrences* adds that not long afterwards someone " mistaken for Mr. Pym " was actually stabbed in Westminster Hall though the murderer escaped. It would be interesting to know whether the criminal was the letter-writer who thus a second time failed to get rid of the public enemy and who also again managed to avoid arrest.

Meanwhile, other events, and suspicions about events, were unsettling men's minds ; in particular there were rumours of a fresh army plot whereby the King was supposed to be trying to raise troops in support of his cause. Then, on 1st November came news of a rising in Ireland on such a scale as to drive every other consideration aside.

[1] II, 295.

The root cause of the trouble was the repeated and long-standing ill-treatment which the Irish had received from their English over-lords. For a time Strafford's iron hand had enforced order, if not peace, throughout Ireland. The removal of that hand, when Strafford was recalled to England and finally executed, had encouraged the renewal of the old disorders with greater rather than less violence for their having been momentarily suppressed. The bitterest opponents of the English Government in Ireland were, of course, the native Irish who had suffered repeatedly both as Roman Catholics and as the victims of the numerous and wide-spread plantations. But many Protestants were only less antagonistic towards England than were their Roman Catholic neighbours. Both alike resented Ireland's being used for the convenience of England whose policy, if Strafford had correctly interpreted it, seemed to be the suppression of all freedom to Irishmen of whatever religious or political creed. Strafford's successor was the Earl of Leicester who, in contrast to Strafford, remained in England. The opportunity was too good to miss : in October 1641 the Irish of Ulster rose, attacked the garrisons, and ill-treated and murdered the English settlers and their families. The numbers massacred are difficult to estimate ; but certainly several thousands perished either through actual violence or through exposure and starvation. What was of scarcely less importance at the time was the widespread belief in a plot for the general massacre of British settlers in Ireland.

News of such a massacre could hardly have reached England at a more opportune moment for the parliamentary leaders. Plans for the outbreak were commonly believed to have been concerted by Roman Catholic priests. This belief intensified Puritan fears of Romanist machinations in England, all the more so because of rumours that Charles was in league with the rebels. The rebellion further brought the political crisis to a head by its necessitating the raising of an army for its suppression. Who was to control such an army ? Constitutionally the King was in command of all armed forces ; yet Pym and his followers realized that to place a large army at the King's disposal would be to ensure the destruction of themselves and of the cause for which they stood. Accordingly, though the Commons voted the raising of men and of money for the suppression of the Irish rebellion, they also took steps to ensure that the King's power was not thereby increased. On 5th November Pym moved that certain instructions to this end should be sent to the committee in Scotland. The Commons regarded the terms of his proposal as so startling that at first they refused to accept it. Not until 8th November was the proposal passed, and then only after prolonged debates and in a modified form. Even so its terms were sufficiently drastic.

After declaring that the great miseries which had afflicted the King's dominions had " issued from the cunning, false and malicious practices " of some of the King's counsellors, and that " those conspiracies and commotions in Ireland are but the effects of the same counsels ", the Instructions thus concluded : [1]

If herein His Majesty shall not vouchsafe to condescend to our humble supplication, although we shall always continue, with reverence and faithfulness to his person and to his crown, to perform those duties of service and obedience to which by the laws of God and this kingdom we are obliged ; yet we shall be forced, in discharge of the trust which we owe to the State, and to those whom we represent, to resolve upon one such way of defending Ireland from the rebels, as may concur to the securing ourselves from such mischievous counsels and designs, as have lately been, and still are, in practice and agitation against us, as we have just cause to believe ; and to commend those aids and contributions which this great necessity shall require, to the custody and disposing of such persons of honour and fidelity as we have cause to confide in.

This was an enunciation, in the most unequivocal terms, of the doctrine of the responsibility of ministers to Parliament. Though taken for granted in modern democratic Britain, it was a revolutionary doctrine in the seventeenth century, so much so that Pym had to fight for the passage of the Instructions through the Commons where they were finally carried by 151 votes to 110.

That the Instructions were thus passed could not blind Pym

[1] *Lords' Journals*, IV, 431, ii.

and his henchmen to the danger implied by that large minority of 110 or by the considerable number of abstentions. The minority included men like Falkland, who had formerly opposed the King, and the existence of a large body of neutrals suggested that others might follow him into the royalist camp. At the moment the supremacy of Pym was evidently precarious, and the whole issue hung in the balance. There can be little doubt that this was the fact which induced the opposition leaders to press on with the Remonstrance on the condition of the Kingdom. Such a Remonstrance had long been projected and might win over more decidedly the support of the people. It is not without significance that the Remonstrance was read on the very day that the Instructions were passed by the Commons.

Details of the Grand Remonstrance, with its two hundred and four clauses, are unnecessary to our purpose. More than half the clauses consist of a recital of grievances. Then follow sixty clauses which enumerate the laws already passed to secure the liberty of the people. The clauses (181–204) referring to religion include the following significant statement :

We do here declare that it is far from our purpose or desire to let loose the golden reins of discipline and government in the Church, to leave private persons or particular congregations to take up what form of Divine Service they please, for we hold it requisite that there should be throughout the whole realm a conformity to that order which the laws enjoin according to the Word of God. And we desire to unburden the consciences of men of needless and superstitious ceremonies, suppress innovations, and take away the monuments of idolatry.

And the better to effect the intended reformation, we desire there may be a general synod of the most grave, pious, learned and judicious divines of this island ; assisted with some from foreign parts, professing the same religion with us, who may consider of all things necessary for the peace and good government of the Church, and represent the results of their consultations unto the Parliament, to be there allowed of and confirmed, and receive the stamp of authority, thereby to find passage and obedience throughout the kingdom.

Our interest in this statement is that it must be taken as representing

Pym's views on the solution of the religious problem as he found it. Evidently a general toleration was no part of his policy. The execution of these clauses of the Remonstrance would, it must be remembered, have abolished not only Arminianism at the one extreme but also the sectaries—the Anabaptists, the Antinomians, and the like—at the other.

The concluding clauses returned to the subject of the responsibility of ministers :

That His Majesty be humbly petitioned by both Houses to employ such councillors, ambassadors and other ministers, in managing his business at home and abroad as the Parliament may have cause to confide in, without which we cannot give His Majesty such supplies for support of his own estate, nor such assistance to the Protestant party beyond the sea, as is desired.

The Remonstrance makes clear that undesirable classes of ministers may include some who cannot be charged with provable offences against the law : evidently the lesson of Strafford's impeachment had not been lost upon Pym and his followers.

The debates on the Remonstrance were long and heated, and occupied eight days between 9th and 22nd November. The clauses which provoked the sharpest division among the Members were those relating to religion.

Meanwhile, evidence was accumulating as to the second army plot, and on 17th November Pym moved and carried a resolution to the effect : [1]

That, upon the examinations now read, there is sufficient Evidence for this House to believe, that there was a Second Design to bring up the Army against the Parliament, and an Intention to make the *Scottish* army stand as neutral.

Whether by design or accident, the resolution was perfectly timed to influence votes for the critical closing stages of the Remonstrance debates. Even so, the final debate on 22nd November was fiercely contested, and the fate of the Remonstrance seemed to hang uncertainly in the balance. Hyde, Falkland, Dering, and Cul-

[1] *Commons' Journals*, II, 318.

pepper all spoke against the Remonstrance. Then Pym rose to answer their arguments point by point. He declared boldly : [1]

> The honour of the King lies in the safety of the people, and we must tell the truth ; the plots have been very near the King, all driven home to the Court and the Popish party. . . . The Popish lords and bishops so obstruct us. . . . We have suffered so much by counsellors of the King's choosing, that we desire him to advise us about it, and many of his servants move him about them, and why may not Parliament ? Altar-worship is idolatry, and that was enjoined by the bishops in all their cathedrals. This declaration will bind the people's hearts to us when they see how we have been used.

Many Members—including Hampden who had come down from Scotland to bring news of Charles' manœuvres there—took part in the debate on the Remonstrance after Pym resumed his seat. The debate had begun that day at noon. When the light failed on that November day, candles were called for ; and not until midnight was the debate concluded and the vote taken. Out of 307 votes, the Remonstrance secured a majority of only 11.

Even then the struggle was not over. Immediately after the vote had been taken, Peard, the Puritan Member for Barnstaple, moved a resolution that the Remonstrance should be printed. Such a resolution showed conclusively what was uppermost in the minds of the supporters of the Remonstrance and was itself revolutionary : the Remonstrance was designed to win back for its advocates the support of the people (the same idea was expressed by Pym in the concluding sentence quoted above); and to publish the terms of a measure before it had been presented to the King was contrary to previous usage. The motion for printing (which in the end was waived) caused a fresh outburst of feeling, as also did a motion by the opponents of the Remonstrance that their names might be entered as protesting against the printing. So high was the excitement that swords were drawn, and only Hampden's calm intervention saved the House from bloodshed : what might have been the upshot of a fracas on the floor of the House none can estimate.

[1] Verney : *Notes of Proceedings in the Long Parliament,* 122-3.

According to Clarendon,[1] when the House met next day :

Mr. Pimm lamented the disorder of the night before, which, he said, might probably have engaged the House in blood, and proceeded principally by the offering a protestation, which had been never before offered in that House, and was a transgression that ought to be severely examined, that mischief hereafter might not result from that precedent : and therefore proposed that the House would the next morning enter upon that examination, and in the meantime men might recollect themselves, and they who used to take notes might peruse their memorials, that the persons who were the chief causers of the disorder might be named, and defend themselves as best they could. And with this resolution the House rose ; the vexation of the night before being very visible in the looks and countenance of many.

The 24th and 25th November were occupied by debates on the conduct of Palmer who had first moved the entry of the protestations, and on the latter day he was committed to the Tower where he remained until 8th December when, following his petition to the House and his acknowledgment of his fault, he was released.

On 25th November Charles returned to London from Scotland. The next move in the game was his ; and upon that move the fate of himself and the State would depend. The struggle over the Remonstrance had revealed, as nothing else had done, the real nature of the difference between King and opposition, and the large following which the King could rally round himself if only he acted wisely.

The question that divided England after the political settlement had been completed in August 1641 was : where lay the greater danger to true religion—in " Jesuiting Popery " or in the " raging sects " ? . . . Strafford's last gift to Puritanism, the Irish Rebellion, provided the answer for a bare majority of the House of Commons, and drove moderate Puritans like Pym and Hampden to accept the radical programme of the younger Vane, Cromwell, and St. John. The result was the Grand Remonstrance. . . . But moderate Churchmen saw greater danger to the Church in the remedies proposed and they finally rejected the identification of the English Church with Rome. The Remonstrance did not

[1] *Great Rebellion*, Book IV, Section 55.

create the two parties of the Civil War, but it defined their attitude to all the issues in addition to religion, and it finally separated the conservative from the revolutionary elements in the opposition.[1]

This summary of the situation is worth quoting at length because it explains precisely on the one hand why Pym, for all his moderation, had been driven to advocate extreme measures, and on the other what was the nature of the crisis created by the Remonstrance. At the moment when Charles returned to his capital, there was a strong reaction in his favour. If he had had the wisdom to avoid any provocative word or act and to allow the reaction to take its course, he might even then have seen his enemies routed. Instead, he conceived his proper policy to be to seize the favourable opportunity and himself to take the initiative. In following this course he, as usual, acted in such a way as to put himself hopelessly in the wrong : the effect was to throw away all that his cause had gained by the Remonstrance, to heal the differences in the ranks of his opponents, and thus to allow the initiative to pass back from himself to Parliament.

The entry of the King and Queen into London on 25th November was a great triumph. The citizens flocked to cheer them ; and the Lord Mayor, the Corporation, and the City Companies in full regalia turned out to give them formal, but not less hearty, welcome. It is not surprising that Charles, and even more Henrietta, should misinterpret this enthusiasm and should imagine that the popular tide had turned in their favour. The King's first action next day was to assert his constitutional command over the armed forces by dismissing the parliamentary guard under Essex. When Lords and Commons protested against this step, the King appointed a new guard temporarily under the Earl of Dorset. How completely Charles had misinterpreted the welcome of the citizens was shown on the 29th when a crowd, rudely armed, swarmed into Palace Yard shouting, "No bishops". So menacing was its attitude that Dorset ordered the guard to fire. Though fortunately, and somewhat mysteriously, the order was not carried out, feeling ran high. In the House, Pym reported the findings

[1] I. D. Jones : *The English Revolution*, p. 51.

of the committee appointed "to draw up Reasons for a Guard". After alluding to disorderly persons in and around the city, to conspiracies in Ireland and Scotland, and to discontented Papists, his resolution concluded : [1]

These several Considerations do move the Parliament to desire a Guard, under the Command of the Earl of *Essex*. . . . But to have it under the Command of any other, not chosen by themselves, they can by no means consent, and will rather run any Hazard than admit of a President so dangerous both to this and future Parliaments.

The upshot was that Dorset's guard was withdrawn.

Another action of the King soon after his return from Scotland, showing the new confidence that his reception by the Londoners had given him, was his dismissal of Sir Henry Vane the elder from the Secretaryship and from his other offices. Thus at last Charles was able to avenge the death of Strafford, against whom the strongest evidence had been that of Vane respecting Strafford's advice to bring Irish troops into "this Kingdom". In December, the younger Vane also was dismissed from the Treasurership of the Navy to which he had been appointed in January 1639. The elder Vane forthwith threw in his lot with the parliamentary opposition ; and father, as well as son, was soon in the full confidence of the parliamentary leader. In August 1642, the younger Vane was appointed by Parliament sole Treasurer of the Navy, an office which he continued to hold for eight years.

It was on 1st December that the Remonstrance was formally presented to the King for his assent. With it was a petition for legislation to exclude the bishops from Parliament. The King's reply was to the effect that he would announce his decision on the Remonstrance as soon as he had considered it, and asking that in the meantime it should not be published.

On 3rd December fresh news arrived of events in Ireland. Armagh had been taken by Sir Phelim O'Neill, who purported to be acting under a special commission from King Charles to restore Roman Catholicism in Ireland. The claim, like the

[1] Rushworth, IV, 435–6 ; *Commons' Journals*, II, 327–8.

" Broad Seal of England " on his " commission ", was doubtless
a mere pretence ; but in the inflamed atmosphere of the time it
served to rouse popular excitement in England to a still higher
pitch. Pym moved and carried a resolution appointing a committee to confer with the Lords on Bills passed by the Commons
for the safety of the country but rejected by the Lords. The
resolution contained the further ominous declaration : [1]

> that this House being the Representative Body of the whole
> Kingdom, and their Lordships being but as particular Persons,
> and coming to Parliament in a particular Capacity, that if they
> should not be pleased to consent to the Passing of those Acts, and
> others, necessary to the Preservation and Safety of the Kingdom,
> that then this House, together with such of the Lords as are more
> sensible of the Safety of the Kingdom, may join together, and
> represent the same to his Majesty.

Several further incidents in the opening days of December showed
how tense the atmosphere was. On 7th December, Haselrig
introduced a proposal to appoint a Lord General with wide powers
to raise, maintain, and command the militia, and to appoint a
Lord Admiral with similarly wide powers at sea. Such appointments would have deeply infringed upon the royal prerogative,
and the Bill met with loud opposition in the Commons ; nevertheless the motion for its rejection was defeated by the considerable
majority of 158 to 125. The Bill received its first reading on 21st
December, and its second reading three days later. The terms of
the Bill show how deeply Charles was already distrusted. On 11th
December a Petition, supposed to bear 20,000 signatures, was
brought to the Commons by a large number of city traders in
support of Pym's policy of excluding the bishops and Roman
Catholic peers from the House of Lords.[2] Four days later the
Commons, tired of waiting for the King's answer to the Remonstrance, voted that its terms should be printed.

The first positive action of Charles was taken on 21st December
when he dismissed Sir William Balfour from the Lieutenancy of
the Tower. Balfour had been the strict gaoler of Strafford and

---

[1] *Commons' Journals*, II, 330.   [2] Ibid., p. 339.

Laud, and his pronounced opposition to the Court was well known. His successor was Sir Thomas Lunsford, whose only claim to fame was the wildness of his life. Clarendon describes him as [1] " a person of great license, and known only by some desperate acts for which he had been formerly imprisoned by the State, and, having made his escape, fled the Kingdom ". Lunsford's appointment at such a juncture was typical of Charles' incapacity to read a situation : the clear implication was that the King intended to send to the Tower certain prisoners who could not be entrusted to anyone sympathetic to the Opposition. On the same day Charles issued his answer to the Petition which accompanied the Grand Remonstrance.[2] To the first part of the Petition, concerning religion, the answer was :

For preserving the peace and safety of this kingdom, from the design of the Popish party, we have, and will still, concur with all the just desires of our people, and in a parliamentary way. That, for the depriving of the Bishops of their votes in Parliament, we would have you consider that their right is grounded upon the fundamental law of the kingdom, and constitution of Parliament. . . .
To the second prayer of the petition, concerning the removal and choice of councillors, we know not any of our council, to whom the character set forth in the Petition can belong. That by those whom we had exposed to trial, we have already given you sufficient testimony, that there is no man so near unto us in place, or affection, whom we will not leave to the justice of the law, if you shall bring a particular charge, and sufficient proofs against him. . . . That for the choice of our councillors and ministers of state, . . . as it is the undoubted right of the Crown of England, to call such persons to our secret counsels, to public employment, and our particular service, as we shall think fit, so we are, and ever shall be, very careful to make election of such persons, in those places of trust, as shall have given good testimonies of their abilities and integrity.

This was Charles I at his best. If only he had continued to act in the kingly, dignified spirit of this declaration, he would have won all England to his side, except perhaps certain small and

[1] *Great Rebellion*, Book IV, Section 102.   [2] Rushworth, IV, 452–3.

extreme factions ; and, from what we have been able to interpret of Pym's mind, we can be certain that Pym would not have been among the factions. But it was ever the way of Charles to throw away every advantage that he won for himself. The effect that the King's reply had had upon the Lords at least was plainly shown : when the Commons asked the Upper House to join with them in petitioning for Lunsford's removal from the Lieutenancy of the Tower, the Lords refused to co-operate. Only when pressure was exerted by the authorities of the city did Charles remove Lunsford and appoint Sir John Byron in his stead. These events, though Pym had no direct share in them, are worth noting as the background of the next scenes in which he was to appear.

The prelude to that appearance was an event of 27th December. As, that day, the Lords were assembling, a mob greeted them with cries of : "No Bishops ! No Papist Lords !" ; and Archbishop Williams of York—the senior member of the bishops' bench now that Laud was in prison—when he appeared, was unpleasantly hustled. On the following day, only two bishops dared to run the gauntlet of the mob and to appear in the Lords' House. The Lords therefore sent to ask the Commons to suggest united action to restore order. The Commons refused the request, and Claren-don notes : [1] "Mr. Pim himself saying, 'God forbid the House of Commons should proceed, in any way, to dishearten the people to obtain their just desires in such a way'." If Pym really did express himself in these terms, it must be remembered that though Lunsford was no longer at the Tower, his command there had suggested an attack upon the Commons' leaders, and that the only protection the leaders had was the London citizens. The Commons' refusal was immediately followed by Archbishop Williams' handing to Charles a formal protest, signed by himself and eleven other bishops, to the effect that, since they were being prevented by violence from attending the Lords' House, anything done during their absence was null and void. Charles encouraged the protest at least to the length of having it passed to the Lords. Here was another typical blunder of Charles. At the very moment

[1] *Great Rebellion*, Book IV, Section 114.

when the Lords were separating from the Commons and were leaning towards the King, Charles associated himself with, or at least did not dissociate himself from, a protest which his friends presumed to make to the Lords as to the legality of the Lords' decisions. The Lords, deeply moved, at once informed the Commons of the Protest and desired " a present Conference, by a Committee of both Houses ",[1] the subject of the Conference being

To communicate the aforesaid Petition of the Bishops to the House of Commons, and to let them know, that, the Petition containing Matters of high and dangerous Consequence, are such as their Lordships are very sensible of, and require a speedy and sudden Resolution ; the Petition extending to the deep intrenching upon the fundamental Privileges and Being of Parliament, this House thinks it fit, the Business concerning the whole Parliament, to communicate with the House of Commons in this affair, of so great and of so general Concernment.

Pym might well have anticipated an exclamation which Cromwell was to utter on a famous occasion and have declared : " The Lord hath delivered them into my hand " ; for, at the moment when the parliamentary prospects were most unpromising, Charles and his friends had walked out of an entrenched position, thereby inviting their opponents to take the offensive against them. Pym was not slow to seize the opportunity. On 30th December, after moving that the doors of the House should be closed, he declared his opinion that the House was in danger of attack and he therefore urged that it should ask for the protection of the city's trained bands. Whatever the facts may have been as to the imminence of an attack, the indirect implications of the Bishops' Protest were serious enough. If the principle were once granted of annulling parliamentary decisions taken under alleged pressure, the way would be open for endless similar annulments in the future : Charles himself might even claim, if his political circumstances improved, that he need take no account of Acts to which he had set his hand under pressure. The Commons, however, chose,

[1] *Lords' Journals*, IV, 497.

rather than appeal to the city, to ask the Lords to join them in asking for a guard. On the immediate issue Pym had no difficulty in carrying the House with him. He moved, and the House agreed, that the twelve bishops who had signed the Protest should be accused " of High Treason, for endeavouring to subvert the fundamental laws of the Kingdom, and the very Being of Parliament, by preferring this Petition, and making the Protestation expressed in the Petition ".[1] The Lords at once concurred. Ten of the twelve bishops were forthwith committed to the Tower ; and the other two, on account of old age, were entrusted to the guardianship of the Usher of the Black Rod. Thus the Tower sheltered both archbishops at once—a situation rendered the more ironical by the fact that the two men had been on anything but friendly terms. On 31st December the Commons adjourned till 3rd January but decided that a committee of the whole House should meet at the Guildhall, thus securing the protection of the city.

On New Year's Day the King sent for Pym to offer him the Chancellorship of the Exchequer.[2] The incident is still shrouded in mystery. About both the King's motive for making the offer, and the nature of Pym's response to it, we are completely ignorant. Whatever may have prompted Charles to offer the post, the strained conditions of the moment, apart from any other consideration, would have made Pym's acceptance impossible. Next day, Culpepper was appointed to the Exchequer, and Falkland became Secretary of State.

Then the scene underwent a dramatic change. As soon as the Lords met on 3rd January, the Attorney-General, Sir Edward Herbert, acting on the personal instructions of the King, laid a charge of impeachment against one Member of the Lords' House and five Members of the Commons.[3]

Articles of high treason and other misdemeanours against the Lord Kimbolton, Mr. Denzil Holles, Sir Arthur Haslerigg, Mr. John Pym, Mr. John Hampden and Mr. William Strode.

[1] *Commons' Journals*, I, 363, i.
[2] Dering to Lady Dering—quoted by Gardiner : *History of England*, X, 127.
[3] *Lords' Journals*, IV, 500–1.

1. That they have traitorously endeavoured to subvert the fundamental Laws and Government of the Kingdom of England, to deprive the King of his royal power, and to place in subjects an arbitrary and tyrannical power over the lives, liberties and estates of His Majesty's liege people.

2. That they have traitorously endeavoured (by many foul aspersions upon His Majesty and his Government) to alienate the affections of His people, and to make His Majesty odious unto them.

3. That they have endeavoured to draw His Majesty's late army to disobedience to His Majesty's commands, and to side with them in their traitorous designs.

4. That they have traitorously invited and encouraged a foreign power to invade His Majesty's kingdom of England.

5. That they have traitorously endeavoured to subvert the rights and the very being of Parliaments.

6. That, for the completing of their traitorous designs, they have endeavoured (as far as in them lay) by force and terror to compel the Parliament to join with them in their traitorous designs, and to that end have actually raised and countenanced tumults against the King and Parliament.

7. And they have traitorously conspired to levy, and actually have levied, war against the King.

The reason for the King's suddenly changed attitude to Pym is not difficult to explain. In well-informed circles it was commonly reported that the parliamentary leaders were planning to impeach the Queen whom they regarded as a chief source of mischief both religious and political.[1] Certainly, they would have had no difficulty in finding evidence enough to win a verdict. The King, therefore, so it would seem, decided to forestall the attack on his wife by turning the tables on the attackers.

The Attorney-General, after preferring the charge, asked for the arrest of the six accused. But the position was not very regular : properly, the Commons should be the accusers in an impeachment ; and the Lords therefore appointed a committee to consider their reply to the Attorney's demand.

Meanwhile there was some excitement in the Commons. First, an answer was received from the King to the Commons' request

---

[1] Gardiner : *History of England*, X, 128.

for a guard : while promising, on the word of a king, that no harm should come to the Members, the answer evaded any definite promise of a guard. The Commons then sent to the city to ask for the trained bands.

Next, Pym rose to announce that the studies of himself, Holles, and Hampden had been sealed up by the King's orders. The Commons voted this to be a breach of privilege and invited the Lords to pass a similar resolution. At this juncture the Sergeant-at-Arms entered to arrest the five Members of the Commons. Once again Charles had chosen the wrong way to effect his purpose, a way that seemed intended to offend both Commons and Lords. The Commons, regarding the attempt to arrest in such circumstances to be a breach of their privileges, answered that they would consider the King's demand and send him word of their conclusions. At the same time they ordered the five Members to attend in their places in the House. The Lords, whose committee was still considering the position, regarded the King's action as an affront. The result was that they joined with the Commons in demanding a guard and ordered the sealed studies to be opened : [1]

Ordered, that the Chambers, Studies and Trunks, that are sealed up, or locked, belonging to Mr. Hollis, Mr. Pym, Mr. Hampden, or to any other Member of Parliament, shall be forthwith unsealed, unlocked, and left for their free use and disposure.

Not even these reactions were pointed enough to convince Charles of the folly of the course he was pursuing. He seems to have been blind to the significance of the changed attitude of the Lords. Hitherto his hope had lain in the growing division between Lords and Commons. With both Houses united against him, his chance of final success was faint indeed. Yet he went heedlessly on from folly to folly. Since his Sergeant had failed to arrest the delinquents, only one course remained—he must arrest them himself. The fateful decision was taken on the night of 3rd January.

Next morning Charles was subject to one of his usual fits of vacillation, and quite possibly, if left to himself, would never have

[1] *Lords' Journals*, IV, 502.

carried through the design. But he was not left to himself. His evil genius, the Queen, urged him on. The remark attributed to her—" Go, you coward, and pull these rogues out by the ears, or never see my face more "—is exactly typical of Henrietta : without any understanding of English constitutional tradition, she saw traitors insolently defying their sovereign. And Charles' reaction to her charge was equally typical. He was devoted to his wife, and he was no coward : these personal factors outweighed for him the larger issues, and, blind to the inevitable results, he went forward to the crowning blunder of his life.

If the inspirer of the blunder was the Queen, she also was the means of its failure. The prospect of the arrest of the archenemies, and the consequent royal triumph, raised her excitement to such an uncontrollable pitch that, even before Charles left Whitehall for the House of Commons, she had confided the plan to her friend the Countess of Carlisle. Around the activities of the latter lady there still hangs some mystery. That, as Lady Lucy Percy, daughter of the ninth Earl of Northumberland, she had eloped in 1617 with James Hay, a Scottish courtier who had come to England with James I and who, the year after their marriage, was created Lord Doncaster and later the Earl of Carlisle ; and that she became one of the beauties and wits of the Court and the confidante of Henrietta Maria—all these are well-known facts. But these facts render all the less explicable her friendship with two other men, neither of whom belonged to the Court circle. The first was Strafford. During Strafford's most difficult days, in Ireland and later in England, there was constant communication between them : whoever else failed him, Strafford could rely upon Lady Carlisle for information, advice, and mediation with Charles and Henrietta. The second object of her friendship, after Strafford's execution, was John Pym. If it is difficult to account for her attachment to Strafford, it is more difficult to understand why she transferred that attachment to his chief enemy. There is, of course, one easy explanation which some contemporaries smilingly passed from one to another, and which later detractors have not failed to repeat. Lady Carlisle was commonly reputed to be the mistress first of Strafford and later of Pym. But the apparent is not always the true explanation of the motives behind the actions of individuals. The Earl of Carlisle had died in 1636, and if his beautiful and witty widow had been disposed to exercise her charms illicitly, there were many more attractive gallants both at Court and outside it than either Wentworth or John Pym. Of late, this estimate of Pym as a philanderer has been revived.

When the Long Parliament met, Pym was in the middle fifties, and was said to have been " indifferent neither to Bacchus nor to Venus ". Indeed, he appears to have been that extremely unpleasant type, a *faux bonhomme*. As a political tactician he has rarely been equalled, and he knew how to turn his very weaknesses to account, for through his mistress, Lady Carlisle, he learnt the secrets of the Court.[1]

To repeat scandal without adducing proof is neither good taste nor good scholarship. If Pym had such " weaknesses " it is well that we should know of them in order to a just estimate of his character ; but we have no right to accept as a fact what can be only conjecture. And no shred of evidence exists to prove that Lady Carlisle was unfaithful to her husband either before his death or afterwards, or that Pym was thus untrue to the memory of his wife whom he had lost twenty years before. There are other possible explanations of the relationship between Lady Carlisle and Pym which, though also conjectural, more nearly accord with what we know of the general character and circumstances of both of them. There is nothing to suggest that Lady Carlisle was attached to the political principles of any party as such. Gardiner's estimate of her that " she loved to mingle political intrigue with social intercourse " and that " without any deep feelings herself, she loved to be of importance, and she was shrewd enough to make herself useful to the real leaders of men " is sufficient to account for her secret alliance with both Strafford and Pym ".[2]

Whatever her motives, there seems no doubt that after Strafford's death Lady Carlisle was the source of much of Pym's information

---

[1] Sir Charles Petrie : *The Stuarts*, pp. 137–8.
[2] *History of England*, IX, 85, 376.

about the activities and intentions of the Court. Certainly it was she who, on 4th January 1642, managed to send information through the Earl of Essex that the King intended to go in person to the Commons.

Yet his coming to the Lower House, being betrayed by that busy Stateswoman, the Countess of Carlisle (who had now changed her gallant from Strafford to Mr. Pym, and was become such a She-Saint, that she frequented their sermons, and took notes) he lost the opportunity of seizing their persons.[1]

It was about three o'clock that Charles, accompanied by his nephew, Charles Lewis, the Elector Palatine, set off from Whitehall for the House. Charles himself went by coach accompanied by between 300 and 400 armed followers. The news of his coming travelled faster than he, and the five accused Members withdrew and made their way by water to the city. The consequent scene in the House has often been described—the armed men remaining at the door, Charles advancing to the Speaker's chair, his failure to see the men whom he came to arrest, the silence when he called their names, Speaker Lenthall's reply : " May it please your Majesty, I have neither eyes to see, nor tongue to speak in this place but as this House is pleased to direct me, whose servant I am here," the King's remark : " I see all the birds are flown. I do expect from you that you shall send them unto me as soon as they return hither. If not, I will seek them myself; for their treason is foul, and such a one as you will thank me to discover," and finally his withdrawal amid shouts of " Privilege ! Privilege ! "

The King's failure was disastrous to his cause. For a king to enter the Commons' House was without precedent in history. To enter with violent intent was to break beyond repair the loyalty of Members which had long been subject to terrific strain. And to fail in the violence meant a loss of royal prestige in the nation at large. On the other hand, if the five Members had not been forewarned, or if, notwithstanding the warning, they had remained in their places, the result would have been even more disastrous for both the King's cause and the nation. Their fellow-

[1] Sir Philip Warwick : *Memoires of the Reign of King Charles I.*

Members would almost certainly have resisted the arrest, the soldiers would have entered, and bloodshed, even a massacre, on the floor of the House must have resulted. What terrible consequences would have ensued is beyond calculation.

Immediately after the King's withdrawal, the House adjourned. Next day Charles went into the city, and at Guildhall demanded that the traitors should be given up. The mind of the City Council was divided, but both on his way and at Guildhall the King was greeted with cries of " Privileges of Parliament ! ", and finally he returned to Whitehall baffled once again. Meanwhile both Houses were in session, but the Commons appointed a committee to meet at Guildhall and then they formally adjourned until 11th January.

On 10th January, the trained bands of the city were put under the command of Captain Skippon who was henceforward responsible for guarding the Houses. As soon as the Commons were securely guarded, the five Members—whom the King's officers had failed to find—entered Guildhall where their fellow-Members welcomed them with cheers.

That same morning Charles and Henrietta Maria had left Whitehall. The reasons for the move are not difficult to guess. To remain to witness the return of the Commons—including the five who had defied the King's attempts at arrest—would have been to suffer a still further blow to royal prestige. Further, almost certainly as soon as the triumphant Commons reassembled, they would continue the plan of impeaching the Queen. Hence, Charles, his wife and children, left for Hampton Court. The next time Charles would see Whitehall would be some seven years later when on the point of execution.

Though in 1642 that tragic end was beyond prediction, the withdrawal of Charles from his capital had an obvious significance. It had about it more than a suggestion of abdication. Though he remained to the end of his life the King of a loyally devoted section of the people, after his withdrawal on 10th January 1642 he ceased to be King of the nation as a whole. The events of the next day left no doubt who had replaced him, so far as any individual could replace him. On 11th January, the Commons reassembled in their House, the five Members being accorded a triumphant return by the citizens. In that moment no one could doubt where the leadership lay. Henceforward, until his death nearly two years later, it was Pym who was the director of the State. The country gentleman's son of Brymore, an orphan almost from babyhood, had become King Pym. He had come to his uncrowned throne at an hour as pregnantly critical as any in English history. The supreme question, for the nation as for Pym himself, was whether his statesmanship would be equal to the task of finding a permanent solution to the complex constitutional problems for the raising of which he had himself been largely responsible.

Part IV

"KING PYM"

CHAPTER X

PRELUDE TO WAR

January to August 1642

THE embitterment produced by Charles' unsuccessful attempt to arrest the five Members was soon evident in the actions of both King and Commons. By the King's orders, the munitions of the disbanded northern army had been sent to Hull. On 11th January—the very day of the return of the five Members to the House and of the royal family's removal to Hampton Court—the King appointed the Earl of Newcastle to be Governor of Hull. News of this appointment, like news of most of the King's plans, leaked out to Pym; and the Commons forthwith countered the King's move by appointing Sir John Hotham to the governorship. Next day, Major-General Skippon, whom the Commons had recently placed in command of the London train-bands, was ordered to place a guard around the Tower. Such acts did more than indicate the trend of events: they widened the breach between the two sides.

Charles soon realized that the only way to maintain his independence of action was to place as great a distance as possible between himself and the Parliament at Westminster. As the first stage in this removal, after staying only a couple of days at Hampton Court, he passed on to Windsor. While there he exchanged several notes, on matters at issue, with the Commons. In so far as the Lords were involved in this paper conflict, they showed themselves less generally antagonistic than the Commons towards the King. Thus when, on 24th January, the Commons formally requested that the militia and the forts should be put " into such hands in whom the Parliament may confide ", the Lords would not associate themselves with the resolution. The upshot was that on the following day a conference was held between the two Houses, the conference being managed, on the Commons' side, by Pym,[1] who used the occasion as an opportunity for expounding the dangers in which the country then stood. He began by presenting four Petitions which had been sent to the Commons by London and by the counties of Middlesex, Essex, and Hertfordshire respectively, and which requested that the bishops and the popish peers might be removed from the Lords' House and that the defences of the Kingdom might be entrusted to officers whom the people could trust. Said he :[2]

My Lords, In these foure Petitions you may hear the voice or rather the crie of all *England,* and you cannot wonder if the urgencie, the extremitie of the condition wherin we are, do produce some earnestnesse and vehemencie of expression more than ordinarie ; the Agonie, terror, and perplexitie in which the Kingdom labours, is universall, all parts are affected with it, and therefore in these, you may observe the groanes and miserable complaints of all.

Using this as a text, Pym proceeded to detail, in his own orderly fashion and at considerable length, the " Divers reasons why those diseases which are Epidemicall are more dangerous than others". So far as contemporary England was concerned, he observed :

The common and epidemicall disease wherein this Commonwealth lies now gasping hath a superior and universall cause from the evil Counsels and designes of those, who under his Majestie bear the greatest sway in Government.

2. It hath a contagious and infectious qualitie, whereby it is diffused and dispersed through all parts of the Kingdom.

3. It is apt to take in the discontents, evil affections, and designes of particular persons to increase and fortifie it self.

Next he elaborated the " variety of *Dangers* to which this Kingdom is now subject ". The causes of these dangers he traced to a number of " obstructions " ; for in the body politic, as in the natural body,

[1] *Lords' Journals,* IV, 540-3.
[2] *A Speech delivered at a Conference with the Lords, January XXV, MDCXLI,* printed by R. Oulton and G. Dexter for John Rothwell, 1641, by Order of the House of Commons.

Reade in this Image him, whose dearest blood
Is thought noe price to buy his Countryes good,
Whose name shall flourish, till the blast of ffame
Shall want a Trumpet; or true Worth, a name.

Edw: Bower pinxit   G: Glouer fecit

John Pym from a contemporary pamphlet

" Whensoever nature is hindred in her proper operations and faculties, distempers will necessarily follow." This led naturally to a description " of the chiefest of these obstructions ", namely " the obstruction of Reformation in matters of Religion ", " an obstruction in Trade ", " the obstruction in the Reliefe of Ireland ", " the obstruction in the prosecution of Delinquents ", " a generall obstruction and interruption of the proceedings of Parliament ", and, finally, " the obstruction in providing for the defence of the Kingdome ". So he wound to his peroration :

I am now come to a Conclusion, and I have nothing to propound to your Lordships by way of Request or desire from the House of Commons ; I doubt not but your judgments will tell you, what is to be done ; your Consciences, your Honours, your Interests will call upon you for the doing of it ; The Commons will be glad to have your helpe and concurrence in saving of the Kingdome ; but if they should faile of it, it should not discourage them in doing their dutie. And whether the Kingdome be lost or saved (as through God's blessing I hope it will be) they shall be sorry that the story of this present Parliament should tell Posteritie, that in so great a Danger and Extremitie, the House of Peeres should have no part in the honour of the preservation of it, you having so great an Interest in the good sucesse of those endeavours, in respect of your Estates, and high degrees of Nobilitie.

These were plain words which admitted of only one interpretation. In the sense that they were a virtual declaration that the Commons were prepared to act independently of the Lords, as though the Commons of themselves constituted Parliament, they were revolutionary words. Yet the whole speech shows that Pym and his party were honestly convinced that the dangers of the State were such as to leave them no alternative. We, after the passage of three centuries, may regard some of Pym's modes of expression as strange and harsh, and even extreme ; but who can say that, in his main contention, he was wrong ? In such circumstances, we ought to hesitate before labelling him as a revolutionary in the ordinarily accepted sense of the term. He was a statesman, maintaining long-accepted principles in unprecedented circumstances and therefore expressing them in unprecedented form.

Meanwhile the tide of feeling against the King was rapidly rising. Crowds of Londoners, both women and men, were constantly thronging the precincts of both Houses. Even the Lords could no longer be relied upon to support the King, and on 1st and 2nd February they joined with the Commons in two Petitions to His Majesty. The first related to the charges against the five Members : [1]

We think it our Duty once again to beseech Your Majesty to give Directions, that Your Parliament may be informed, before *Friday* next, what Proofs there is against them, that accordingly they may be called to a legal Trial, it being the undoubted Right and Privelege of Parliament, that no Member of Parliament can be proceeded against without the Consent of Parliament.

The second related to the forts and militia : [2]

We most humbly beseech Your Majesty, that You will be pleased forthwith to put *The Tower of London*, and all other Forts, and the whole Militia of the Kingdom, into the hands of such Persons as shall be recommended unto Your Majesty by both Houses of Parliament ; which, they assure themselves, will be a hopeful Entrance into those Courses which, through GOD's blessing, shall be effectual for the removing all Diffidence and Misapprehension betwixt Your Majesty and Your People.

On 6th February, the King replied that : " When he should know the extent of power which was intended to be established in those persons whom they desired to be commanders of the militia . . . then he would declare that he would be content to put in all the forts and over the militia such persons as both Houses of Parliament should either approve or recommend to him." A few days later, at the request of the Parliament, Charles agreed to the removal of Sir John Byron from the Lieutenancy of the Tower and to the appointment of Sir John Conyers in his place.

Though Charles and Parliament had thus reached a settlement on these hitherto outstanding matters, Charles was still feeling aggrieved at certain passages in the speech which, on 25th January, Pym had delivered at the Conference between the two Houses.

[1] *Lords' Journals*, IV, 556.   [2] Ibid., pp. 559–60.

Accordingly, on 7th February, Charles sent a message to the House of Commons on the subject : [1]

His Majestie taking notice of a Speech, pretending in the Title to have bin delivered by *Mr. Pym* in a Conference, and printed by Order of the House of Commons, in which it is affirmed, That since the stop upon the Ports against all *Irish* Papists by both Houses, many of the Chief Commanders, now in the head of the Rebels, have bin suffered to passe by his Majesties immediate Warrant ; and being very certain of having used extream Caution in the granting of Passports into *Ireland* ; So he conceives, either this Paper not to have bin so delivered and printed as it pretends, or this House to have received some mis-information.

His Majestie would be resolved, Whether this Speech were so delivered and Printed, and if it were, would have this House to review upon what Informations that particular was grounded, that either that may be found upon re-examination to have bin false, and both this House and His Majestie injured by it ; Or that His Majestie may know by what means, and by whose fault, His Authoritie hath bin so highly abused, as to be made to conduce to the assistance of that Rebellion, which he so much detests and abhors, and that Hee may see Himselfe fully vindicated from all reflections of the least suspition of that kind.

Accordingly, the Commons replied, furnishing names in justification of the charges contained in Pym's speech and concluding their reply with a somewhat ironical paragraph :

And your Majesties most faithfull Subjects are very sorry, that the Extreame Caution which your Majestie hath used, hath been so ill seconded with the diligence and faithfulnesse of your Ministers, and that your Royall Authority should be so highly abused, Although, as it was exprest in that speech by Mr. *Pym* wee believe it was by the procurement of some evill instruments too neer your Royal person, without your Majesties knowledge, and intention ; And wee beseech your Majesty to take such course, that not only your Honour may be vindicated for the time past, but your Kingdome may be secured from the like mischiefe for the time to come.

Even this did not end the dispute. A fortnight later the King sent

[1] *The Kings Majesties Message . . . with the House of Commons Humble Answer*, printed for John White, 1641.

a lengthy reply stating that he could not rest satisfied with the Commons' explanation and that he expected them either to furnish him with the names of individuals who had entered Ireland by royal licence and passed into the land of rebels, or failing this, that they would publish a declaration of their error. In accordance with this request, the Commons supplied certain names which the King challenged, and so the matter was never brought to a satisfactory issue.

Meanwhile another matter, which had hung fire for a long time and in the earlier stages of which, as we have seen, Pym had played a large part, was at last coming to a head. This was the position of the bishops in the House of Lords. On 5th February the Lords had finally passed the Bishops' Exclusion Bill.[1] Charles was thereby placed in a painful dilemma, for his attachment to the Church was deep and unfaltering. Added to this was the further consideration that hitherto the King had been able to rely upon the bishops to cast their votes in the Upper House almost invariably in his support : hence the exclusion of the bishops from that House would deprive the King of votes whose value would have grown as the disputes between King and Parliament intensified. The King might well hesitate, therefore, before giving consent to the Bill. According to Clarendon,[2] it was the arguments advanced by the Queen which finally overcame the King's hesitation. The Queen was persuaded not only

that indeed the Church could be only that way preserved. . . . but that her own safety very much depended upon the King's consent to that bill, and that if he should refuse it her journey into Holland would be crossed by the Parliament, and possibly her person in danger, either by the tumults which might easily be brought to Windsor from Westminster, or by the insurrection of the counties in her passage from thence to Dover, where she intended to take shipping. . . . These insinuations and discourses so far satisfied the Queen, and she the King, that, contrary to his most positive resolution, the King consented, and sent a commission for the enacting

[1] *Lords' Journals*, IV, 564.
[2] *Great Rebellion*, Book IV, Sections 297–305.

of the Bill (14th February). This is but one example out of many of Charles' actions being determined by his genuine affection for his wife, and too often determined to his own—and her—hurt.

On 23rd February, Henrietta Maria and her daughter set sail for Holland. She took with her the Crown Jewels which might be useful, in case of necessity, as a means of raising money. Henceforward the King, no longer hampered by considerations of the Queen's safety, was free to move and act as he thought best. His general plan seems to have been to make for the north of England where (as the Civil War was to show) the main body of loyalists was to be found. Thence he could defy the Parliament to do its worst. A reaction in his favour was far from impossible ; and if the worst came, the road would be open to the Continent. The farther north he went, the more acidly independent was the tone he adopted towards Parliament.

He began, on 28th February, by sending a lengthy reply to Parliament's request about the Militia.[1] Although " His Majesty calls the Almighty GOD to witness that He was so far from any Intention or Thought of Force or Violence ", he declared that

He cannot consent to divest Himself of the just Power which GOD and the Laws of this Kingdom have placed in Him for the Defence of this People, and to put it into the Hands of others for an indefinite Time.

Next day the Houses replied, protesting against the unsatisfactory nature of the King's statement and, not less, against the King's plan—which was common knowledge—to leave London. On this latter subject they begged the King

that, for the Dispatch of the great Affairs of the Kingdom, the Safety of Your Person, the Protection and Comfort of such Subjects you will be pleased to continue Your Abode near to *London* and the Parliament, and not to withdraw Yourself to any the remoter Parts ; which, if Your Majesty should do, must be a Cause of great Danger and Distraction.

The King's retort, on 2nd March, to those presenting this petition,

[1] *Lords' Journals*, IV, 617-18 ; *Commons' Journals*, II, 459-60.

was that : [1] " For My Residence near you, I wish it might be so safe and honourable, that I had no Cause to absent Myself from *Whitehall*. Ask Yourselves whether I have not ? " Within a week of that date the King was at Newmarket ; thence he moved northwards, and on 19th March he entered York.

From that moment, England was virtually without a government. Hitherto the monarch had ruled the country with the advice and consent of Parliament. The action of Charles—though doubtless he did not then realize its significance—was tantamount to an abdication. Pym and his supporters were thereby left with no alternative but gradually to improvise a method of government without the King. In this sense, Charles must bear at least equal responsibility with Pym for any revolutionary character which the new form of government necessarily developed.

The sense of an impending struggle made both sides anxious to gain control of the armed forces. On 5th March, Parliament issued a Militia Ordinance,[2] nominating the Lords Lieutenant of the counties who were to " have power to assemble and call together all and singular His Majesty's Subjects . . . that are meet and fit for the Wars ; and them to train, exercise and put in Readiness ". Three weeks later the King issued a proclamation [3]

forbidding all His Majesty's subjects belonging to the trained bands or militia of this Kingdom to rise, march, muster or exercise, by virtue of any Order or Ordinance of one or both Houses of Parliament, without consent or warrant from His Majesty, upon pain of punishment according to the laws.

Meanwhile, the Houses were convinced that one reason for the King's journey to York was to enable him to get control of the port of Hull and of the store of ordnance there. Accordingly, on 19th March they issued orders to the Governor [4] " that he receive no *English* or other Forces into that Town but such as by the Wisdom and Authority of both Houses of Parliament shall be advised and directed to be received into that Town ". Here was the first

---

[1] *Lords' Journals*, IV, 621–2.   [2] Ibid., pp. 625–7.   [3] Ibid., p. 587.
[4] Ibid., pp. 655–6.

manœuvre between King and Parliament for military advantage and, as such, it was a recognition that a breach, involving a resort to armed force, was possible if not inevitable. A week later, Parliament instructed Hotham to reinforce his garrison. On the other hand, a small but growing band of loyalists began to gather round the King at York. The stage was being prepared for a civil war.

One series of events will illustrate how rapidly the situation was developing : on 2nd April both Houses requested the King to consent to the removal of the magazine from Hull to the Tower of London ; on 16th April Charles replied by pointedly quoting from Pym's speech at the trial of Strafford emphasizing the necessity for maintaining the law (" If you take away the law, all things will fall into a confusion, every man will become a law unto himself ") ; [1] and on 18th April Parliament, defying the King, ordered that the magazine should be removed to London. On 23rd April Charles himself appeared before Hull with several hundred horsemen and demanded that Hotham should admit him to the town. Hotham's retort was to raise the drawbridges. That the commander of armed forces within the Kingdom should refuse to obey the King's command was an act of rebellion. Civil War had begun. The King, not yet ready to precipitate matters by using force, could only proclaim Hotham a traitor and then retire baffled.

After this episode, events marched rapidly towards open conflict. On 7th May Parliament renewed its order that the Hull Magazine should be removed to the Tower, an order which was shortly carried out by ships under the command of the Earl of Warwick. On 10th May, the Parliament's

own new officer, sergeant-major-general Skippon, appeared in Finsbury Fields, with all the train-bands of London, consisting of above eight thousand soldiers, disposed into six regiments, and under such captains and colonels as they had cause to confide in. At this first triumphant muster the Members of both Houses appeared in gross, there being a tent purposely set up for them,

---

[1] Ibid., pp. 722–3 ; *Commons' Journals*, II, 532.

and an entertainment at the charge of the city to the value of near a thousand pounds.[1]

Ten days later, Parliament drew up a Petition to the King [2] which, after reviewing the King's measures for the collection of armed forces, proceeded to declare

the Continuing and Increase of which Forces is to Your Parliament, and must needs be, a just Cause of great Jealousy and Danger to Your whole Kingdom. Therefore we do humbly beseech Your Majesty to disband all such Forces as, by Your Command, are assembled ; . . . otherwise we shall hold ourselves bound in Duty towards GOD, and by the Trust reposed in us by the People and the fundamental Laws and Constitutions of the Kingdom, to employ our Care and utmost Power to secure the Parliament, and to preserve the Peace and Quiet of the Kingdom.

On the King's side the weeks following his rebuff at Hull were marked by a steady increase in the numbers of his supporters who continued to gather at York from all parts of the country. These supporters included the Lord Keeper Littleton (who took with him the Great Seal), and Edward Hyde who was destined to be the Lord Keeper to the King's son, Charles II.

The two Houses moved the dispute one stage farther when, on 2nd June, they despatched to the King a summary of their views in the form of " The Nineteen Propositions ".[3] These included the petitions that the great Ministers of State should be " such as shall be approved of by both Houses of Parliament " ; that " the votes of Popish lords in the House of Peers may be taken away " ; that " your Majesty may be pleased to consent that such a reformation be made in the Church government and liturgy, as both Houses of Parliament shall advise " ; that " your Majesty will be pleased to rest satisfied with that course that the Lords and Commons have appointed for ordering the Militia " ; and that " your majesty will be pleased, by Act of Parliament, to clear the Lord Kimbolton and the five members of the House of Commons, in such manner that future Parliaments may be secured from the consequence of

[1] Clarendon : *The Great Rebellion*, Book V, Section 139.
[2] *Lords' Journals*, V, 77.   [3] Ibid., pp. 97–9.

that evil precedent ". The significance of the Propositions for our purpose is that they express the considered views of the Parliamentary opposition—including particularly those of John Pym—on the problems at issue between themselves and the King. One of the striking features of the Propositions is the accuracy with which they anticipated the final solution which later generations would apply to those problems, notably the responsibility of ministers to Parliament. Nevertheless, the Propositions constituted what, for the middle of the seventeenth century, was a revolutionary document in that they would have transferred the executive power from King to Parliament. To such a suggestion Charles could not be expected to agree, certainly not while any alternative existed. On the other hand, the Propositions prove conclusively that Pym and his fellows had ceased to trust Charles and had come to the conviction that the only hope of stable government was by the common acceptance of a written constitution which would define the relations of King and Parliament and would ensure, in the last resort, the supremacy of the people's will over that of the monarch. As a contribution to an immediate settlement, the Nineteen Propositions were valueless ; but as a statement of Parliament's views at the outbreak of the conflict, shaped as those views very largely were by Pym, they are of the highest significance.

From that point onwards, both sides gathered their resources and manœuvred for advantages in ways that, for the most part, do not concern us. On 4th July, the two Houses appointed a committee of fifteen members as a Committee of Safety " to take into Consideration whatsoever may concern the Safety of the Kingdom, the Defence of the Parliament, and the Prevention of the Peace of the Kingdom, and of opposing any Force whatsoever which may be raised against them ".[1] The five peers on the committee were Northumberland, Essex, Pembroke, Holland, and Saye ; and the ten commoners were Holles, Sir Philip Stapleton, Martin, Sir John Meyrick, Fiennes, Hampden, Pierpoint, Glyn, Pym, and Sir William Waller. On 11th July the two Houses agreed to a lengthy declaration [2] which reviewed in detail the

[1] Ibid., p. 178 ; *Commons' Journals*, II, 651.   [2] Ibid., pp. 200–2.

military actions of the King, proving that it was he who had begun the war and stating that

The War being thus by His Majesty begun ; the Lords and Commons in Parliament hold themselves bound in Conscience to raise Forces, for the Preservation of the Peace of the Kingdom, and Protection of the Subjects in their Persons and Estates.

Next day the Houses appointed the Earl of Essex as the commander of the Parliamentary army. Finally, on the afternoon of Monday, 22nd August, Charles took the fateful step of erecting his standard at Nottingham Castle. The outcome of the war thus begun was —as in every war—beyond human power to predict. One thing however, was certain, namely, that the high quality of statesmanship which distinguished Pym, and his administrative ability, would make him the centre of the Parliamentary organization.

CHAPTER XI

PRELIMINARIES OF WAR

August 1642–June 1643

THE full significance of the raising of the royal standard at Nottingham was immediately understood, so far as can be judged, by only a minority of the nation. Parliament, largely under Pym's direction, had taken one step at a time in its struggle against the King without always appreciating the point that it had reached, and without understanding whither its path was leading. Parliament had never desired or intended to alter fundamentally the powers of the monarchy in general or to make any irreparable breach with Charles I in particular. Not only was the King's challenge at Nottingham taken up reluctantly, but, even then, it is doubtful whether there was any general understanding that resort to arms meant war on a large scale or that, in the nature of the case, war put an end to any hope of a compromise or a bargain. Not until hostilities had been in progress for several months did Parliament grasp the fact that war must be continued until one side or the other was completely and finally defeated.

If we use our terms accurately, we cannot thus differentiate between "Parliament" and "The King" because substantial numbers of both Houses of Parliament supported the King. Within the Commons, the rift revealed by the debates over the "Root and Branch Bill" and over the exclusion of the bishops from the Lords had widened into a breach and become permanent. Hence, though the attitude of some Members of the Commons was never very definite and though some others changed sides as the war went on, in general terms we can say that about a hundred and seventy-five of the Commons threw in their lot with Charles, leaving about three hundred to support "Parliament" in the House and on the field. The peers also were divided, though in different proportions : perhaps thirty of them could be labelled as "Parliamentarians", and eighty as Royalists, while about twenty remained neutral. "Parliament" and "Parliamentarians" must thus be understood as merely conventional terms to indicate opponents of the Royalists.

Parliament's first reaction to the King's resort to open war was one of surprised indignation. Three days after Charles had raised his standard, he sent the Earl of Southampton and Sir John Culpepper to the Lords and to the Commons respectively with the object of opening up negotiations for peace. Charles' motive in so doing, as explained by Clarendon, is less creditable than on the surface it appears to be : [1]

That which prevailed with his majesty very reasonably . . . was that it was most probable . . . that, out of their contempt of the king's weakness and want of power, the Parliament would refuse to treat ; which would be so unpopular a thing that, as his majesty would highly oblige his people by making the offer, so they would lose the hearts of them by rejecting it ; which alone would raise an army for his majesty.

On 27th August the Lords received Southampton's message. In the Commons, that same day, an extraordinary scene took place. The appearance of Culpepper worked up a section of the Members to a state of high fury, and Strode advanced towards the offending Royalist as if to remove him forcibly from his seat. This, incidentally, was typical of Strode's impetuous nature. The same trait had shown itself when the warning had been given that the King was on his way to the Commons to arrest the five Members : Strode had then been the only one of the five to wish to remain in the House to face Charles, and his friends had to drag him out by force. Now, the more moderate Pym rose to calm the House and to urge that the King's message be received. [2]

[1] *Great Rebellion*, Book VI, Sections 10–15.
[2] Rushworth, IV, 784 ; *Lords' Journals*, V, 326 ; *Commons' Journals*, II, 739–40.

Not any man spake against his expelling in due time, but only against the doing of it at this time when hee had brought a message from his Ma'ty yet some fiery spiritts were soe hot upon it as they would scarce permitt Mr. Pym himselfe to speak for Sir John Culpepper.[1]

Thus even Pym was powerless against the deep resentment felt at Charles' action. In the end, Culpepper was allowed to deliver his message in writing at the bar of the House. "This message", writes Clarendon, "had the same reception his majesty believed it would have." That is to say, the two Houses, after a conference, replied that : [2]

until your majesty shall recall those proclamations and declarations whereby the earl of Essex and both Houses of Parliament, and their adherents and assistants . . . are declared traitors, and until the standard set up in pursuance of the said proclamations be taken down, your majesty hath put us into such a condition that we cannot . . . give your majesty any other answer to this message.

On 9th September the Earl of Essex, who as far back as 12th July had been appointed Parliamentary General, bade formal farewell to the Houses and set off towards Northampton to join the army under his command. Thenceforward his contact with Parliament was maintained chiefly by means of communications with Pym who, as the most forceful member of the Committee of Safety appointed in the previous July, soon became the head, and even the personification, of the executive government of the State, just as years before he had been the real executive of the Providence Company. Incidentally, it is interesting to note that no less than five of the fifteen members of the Committee of Safety had been connected with that company—Holland, Saye, Pym, and Hampden had been members of the company, while Nathaniel Fiennes was the son of Lord Saye.

Towards the end of September the Houses sent, by the Earl of Essex, a combined request to the King that he would return to Westminster, to which Charles replied that he would not " receive

---

[1] D'Ewes *Journal*, Harl. MSS. 163, f. 303*b*.
[2] *Great Rebellion*, Book VI, Section 14.

any Petition by the Address of the Lord General ; he being the Principal of those Traitors that are named by His Majesty ".[1]
The result was that, on 20th October the Commons resolved and declared [2]

> That they will oblige themselves to a mutual Assistance of one another, and of the whole Kingdom, for Defence of the Protestant Religion, the Privilege of Parliament, and the Liberty and Property of the Subject : and that a strict Association be prepared and entered into by the whole Kingdom to this purpose.

Charles' refusal to have dealings with Essex seems to have convinced Pym that the day of argument and compromise was at an end. The scheme of Association, which was the subject of the Commons' resolution mentioned above, and to the idea of which Pym had more than once alluded in his speeches, was evidently modelled on the Scottish Covenant. At a Conference the same day, the Lords concurred with the Commons in advocating the Association.[3] For the moment, the scheme was not carried into effect, but it would bear fruit later.

Meanwhile Charles, at the head of his army, was moving south towards London. Three days after the proposal for the Association —on 23rd October—Essex intercepted the Royalists at Edgehill. Regarded as a military action, this first battle of the Civil War was indecisive ; neither side was completely routed, and consequently both sides claimed the victory. In one respect the King was the victor, since he was able to continue his march, though he deflected it from London to Oxford. The advantages which Parliament gained from the battle were less obvious but more real. The King's inability to enter and hold London was perhaps the decisive factor in the war : from this time onwards, London— with all its advantages of prestige, strategic position, man-power, and wealth—was safely in the hands of Parliament.

The immediate effect of the clash of arms seems to have been to bring home to men's minds the reality of war and to evoke a desire for measures of peace before the spread of hostilities and

---

[1] *Commons' Journals*, II, 816, i.   [2] Ibid., 816, ii.
[3] *Lords' Journals*, V, 411–12.

the bitterness of partisanship should make such measures more difficult. On 9th November the Speaker of the House of Lords reported the result of a conference between the two Houses as follows : [1]

That Mr. *Pym* said, he was sent by the House of Commons, to communicate to their lordships some Votes, which are different to a former Vote, which were read, as follows : *videlicet,*
Resolved, upon the Question,
That the Petition be sent to His Majesty.
Agreed to.
The Reasons that induced the House of Commons to make this Vote were these :
1. The great Advantage we should have by a well-settled Peace ; for thereby, we should the better intend the War in *Ireland,* and it would unite the King and the Kingdom more closely, and prevent the Loss of our Religion and the Liberties of the Subject ; for other Peace than that, they are resolved never to accept.
2. The House of Commons did consider the Danger which the King's person was in at the last Battle.
3. The great Mischiefe that War hath already brought upon the Commonwealth, which would be increased if the War should be continued, so much blood being already spilt in the last Battle, and many of great Quality being lost.

As an expression of the Commons' unwillingness to go to war, and of their feelings towards the King, this Petition is not without its significance. Next day, in order to calm the fears of the Londoners about the meaning of this peace move, Pym went down to Guildhall. After explaining the negotiations which the Parliament had already tried to open up with the King, he assured the city that, while Parliament would always be anxious to bring the war to an end at the earliest possible moment, a peace that did not secure the liberties of the nation would be no peace but only a delusion. He therefore appealed to the City to continue its support of Parliament both with men and with money. Following a speech by the Earl of Holland, Pym said : [2]

My Lord Mayor, and you Gentlemen of this famous City of *London,* . . . there is little to be added to that that was said by

---

[1] Ibid., 439, ii.   [2] B.M. *Thomason Tracts,* E 126 (48).

this noble Lord, who hath represented to you the sence of both Houses, and the reasons and motives upon which they did desire peace, motives indeed that have wrought with us from the beginning of this Warre to this time, for we should never have step'd one step towards Warre if we might have had, or hoped for such a peace as might have secured Religion and Liberty, and the publicke good of the Kingdome ; but truely ill counsell did exclude us from such hope ; we now conceive that the King having seene the courage of his Subjects, having seene the danger of his owne Person, so much blood shed about him, will be more tractable to good conditions of Peace, then he would have beene before, and that is the reason, why we do thinke fit to try him, once more after this battle that hath beene lately fought, before it come to another battle againe. . . . Therefore wee shall put it to a very quicke issue, if the KING receive the Petition, to make such propositions whether you shall bee secur'd in your Religion, in your Religion with a hope of Reformation, such a Reformation as may maintain the power of Religion, and the purity of Religion, as well as the name of Religion. . . . And we shall pursue the maintenance of our Liberties, Liberties that may not onely be the Laws and Statutes, but Liberties that may be in practice, and in execution ; . . . For to have printed Liberties, and not to have Liberties in truth, and realities, is but to mock the Kingdom ; . . . And we shall take care to maintain the Dignity, and the Honour of Parliament, for that is that that will be a lasting security to you in your Liberty and Religion. We shall take care in the fourth place, to Answer the affections of the City of London, That we will not consent to anything that shall be prejudiciall to them. . . . Therefore, I shall commend to you, that you would not let fall any part of your contributions, for it is that that must maintain the Army ; and entertain noe ill apprehensions of the Parliament, but goe on so as you have done, and I hope it will be such an end as God may have all the glory, and you all comfort.

At the moment the King, believing himself to be on the verge of victory, refused to treat ; but after 13th November, when he found his way towards London barred by the trained bands at Turnham Green, he agreed to negotiate. Pym's proposal was that both sides should disband their armies so that negotiations might be unprejudiced by military conditions.[1] The proposal met with

[1] Yonge's *Diary*, B.M. Add. MSS. 18777, ff. 64–6 (quoted by Gardiner : *History of the Great Civil War*, I, 62).

no general support ; and, no other tangible proposal being forth-coming, the attempt to renew negotiations came to nothing.

Nevertheless, the nation, instead of growing accustomed to the war, as might perhaps have been expected, became more and more clamorous for peace. The hope that Charles might, at that early stage in the war, agree to terms acceptable to the people, was illusory. Until he was beaten in the field he was not likely to make concessions. Moreover, whatever compromise he might make on the political issues, there was not the remotest chance of his granting the religious claims of the Puritans. That the desire for peace should have blinded large numbers of responsible men to these obvious facts shows how intense their desire must have been. On 26th December both Houses agreed to make yet another effort to renew negotiations with Charles. Yet before even this resolution could take effect, the Common Council of the City sent to Oxford to Petition Charles to return to London. The only reply that Charles deigned to send them (on 13th January) was to ask : [1]

what hope His Majesty can have of safety there, whilest Alderman *Pennington*, their pretended Lord Mayor, (the principall authour of these Calamities which so neerely threaten the ruine of that famous City) *Ven*, *Foulke* and *Mainwaring* (all persons notoriously guilty of Schisme and High Treason) commit such Outrages in oppressing, robbing and imprisoning, according to their discretion, all such His Majesties loving subjects, whom they are pleased to suspect but for wishing well to His Majesty. . . . If his good Subjects of that His Citie of London shall first . . . apprehend and commit to safe custody the Persons of those foure men, . . . that His Majestie may proceed against them by the course of Law, as guilty of high Treason, His Majestie will speedily return to them with His Royall, and without His Martiall Attendance.

Pym, who was present at Guildhall, along with other Members of Parliament, to listen to the King's answer, was quick to see the advantage which the terms of that answer gave to him and his party. He at once rose to reply, point by point, to the King's argument. It was a vigorous, fighting speech exactly suited to

[1] *Two Speeches* printed for Peter Cole January 1642.

the temper of his audience, so much so that the printed form of the speech declares that :

At the end of every period of this Speech, the applause was so great, that he was fain to rest till silence was again made, and at last (the Company ready to be dissolved) after some pause and consultation with the Committee of Lords and Commons then present, and by their direction (silence being made) he closed all with the words following :

Worthy Citizens, you have understood the sense of both Houses of Parliament, concerning my Lord Mayor here, and those worthy Members of your City, that are demanded ; You have heard the Parliament declare, that they will protect them in that which they have done by direction of both Houses, and they expect that you should express it your selves likewise, that if any violence be offer'd to them, you will secure and defend them with your uttermost force ; and you shall alwaies find, that this protection of the Parliament shall not onely extend to these, but to all others that have done any thing by their command.

Which words were no sooner uttered, but the Citizens with one joynt harmony of mindes and voices, gave such an acclamation as would have drown'd all the former, if they had been then breathing, which after a long continuance resolved itself into this more articulate and distinct voice, We will live and dye with them, We will live and dye with them, *and the like.*

The King's answer to the city must have convinced even the staunchest friends of peace among the Parliamentarians that the King had no intention of making peace on the basis of a compromise. Pym and his party were thus free to concentrate upon the clearly defined task of organizing their resources and prosecuting the war to a point at which Charles would be compelled to make concessions, both religious and political, acceptable to Parliament.

Already, in the early part of December 1642, Parliament had levied taxation on the city though it met with much opposition. For Parliament to levy taxes without the assent of the King was, according to the letter of the law, as irregular as for the King to levy them without the consent of Parliament. Yet, until Parliament had devised regular and adequate monetary supplies, its activities on the field would be hopelessly handicapped. Not until

February 1643 did the Commons seriously tackle the problem.
Even then the debates were long and heated. Finally, on 24th
February, the Committee for Advance of Monies in London was
" especially recommended . . . to take Care for the effectual and
speedy Putting in Execution the Ordinance for the weekly Assessments ; and for the Dispersing of them ".[1] That same day it was
further ordered that the Knights and Burgesses of twelve counties
together with the Burgesses of Westminster " do meet this Afternoon, to consider of the most speedy and effectual putting in
execution the Ordinance for the weekly Assessments ".[2] The
business of the commissioners was to assess, for taxation purposes,
the value of property within their respective jurisdictions. Even
so, there was widespread resistance to the commissioners' demands,
and the payments were both slow and meagre.

The fact was that English folk, however irksome they might
find the tyranny of the Stuarts, would, with typical illogicality,
need a long time to grow accustomed to a form of government
from which the Stuarts were eliminated. All the time, a large
body of Members of both Houses, even of those who had not
thrown in their lot with Charles, were constantly hoping for peace
and were urging an accommodation with him. Thus, in spite
of the failure of negotiations in December 1642, on 18th March
1643 the two Houses, through their commissioners at Oxford,
made fresh overtures. The proposal was for a truce during which
the King should place the forts and ships in the hands of his own
nominees, provided these latter should have the confidence of
Parliament.[3] Charles' answer was that the only condition on
which he would agree to a truce was that the forts and ships should
be restored to the hands of those who had held them under his
authority at the outbreak of the war. This answer once more dis-
sipated any hopes for a cessation of hostilities, and provided Pym
with an opportunity to urge afresh that adequate and reliable
sources of revenue must be found for the Parliamentary exchequer.

Pym appears to have been one of the very few Parliamentarians

---

[1] *Commons' Journals*, II, 977, ii.   [2] Ibid., 978, i.
[3] Rushworth, V, 175-7.

clear-sighted enough to realize that such a revenue must be a decisive factor—and might be *the* decisive factor—in the struggle. To this conclusion he was doubtless helped by his experience in the Exchequer. On 27th March, Parliament took the step of issuing an " Ordinance for seizing the Estates of notorious Delinquents ".[1] Next day—which was the very day on which the Houses received Charles' reply to their proposal for a truce—Pym introduced what was certain to be an unpopular proposal, namely, an excise levied on the sale of all goods. If the property tax was unpopular among landowners, an excise would be unpopular among every class of the community, from the richest merchant to the poorest labourer. This was clearly reflected in the reception that Pym's motion was given in the Commons : [2]

Mr. Pym then stood upp and proposed another way for the speedie raising of money and that was by laying an Excise or Taxe that was to be paid out of commodities bought and sold which motion though it would have been thought about two yeares since to have tended no lesse then to the ruine of the Kingdome if it had beene then moved yet did some indiscreet men say it was well moved which made old Mr. Cage one of the Burgesses for Ipswich in the Countie of Suffolk to stand upp and say plainly

That hee wondered that any man should make such a motion as this was. . . . Mr. Pym then stood upp againe and thought to have amended the matter somewhat by saying that hee only intended to have this Excise laid upon superfluous commodities that were imported into the Kingdome.

Mr. Cage thereupon stood upp againe and said that hee considered that this motion was of little lesse dangerous consequence than the former. . . . Others spoke to this matter and most of them opposed both Mr. Pyms second and first motion wondering that hee who pretended to stand so much for the libertie of the subiect should propose such an uniust scandalous and destructive a proiect. I came out of the howse wherein I left the Grand Committee sitting betweene one and two of the clocke in the afternoone and understood that both these proiects of Mr. Pym were reiected.

---

[1] *Lords' Journals*, V, 672–3 ; *Commons' Journals*, III, 21, i.
[2] D'Ewes *Journals*, Harl. MSS. 164, f. 346*b*.

Notwithstanding the summary rejection which Pym's proposal for an excise then received, within four months such an excise was actually imposed. In this instance, as in numerous others, Pym's understanding was far ahead of that of any of his fellows. Had Parliament seen with Pym's eyes, and acted promptly upon his guidance, instead of much later when the significance of events had slowly convinced them of the soundness of his judgment, valuable months of campaigning would have been saved. Doubtless he often wished that he was free to apply to the affairs of State the same personal initiative as he had exercised as Treasurer of the Providence Company. But his position as the executive official of a private company was one thing, and as leader of something like a democratic assembly was quite another.

Pym's next move was of a different kind. On 2nd May the two Houses agreed, at his instigation, to send commissioners to Holland and to Scotland so as to carry information of the true position of English affairs, in the hope, doubtless, of obtaining help of either money or men or both.[1] The Commons agreed to the proposal—at least to that part of it relating to Scotland—though nothing was done immediately to carry it into effect. Almost at the same time, Pym was secretly in communication with the Queen, though Saye, Manchester, Salisbury, and Hampden were privy to the move. His object appears to have been that Henrietta might persuade Charles to reconsider the truce terms that he had already rejected. Whether Pym was serious in his dealings with the Queen, or whether he had some ulterior motive, is not clear. Whatever his purpose, the negotiations yielded no tangible result—which was in keeping with all that we know of the character of Henrietta Maria.

While Pym was thus trying, by financial and diplomatic measures, to place the Parliamentary resources on a sound foundation, the King's friends were plotting to undermine the Parliament's position at its pivotal point—the city of London. In spite of the City's strong loyalty to Parliament, many citizens were known to be sympathetic to the King ; and as early as March 1643, commissions

[1] *Commons' Journals*, III, 67 ; *Lords' Journals*, VI, 25, ii.

of array had been drawn up at Oxford authorizing the appointment of officers and the training under them of loyal citizens. The commissions, however, were kept in abeyance until a suitable season. In May of the same year that season was judged to have arrived. To prepare the way for the operation of the scheme, a plot was formed to secure control of the city's strongholds—including the gates and the Tower—and to seize the Parliamentary leaders, notably Pym and Hampden. A prominent part in the plot was taken by the poet Edmund Waller, Member of Parliament for St. Ives, who had been a consistent supporter of the King through all the long Parliament's debates, in concert with his brother-in-law named Tomkins and with the royalist Lord Conway. Clarendon's account of the plot is that [1]

a servant of Mr. Tomkins, who had often cursorily overheard his master and Mr. Waller discourse of the argument we are now upon, placed himself behind a hanging at a time they were together, and there, whilst either of them discoursed the language and opinion of the company they kept, overheard enough to make him welcome to those whom he thought concerned, and so went to Mr. Pimm, and acquainted him with all he had heard, or probably imagined. The time when Mr. Pimm was made acquainted with it is not known, but the circumstances of the publishing it were such as filled all men with apprehension. It was on Wednesday the 31st of May, their solemn fast-day, when being all at their sermon in St. Margaret's Church in Westminster, according to their custom, a letter or message is brought privately to Mr. Pimm, who thereupon with some of the most active members rise from their seats, and after a little whispering together remove out of the church : this could not but exceedingly affect those who stayed behind : immediately they send guards to all the prisons, as Lambeth-house, Ely-house, and such places where their malignants were in custody, with directions to search the prisoners ; and some other places which they thought fit should be suspected. . . . A committee was appointed to examine all persons they thought fit, and to apprehend some nominated at that time. And the same night this committee apprehended Mr. Waller and Mr. Tomkins, and the next day such others as they thought fit.

[1] *Great Rebellion*, Book VII, Section 62.

There was at the time a widespread conviction—which subsequent investigations have done nothing to shake—that the city had narrowly escaped a serious catastrophe. Tomkins and an accomplice named Chaloner were hanged for their part in it. Waller himself, as a Member of the Commons, was expelled the House and imprisoned for several months : that his life was spared was probably due to the information which, through abject, craven fear, he gave against his fellow-conspirators.

Our main concern, however, is not with the fate of the plotters but is rather with the reaction of the plot upon the career and influence of Pym. On 6th June Pym reported to the Houses the result of investigations into the plot. These established beyond doubt the active complicity of the King in violent designs upon the city and upon the persons of Members of Parliament. Clearly, the King regarded his opponents as rebels whom it was neither illegal nor immoral to destroy by any means in his power. Equally clearly, while the King held such views there could be no possibility of negotiating terms of peace with him : a king could never negotiate with rebels, or, if he did, he would not feel any obligation to keep faith with them. Only one course, therefore, remained, namely, to organize a large-scale, effective offensive against him so as to compel him to accept Parliament's terms. Pym's motion for an association—mooted in October of the previous year—was therefore revived and this time received an almost unanimous vote in the Commons.

The Parliament, upon this Discovery, formed an *Oath* or *Vow* to be taken by the Members of both Houses, and by their Army, and appointed a general Thanksgiving to be kept throughout the Kingdom, at which time a printed Narrative of this Design was to be read, and the said Oath or Covenant to be tendered to all Persons, (but no Penalty set on the Refusers).

Accordingly a Covenant was framed, each signatory to which undertook

that in order to the Security and Preservation of the true reformed Protestant Religion, and liberty of the Subject, I will not consent to the laying down of Arms, so long as the Papists, now in open War against the Parliament, shall by force of Arms be protected from the Justice thereof.[1]

Once more the prescience of Pym had been justified by events ; once more the Commons were driven by events to adopt a policy which months earlier Pym had advocated in vain. Waller's Plot had at last convinced Parliament of the wisdom of Pym's leadership. Henceforward thoughts of compromise and negotiations were abandoned. Parliament set itself to muster all its resources for the one purpose of defeating the King so completely that it should be he who would wish to negotiate. The unquestioned leader, and at the same time the pivot, of the process, for the few remaining months of his life, was Pym. The preliminaries of war were over. War in dead earnest on both sides was about to begin.

[1] Rushworth, V, 325.

CHAPTER XII

CONDUCT OF THE WAR

June–December 1643

THE main period of the war began with a terrible misfortune for Pym personally and, scarcely less, for the whole Parliamentary cause. On 18th June, following a foray by some of Rupert's troops in the neighbourhood of Oxford, a skirmish took place at Chalgrove, some eight miles east of Abingdon. The fight had scarcely begun when Hampden—who, being in the district by chance, had joined his fellow-Parliamentarians on the spur of the moment when the alarm was sounded—had to ride off mortally wounded. Six days later he died at Thame. Hampden's death was the severest political blow that Pym ever sustained. Hampden seems to have been the one man who shared Pym's views in every detail, both as to principles and to procedure. For several years, Hampden had been Pym's closest friend and confidant, both in the House and out of it. Now, at the very moment when the main stress of the conflict was beginning, Pym had to face his political responsibilities, and his physical trials, alone. Already Pym must have been in the grip of the fell disease which, only six months later, was to bring death to him too. To what extent his end was hastened by the loss of his friend we can only guess.

Pym was given but little time either to mourn the loss of a friend or to nurse his own sickness. His most urgent problem was that of leadership for the Parliamentary forces. The Earl of Essex had been appointed to the command in 1642 not because he was a military genius but because, in rank and prestige, there seemed no one more fitted for the post. Events were to show that Essex's outstanding virtue was his loyalty. Lack of military preparations—in men, munitions, and plans—made his task a thankless one. Upon him fell the blame for every failure in the field. Only too often the blame was just ; but if he had not undertaken the command, or if he had resigned in disgust, it is difficult to see who could have replaced him. Yet in spite of all the difficulties and censures of the opening months of the war, his loyalty to the Parliamentary cause never faltered. Nevertheless, we have to confess that Essex's military qualifications were in the realm of good intention rather than of accomplishment. No one can have been more acutely aware than Pym of the short-comings of the Parliamentary General. Here, for example, is a letter written by Essex to Pym on 5th November 1642 : [1]

For my honoured friend John Pym, with haste.

Sir, now wee are upon ower march to St. Albons ower long and late marches hath made ower regements som thing thin, but wee hope many will come up within a day, but if the cavelirs march towards you, wee shall march to barnet, tomorrough upon necessety, or otherwise on mounday, I doubt many are gone to London to visit theare frends, but I am confident thos that fought guallantly will not quite quit thear coulours, if thear bee a search made, in London, and Essex I beleev many will returne, the army is marching thearfore I end with this desier that wee may have spare arms of picks and muskets, I have often wrote for them, I am

Your faythfull frend,

ESSEX.

MARGET STREET,
5th of November 1642.

That same night, Essex wrote another letter endorsed : [2]

For the Lords of the close Committee these with haste. Haste, haste, Posthaste.
5th. No. 1642

St. Albans
London

10 att night
Essex

[1] B.M. Bouverie MSS., Add., 11692, f. 27.
[2] Ibid., f. 29.

This letter begins :

My Lo :

I receaved a letter from you, of a desier to have hors and dragoneers sent to Oxenfourd and thear abouts, I dismissed not the hors till it was late, (but long before your messenger came) to thear several quarters soe that I could not have sent any considerable body time enough.

And it concludes with a reference to " prince Rubert troops " :

I confes you can not bee too watchfull, but a treaty and plundring of the subburbs have noe great coherence to guether. My lo. I am to geave you humble thanks for your care about the officers, wee have some goud, but more bad. My Lords, I am your humble servant,

ESSEX.

These letters are a perfect reflection of the ingenuousness of the writer : large, open handwriting (not scribbled, in spite of his " haste ", but carefully corrected here and there), uncertain spelling, naïve surprise expressed that " Rubert " should plunder the " subburbs " after making a treaty, and the equally naïve reflection on the quality of his own officers. To read them is to understand the slow, unmilitary General who sorely tried the patience of the Parliamentary leaders. " Haste " seems to have been a characteristic of Essex's despatches. Thus, from Windsor on 10th December 1642 Essex addressed a letter : [1]

For the Committee of the Lords and Commons for the safety of the Kingdome.

Under the above endorsement he added :

> Hast, hast, hast
> post, post,
> hast, hast, haste

But haste was no characteristic of his tactics. On 25th June, the day following Hampden's death, a squadron of Royalist cavalry plundered Wycombe almost unhindered, and were believed to be even threatening London. Next day, at the direction of the Commons, Pym addressed to Essex a severe remonstrance : [2]

[1] Ibid., f. 35.   [2] *Commons' Journals*, III, 144, ii.

Ordered, That Mr. *Pym* do prepare a Letter for Mr Speaker to write unto my Lord General, to acquaint him from what the Countries suffer, by Parties of the King's Forces, that come forth and spoil and rob the Countries ; and to desire him to take some Course to prevent it ; and likewise to desire him to tender the Covenant to all the Officers and Soldiers in his Army ; and forthwith to certify the Names of such as refuse.

Essex took the obvious course of tendering his resignation ; and Parliament the equally obvious one—since it could not replace Essex—of refusing to accept it.

For the campaign of 1643, the Royalists had made a comprehensive plan for a threefold attack—from the north, the Welsh border, and the south-west—to converge on London. Ultimately, the plan was frustrated by the loyalty of Hull and Plymouth to Parliament ; but, in the meantime, the King's forces inflicted numerous defeats on Essex and his subordinates—at Chalgrove Field where Hampden was wounded on 18th June, at Adwalton Moor where the Fairfaxes were routed on 30th June, and at Roundaway Down where Sir William Waller was defeated on 13th July. The result was a renewed, widespread desire among the Parliamentarians for peace. Essex himself was one of the advocates of a peace policy, and on 9th July he addressed to the Lords a letter [1] urging that negotiations should be reopened with the King. On 11th July Pym countered this proposal in a speech to the Commons, pointing out that all previous negotiations had been futile and that there was no fresh circumstance to suggest that new ones would be more profitable than the old. Pym was still convinced that, before negotiations could be profitable, the King must be beaten decisively in the field. To this end the Parliamentary armies had two supreme needs—substantial reinforcements of troops, and a reorganization of the higher command.

The battles already fought had shown—as others were to show still more clearly—that the Parliamentary forces were hopelessly inadequate for the task of a large-scale campaign that would

[1] *Lords' Journals*, VI, 127.

inflict upon the Royalists such irreparable and final defeat as Pym envisaged. Only one resource seemed to remain, a resource which Pym had repeatedly urged should be tapped, namely, the Scots. On 1st May, as we have seen, he had urged that commissioners should be appointed to negotiate for Scottish intervention in favour of Parliament. On 19th July, six commissioners were actually appointed, two being peers and four Members of the Commons. In practice, neither of the peers carried out his commission ; and of the four Commoners the only one of note was the younger Sir Henry Vane who became virtually Parliament's mouthpiece to the Scots. These four arrived in Edinburgh on 7th August, so that discussions opened on the 8th, which was the very day on which the Commons were rejecting the Lords' propositions for peace. For ten days there were continuous debates between the English commissioners and the Scots as to the conditions on which a Scottish army should be allowed to cross the Border in the interests of Parliament. To one condition the Scots inflexibly adhered, namely, that there should be " a reformation of religion in the Church of England, according to the example of the best reformed Churches ", which, of course, meant the establishment of a Presbyterian Church system in England. The English commissioners, knowing that such a system would be unacceptable to the great majority of English folk, struggled hard and long against the terms, but the Scots remained adamant. The most that Vane could secure was an amendment which allowed " the reformation of religion in the Church of England according to the same Holy Word [of God] and the example of the best reformed Churches ". The Scots could not object to the Word of God as a basis of religion, yet the amending clause turned a hard-and-fast definition into one that allowed of various interpretations. This kernel of dispute being settled, the rest was not likely to be difficult. Both parties, for example, easily agreed that Episcopacy should be abolished. The final terms were drawn up into The Solemn League and Covenant, which the Scottish Estates ratified on 17th August.

The Covenant first came before the English House of Commons

on 1st September. Its terms met with opposition from men of various shades of opinion, from those who disliked Presbyterianism at least as much as from those who disliked Episcopacy. To those of the Commons to whom Presbyterianism was distasteful, Pym presented the question whether a sick man threatened by a murderer would " cast away his medicine and betake himself to his sword, or take his medicine and suffer himself to be killed ? " [1] When the dilemma was thus nakedly presented, there was no doubt upon which horn the Commons would choose to be impaled. After some further debates, both Houses finally adopted the Covenant. The conditions were harsh, and so were the financial demands—£30,000 a month paid by the English Parliament, with an advance of £100,000 before a Scottish army would enter England—but, faced with the high probability of a Royalist victory apart from Scottish help, Parliament had no alternative to accepting. On 25th September 1643 the Commons attended service in St. Margaret's, Westminster, and swore their acceptance of the Covenant.

While these negotiations and debates were taking place, the other problem—that of Generalship—was receiving attention. Indeed, the Generals saved Pym trouble by raising the issue themselves. Essex was the subject of widespread distrust. He was commonly regarded as both indolent and incompetent, and the numerous Royalist victories were attributed to his inefficient organization. Waller, on the contrary, in spite of his defeat at Roundaway Down, remained a popular figure. For that defeat, Essex and Waller blamed each other. The jealousy thus provoked between them was increased when Waller, only a fortnight after Roundaway, was appointed by the Houses to command a new force which the city was to recruit. This gave Essex his chance : on 31st July he furnished the Lords with details of the numbers of men under his command—numbers too ludicrously small to make possible the planning and execution of any comprehensive campaign—and he further claimed that no new com-

[1] Yonge's *Diary*, B.M. Add. MSS. 18778, f. 29 (quoted by Gardiner : *History of the Great Civil War*, I, 233).

mander should be appointed except by the Lord General.[1]   Once
again Essex had shown himself completely unruffled and loyal in
circumstances that would have driven most men, if not into the
opposite camp, at least to inactive neutrality.   His two contentions
would not be gainsaid ; nor, in spite of Essex's dilatoriness, was
any more efficient General available.   Pym therefore, recognizing
the realities of the situation, stepped in to prevent further division in
the Parliamentary ranks.   He was the manager, on the Commons'
behalf, of several conferences with the Lords, and on 31st July
he presented certain proposals to the Commons on the lines of
Essex's demands : [2] more troops were to be raised ; and Waller,
though retaining his command of troops for the defence of London
and the adjoining counties, was to hold his commission from
Essex.   Next day the Lords, among whom was a strong peace
party, sent representatives to try to win Essex to their side.   The
Commons, not to be outdone, at once sent representatives of their
own, including Pym,[3]

to express the Confidence of this House in my Lord General,
and the Army, and their Respects unto him and them ; and
to acquaint his Excellency with the Votes of this House upon
his Propositions, and the Reasons thereof ; . . . and to assure
his Excellency and the Army of all Encouragement from this
House : and to desire his Lordship to grant a Commission to
Sir *Wm. Waller* according to the former Desire of both Houses.

Clearly, Pym had persuaded the House to his view about the
army command.

Nevertheless, the Lords were not to be easily put off.   They at
once requested, and obtained, a conference with the Commons on
the Lords' proposals for a peace with the King.   Though the
proposals amounted to a complete surrender to Charles, they
occasioned fierce and long debates.   In the city there seems to
have been a widespread fear that the Commons would support the
Lords' proposals.   The result was that on 8th August a mob,
several thousands strong, surged into Palace Yard demanding that

---

[1] *Lords' Journals*, VI, 160.   [2] *Commons' Journals*, III, 188–9.
[3] Ibid., p. 193.

Parliament should not make peace. Even so, the Commons rejected the propositions by a majority of only seven in a House of a hundred and seventy. Next day, writes Clarendon : [1] " A great multitude of the wives of substantial citizens came to the House of Commons with a petition for peace." (It is interesting to note that Clarendon describes as " a rabble " the crowd of men who asked for a continuance of the war, while the women asking for peace were " wives of substantial citizens " !) In partcular they clamoured for " that dog Pym ! " So persistent and menacing were they that soldiers were called in. A general scuffle ensued so that the soldiers were obliged to drive off the crowd by using first the flat and then the edge of their swords so that there were one or two deaths.

The matter of immediate peace being thus disposed of, Pym was free to devise measures for an energetic prosecution of the war. While Parliament had been divided in its mind, Colonel Oliver Cromwell had been conducting a campaign in Lincolnshire where, as a cavalry commander, he first displayed the qualities which were to make him famous. For the moment, lack of adequate forces limited his operations and more than once compelled retreat. On 9th August, therefore, the Commons appointed the Earl of Manchester as the commander of the Eastern Association and voted that the number of the troops in the Association should be raised to 10,000. Thus the Parliamentary forces were in three armies : Waller's in the Home Counties, the Eastern Association under Manchester, and the main army under Essex.

The first task that Essex set himself after this reorganization was the relief of Gloucester which the King was besieging. Essex's arrival with 15,000 men compelled the withdrawal of the Royalist troops when the city was at the very end of its resources. The King then tried to bar the return of Essex to London. At Newbury, on 20th September, the two armies met. The battle was indecisive : Charles, retiring from the field because his ammunition was spent, entered Oxford ; and Essex, as he made for Reading, was unable to hold his army together.

[1] *Great Rebellion*, Book VII, Section 171.

This latest proof of the inability of the Parliamentary armies to inflict decisive defeat upon the King was an additional proof of the wisdom of Pym in coming to terms with the Scots. Five days after Newbury, the Commons, as we have seen, accepted the Covenant. On 15th October, the Lords also—that is, those few of them who remained still at Westminster—took the Covenant.

Thus the two objects immediately necessary, if the Parliamentary cause was to succeed in the field, had been achieved—the settlement of the problem of Generalship, and the agreement with the Scots for the supply of man-power. Much remained to be done, and many obstacles remained to be overcome, before the final victory : a more capable and vigorous General than Essex would need to be found, and the rank and file of the English Parliamentary army would need to be expanded and organized. But the foundations for that future development had been laid, and the man who had laid them was John Pym. To build upon those foundations was not to be given to him. His work was done.

On 7th November 1643 Parliament made Pym the Master of the Ordnance, that is, of the arms stored in the Tower : [1]

Ordered, That *John Pym* the elder, Esquire, shall be Lieutenant of the Ordnance, and shall execute the said Place, in all the Duties thereof ; and shall receive all the Profits and Advantages thereunto belonging, in as ample Manner, as any other Lieutenant of the Ordnance formerly had, might, or ought to have done.

A month later, on 8th December, he died at Derby House, Westminster—formerly the property of the Earl of Derby and latterly assigned to Pym as a residence—" worn out by the fearful efforts of the war, by the exciting alternations of danger and success, of defeat and victory ".[2] The Commons showed their appreciation of their dead colleague by voting [3]

That the Body of Mr. *Pym* be interred in *Westminster Abbey*, without any Charge for the breaking open the *Ground* there :

[1] *Commons' Journals*, III, 303.
[2] L. von. Ranke : *History of England*, II, 229.
[3] *Commons' Journals*, III, 336–7.

And that the *Speaker*, and the whole House, do accompany his body to the Interment.

Ordered, That Captain *Alexander Pym* shall have his Arrears forthwith paid him : And that Sir. *Gilb. Gerard* bring in an Order for his Payment forthwith, notwithstanding any former Order.

In the royal Chapel of Henry VII, therefore, the body of John Pym, though uncrowned, was laid to rest on 13th December. An undated letter of Baillie [1] notes that

On Wednesday Mr. Pym was carryed from his house to Westminster, on the shoulders, as the fashion is, of the chieffe men in the Lower House, all the House going in procession before him, and before them the Assembly of Divines. Marshall had a most eloquent and pertinent funeral sermon ; which we did not hear ; for funeral sermons we must have away, with the rest. The Parliament has ordered to pay his debts, and build him, in the Chapell of Henry the VII a statelie monument.

The funeral sermon to which Baillie alludes was preached by Stephen Marshall, a prominent English Presbyterian who had accompanied the English commissioners to Scotland in August. His oration was based on Micah vii. 1 and 2 : " Woe is me, for the good man hath perished out of the earth." It was a typical seventeenth-century funeral panegyric, of some interest as revealing what Pym's admirers thought of him, but otherwise of no particular historical significance.

Rushworth's note on these events is that : [2]

December 8, 1643, died *John Pym*, a Member of the House of Commons at *Derby House*, and on 13th. his Corps, carried by six Members of that House, and attended with most of the Lords and Commons at *Westminster* was interred in the Abbey. But whereas it was reported by some, that he died of that loathsome and ignominious Disease, called by Physicians, *Morbus Pedicularis*, the same was not true ; and for satisfaction therein, his dead Body was for some time exposed to, and viewed by many Hundreds of People ; the true natural cause of his Death seeming to be the great Pains he took, joined with a competent Old Age, and (at best) but an infirm Constitution.

So persistent were the unpleasant rumours as to the cause of

[1] *Letters and Journals*, II, 118.   [2] Rushworth, V, 376.

Pym's death, that a post-mortem examination was held and a certificate issued under the title of *A Narrative of the Disease and Death of that noble Gentleman John Pymm Esquire, late a Member of the honourable House of Commons, attested under the Hands of his Phytitians, Chyrurgians, and Apothecary.* This " Narrative " contains the statement that

The most ignoble part of this lower belly, the *mesentry*, was found, *fundi calamitas*, the shop wherein the instrument of his dissolution was forged ; there being a large abscesse or impostume which wrought itself to such a bulke, as was easily discovered by the outward touch of his phytitians at the beginning of his complaining, and did increase to that capacity, as being opened it did receive a hand contracted, and in it's growth did so oppress the gall and stop its vessels, as occasioned the jaundice. Beside this abscesse (by the matter contained in it) did so offend the parts adjacent, as most of them suffered by its vicinity, yet without any such turbulent symptome, as did at any time cause him to complain of pain ; being sensible only of some sorenesse upon the touch of the region of the part affected. . . . At last, after a long languishment, this impostume breaking, he often fainted ; and soon after followed his dissolution, on December the 8th, 1643, about 7 a clocke at night.

Among the ten signatures to this certificate was that of " Dr. Merevell, President of the colledge of phytitians ".

In short, John Pym was the victim of cancer. No matter how rapidly the malignant growth may have developed, he must have been in its grip for several months at least. Yet through it all, he had continued unfalteringly to lead the Parliamentary cause. Here, surely, is a final proof of the unselfish nobility of his character.

Another indication of his self-denial was the evident poverty, at the time of his death, of both himself and his family. We have seen already the Commons' order of 11th December for the payment of arrears to Pym's elder son, Captain Alexander Pym. How urgent the matter was is suggested by a further order of the Commons on the next day : [1]

[1] *Commons' Journals*, III, 338, i.

That the Committee at *Haberdashers Hall* do forthwith advance, by way of Loan, unto Captain *Alexander Pym*, Two hundred Pounds, to be deducted out of the Arrears due unto the same Captain *Alexander Pym*, for his Entertainment, so soon as he shall have perfected and passed his Account.

Further, the Commons, having set up a committee to examine the condition of Pym's finances, found it necessary, on 13th February 1643/4, to take an wholly exceptional course in order to pay his debts and secure his family from want : [1] " *Resolved*, That this House will undertake the Payment, and satisfying of the Debts, of *John Pym* Esquire, late a Member of this House, and since deceased, not exceeding the Sum of Ten Thousand Pounds." On 5th January 1646, the Commons ensured the execution of that vote by an ordinance which ear-marked certain properties, forfeited by two " delinquents ", to provide the requisite sum.[2] That such provision should have been necessary, in spite of the enormous amount of property that Pym owned, is a further indication of the extent to which he had neglected his private interests in order to serve the State.

Our study of the career of John Pym has singularly failed if the quality of the man himself, in mind and in character, has not therein found its own expression. Perhaps, however, three quotations, two by contemporaries and one more recent, may be allowed as summarizing the position that he occupied—and occupies—in the life of the nation. The first is from a contemporary pamphlet : [3]

This day one of the great Champions of our Religion, Lawes, Lives, and Liberties, Master *Pym* deceased ; He was a member of the House of Commons, but such a member as almost the whole body of them was to be found in him ; the excellent speeches that he made, indefatigable care he took to support these sick and bleeding Kingdomes : shall speak his truest Epitaph and be his best Memorialls.

Seventeenth-century pamphlets are notoriously unreliable as por-trayers of character : this one, however, is unusually moderate

[1] *Commons' Journals*, III, 399, i.   [2] Ibid., VI, 397.
[3] B.M. *Thomason Tracts*, E 78 (15), p. 5.

in tone and is confirmed by the more sober Baillie,[1] in a letter
" For Mr. Spang, August 10th " 1644 :

Since Pyme died, no a state head amongst them : many very
good and able spirits, but not any of so great and comprehensive
a braine, as to manage the multitude of so weightie affaires as
lyes on them. If God did not sitt at their helme, for any good
guiding of theirs, long ere this they had been gone.

Our last quotation is from Sir J. A. R. Marriott[2] who describes
Pym as

The first and perhaps the greatest Parliamentary leader whom
this country has produced. A financier of really first-rate ability ;
a singularly clear and convincing speaker ; a ' consummate Parliamentary tactician ' ; a tireless and vigilant leader, Pym was unques-
tionably the man who impressed upon the House of Commons
its modern aspect, and who went far to define its party system
and its methods of procedure. From the day of meeting until
the day of his death he was the soul of the opposition in Parliament
and outside ; and was, for all practical purposes, the leader not
merely of a party but of the nation.

This is high praise. But can anyone read the story of the pre-
ceding pages without agreeing that it is justified to the full ?

---

[1] *Letters and Journals*, II, 216.
[2] *Life and Times of Lord Falkland*, p. 150.

EPILOGUE

OUR difficulties in obtaining exact information about Pym and his family are increased by the fact that, owing doubtless to the unsettled national conditions at the time of his death, his will, so far as is known, is no longer in existence. About his immediate descendants our knowledge is reliable only within limits. The two genealogical tables reproduced at the end of the book, though having certain features in common, show numerous differences even in the details of Pym's children. Our chief concern is with his two sons, Alexander, the heir, and Charles.

Alexander had followed the family tradition of becoming a student in the Middle Temple where he was admitted on 20th October 1629. Apart from this, little is known of him except what can be gleaned from a letter which his father wrote to him five years later.[1]

To my sonn Alexandre Pym, on of the Gentlemen of Colonells Harbuts Company in the States Army. These with speed.

Alexandre. I lately writ to you by a messenger sent by Allin the poste and delivrd him £10 to be payd unto you by the same messenger. In that letter I gave you leave to goe from the army if you would, and to live in what part you thought good till you should receyve further direction from me. Since that time I have spoken with Mr. Darly and he hath given me a good report of you, wherupon I have conceyved some hope that I shall find you a changed man : wherefore I am very willing to call you home. But because I have not yet compounded with your creditors, thoughe I have set on a worke to treate with two of the greatest of them which I can finde, that is Wroth and Robins. Peck I know not wher to inquier for, the rest I know none but Mr. Darly and Mr. Knightley. That I may have the more time to

[1] B.M. Add. MSS. 11692, f. 1.

compounde with these I would not have you hear till ye end of January, and when you shall lande I would not have you come to me till you hear from me, for if they once take notice that you are reconciled to me I shall bring them to no reason, therefore keepe yourselfe private and send to me before you come, I will then give you directions what to doe. I have delivered Allin £5 more which he hath promised that you shall receyve with this letter. I hope this will be sufficient to bring you home yet least you may have some extraordinary occasion, I have promised him to pay £5 more if you take up so much of his servaunt wch he sayth shall furnish you if there be need. Now let me see by your thrifty and discreet carriadge in this small matter how I may trust you in greater and assure yourselfe as I am very apt to receyve you if you be truly a reformed man, so you will easily fall back into my displeasure, if you bring home your old faults and follyes with you. Thus I pray God direct you in his fear and commend you to his blessing, resting

Your loving father,

Jo. Pym.

London, *21 May 1634.*

Dorse.

I have appoynted Arthur to pay all charges for this and the former mony if you can send me a perfect note of your other debts and wher I may find Mr. Peck to whome you owe £30 I shall the better make all ready for your returne here sooner. I permitt you to come in a privat manner and to be heare by ye end of January.

Not the least interesting aspect of this letter is the side-light that it throws upon the character of the writer, in particular his practical wisdom—not to say craftiness—in not allowing Alexander's creditors to know of the reconciliation between father and son until after the father had reached agreement with them about the amount he would pay in settlement of his son's debts !

What little we know of Alexander in later years suggests that, having sown his wild oats, he settled down to a respectable career, and, as we have seen, became a captain in the Parliamentary army. After John Pym's death, Alexander succeeded to Brymore and, as is shown in several extant deeds, succeeded also to at least some, and presumably all, of the rest of the family properties. The votes of the Commons immediately after his father's death suggest that, for whatever reasons, Alexander inherited not only the property but also considerable debts. The Calendar of the Committee for the Advance of Money shows that various sums continued to be paid to Alexander between 1643 and 1647 " on account of his arrears " as captain of horse. However, the family exchequer must indeed have been heavily depleted if the Parliament's grant of £10,000—which would represent perhaps nearly ten times that amount in present-day value—did not restore solvency. The precise date of Alexander's death is not known ; but the idea, once commonly held, that he did not long survive his father, is certainly wrong. For instance, in 1650–1 Alexander was Sheriff of Somerset. Also, according to William Prynne,[1] Alexander was one of the secluded members of the Long Parliament who were still alive on 7th May 1659 (that is, about the time when the Rump was restored) but who were then refused admission to the Parliament House.[2] The strange fact about this entry by Prynne is that we have no other information that Alexander Pym was ever a Member of Parliament ; and, even if Prynne's information is correct, we do not know which constituency he sat for. The last mention of Alexander in official records seems to be his appointment to the Commission of Assessments for Westminster on 10th February 1660. Alongside this can be set several deeds bearing his signature, the latest being an indenture between Alexander Pym of Brymore and William Gapper of Sutton Malet in Somerset dated 10th September 1660, the twelfth year of Charles II. We must therefore conclude that Alexander Pym died towards the close of 1660.

Since Alexander died without issue, he was succeeded by his brother Charles. In 1641 Charles had been elected to the Long Parliament as Member for Beeralston, some eight miles from Plymouth. He, like his brother, served in the Parliamentary army and was excluded from Parliament in 1648 ; but, unlike his

[1] *Conscientious, Serious, Theological and Legal Quaeres*, p. 46.
[2] A useful summary of these details is given in *Notes and Queries*, Series IX, Vol. vii, pp. 181–2 (March 1901).

brother, he returned to the House in March 1660. In the Convention Parliament of the same year he sat as Member for Minehead. Charles is sometimes stated to have been created a baronet by Richard Cromwell,[1] but reliable confirmation of this creation seems to be lacking. Other records show Charles as having become a " Knight Bachelor " on 14th February 1662–3 ; [2] and, further that " Sir Charles Pym of Brymore, Knight " was raised to the Baronetage on 14th July 1663.[3]

Before we trace the later generations of John Pym's family, attention must be called to the name of Anthony among his sons. Nothing is known of him with any degree of certainty. A letter, dated 29th July 1633, was written by Anthony to his brother Charles : [4]

DEARE BROTHER CHARLES,

I want time and words to expres the greatnes of my affection to thee. I hope I am not now to be assured of thine, yet I entreat thee to show it in this, in praying to God to be merciful unto me.

Let my miserable example make thee avoid all wicked and prodigal courses. I am now going out of England, and doubtful I am, whether ever I see any of you again. I hope I shall therefore the sooner prevaile with you. Keep the favour of God and you will never loose the love of my father.

I know you are of a warm nature, apt to take any impression. Get the impression of Grace, surely fixt, and then you need not feare. Take my counsell, for the counsell of a prodigall may be sometimes good.

So desiring thy prayers and well wishes,

For hast I rest,

Your loving Brother,

ANTH. PYM.

This letter strongly implies that Anthony was a prodigal son going into a far country. Though the country is not specified, there seems a possibility, even a probability, that he was emigrating to the Island of St. Christopher's in the West Indies. Certainly a

[1] See D.N.B. article on *John Pym*.
[2] W. A. Shaw : *Knights of England*, II, 237.
[3] G. E. C. (Ed.), *Complete Baronetage*, III, 281.
[4] MS. formerly at Brymore.

Colonel Charles Pym died at Nevis, St. Christopher's, in 1699 leaving to a son, also called Charles, monies in New England, Nevis, and London. From this second Charles were descended several generations of Pyms whose fortunes we need not trace. There is thus nothing unlikely in the family tradition that the Colonel Charles Pym who died in 1699 was the son of Anthony who emigrated in 1633. What could be more natural than that Anthony should name his son after the brother Charles to whom he wrote so affectionately when on the point of emigrating ?

Of John Pym's daughters we may note that the eldest, Phillipa, married Thomas Symons, a Cambridgeshire gentleman, one of whose daughters, Lucy, married Mr. Thomas Luttrell of Dunster Castle ; and that the second, Dorothy, married Sir Francis Drake of Buckland Monachorum and died childless. Incidentally, these marriages into the families of the Luttrells and the Drakes suggest the high esteem in which the Pyms were held in the West Country.

If we return now to the main line of John Pym's descendants, the remainder of the story can soon be told. His son, Sir Charles, married Katherine, the daughter of Sir Gilbert Gerrard, and had two children, Charles and Mary. When Sir Charles died in 1671 (his will was proved on 8th January 1671/2), his title and property descended to his son who also was named Charles. Sir Charles, the second baronet, died unmarried in 1688, being killed, according to a contemporary diary, in a tavern brawl : [1]

4 May 1688. The same evening also Sir Charles Pymm, baronet, was basely killed by one Waters, a lifeguard man, at the Swan Tavern in Fishstreet ; and since, the coroners inquest have found it wilfull murder.

—an incident likely to have a special interest for the diarist, who, according to the preface of the published diary, was a " gentleman descended from the Luttrells of Dunster Castle, Somerset ". Hence the baronetcy became extinct, and the property devolved upon the second baronet's sister Mary, the wife of Sir Thomas Hales of

---

[1] Narcissus Luttrell : *A Brief Historical Relation of State Affairs from September 1678 to April 1714,* I, 439.

Kent. Her brother had been only twenty-four at the time of his murder, and it may well have been only through the accident of the brawl that the direct heirs of John Pym in England ceased in the second generation of his descendants. Also, by the same accident, the male line of the Pyms, hitherto unbroken during at least sixteen generations, failed at last : and Brymore, which had remained in the Pym family since Elias Pym had acquired it nearly four and a half centuries earlier, passed into the hands of strangers.

One matter connected with Pym has always interested historians, namely, what would have been Pym's solution of the constitutional problem, for the shaping of which he had himself been largely responsible, if he had lived to see the end of the Civil War. Whatever answer is given to this question must be based in part upon conjecture. Pym never issued a statement of what he would do when the war ended. Even if we possessed such a statement it would have only a limited value because, had Pym lived to direct the Parliamentary resources and policy, the war would almost certainly have followed a different course from what it actually did follow. Hence, to guess what Pym would have done in circumstances which did not arise, and which we cannot reconstruct, is an almost impossible task.

But there is one approach which we may follow with some degree of certainty. One prediction can be made with some confidence : no matter in what circumstances the war had ended, Pym, the organizer of the Parliamentary victory, would have enjoyed a position of overwhelming prestige in the nation. The effect would have been a very different distribution of power between the three sections of the victors—Parliament, Army, Scots —from that which actually existed in 1645. Each of the three had its own solution of the constitutional problem. Of the three the Army was decidedly the strongest ; and not a little of its strength was due to the unrivalled personal force of its leader Cromwell. But suppose Cromwell had had a rival. The death of Pym had left Parliament without anyone strong enough to counter the influence of Cromwell or to keep the Army in its proper place as the military instrument of the Government. Pym's successor, as the leader of the Commons, was the younger Vane. This was shown, for example, immediately after Pym's death, by Vane's being repeatedly chosen as the Common's " manager " in conferences with the Lords, a capacity in which hitherto Pym had commonly acted. Sir Henry Vane was a clever man, with considerable political experience and with definite views backed by intense religious convictions. But he lacked both the broad outlook and the solid foundations which were typical of the mind of Pym. Moreover, Vane all along had shared too closely the views of Cromwell and the other Puritan extremists to be likely even to wish to hold the Independents of the Army in check. One of the leading ideas of the whole of Vane's life was religious toleration ; and it was on this issue that, after 1645, Vane finally parted company from the Presbyterian majority in the Commons and threw in his lot with the Independents of the Army. The result was that Parliament was left leaderless, as against the Army, and that early in August 1647 the Army entered London and remained henceforward the masters of the capital and of Parliament.

Such a situation could never have arisen if Pym had continued to lead the Commons. As we have seen, toleration was never part of his programme. The Grand Remonstrance, in which Pym was a prime mover, leaves no doubt on the point :

It is far from our purpose . . . to leave private persons or particular congregations to take up what form of Divine Service they please, for we hold it requisite that there should be throughout the whole realm a conformity to that order which the laws enjoin according to the Word of God.[1]

Such views were quite incompatible with belief in freedom of worship ; and it is inconceivable that Pym could ever have thrown in his lot, as his successor Vane did, with Cromwell and the Independents. Rather, he would have maintained the supremacy of Parliament against the Army as strenuously as he had maintained it against the King ; and he would have had enough prestige in the nation to have opposed it successfully, for events were to show

[1] See above, p. 193.

that the nation hated a tyrannical army at least as much as it hated a tyrannical king.

Another factor which must be remembered in this connection was Pym's consistent loyalty to the monarchy and even to Charles I. Over and over again in the previous pages we have heard this principle emphasized in his speeches and have watched it applied in his actions.   This same note was struck in the lengthy statement that he issued to counteract charges that were being circulated against him :

A Declaration and Vindication of John Pym, Esquire : Concerning The divers aspersions which have been cast upon him by sundry base and scandalous Pamphlets, and by divers Malignants, and people ill-affected to the good of the Commonwealth. Showing His continuall fidelitie and integritie towards His Majesty, and the High Court of Parliament, for the good of this Kingdome, and other His Majesties Dominions.

> Printed March 4.   Anno D. 1643.

In particular the *Declaration and Vindication* was directed against

that mountaine of scandalous reports that have been inflicted on my integritie to his sacred Majesty : some boldly averring me for the author of the present distractions between His Majestie and his Parliament.

To which reports he answered :

I take God and all that know my proceedings, to be my Vouchers ; that I neither directly nor indirectly, ever had a thought tending to the least disobedience, or disloyaltie to His Majesty, whom I acknowledge my lawfull King and Soveraigne, and would expend my bloud as soone in his service, as any Subject he hath.

Referring to the aspersion " that I have promoted and fomented the differences and schismes now abounding in the English Church " Pym declared :

How unlikely this is, and improbable, shall to every indifferent man be quickly rendred perspicuous : for that I am, and ever was, and so will dye a faithfull son of the Protestant Religion, without having the least relation in my beliefe to those grosse errours of Anabaptisme, Brownisme, and the like, everie man that hath any acquaintance with my conversation can beare me righteous witnesse.

Having now followed Pym's career through to its close, we can agree that all that we know of him bears out the truth of these assertions about his loyalty to both Church and King. To state categorically that in no circumstances would Pym ever have modified his adherence to the Crown would be absurd. Even Cromwell did not set out with any idea of being a regicide. Nevertheless, from the very beginning of Pym's parliamentary career to the end of it, consistency of principle was one of his characteristics. Of this characteristic several notable examples might be adduced. One of the most striking is to be found in the fact that his idea of an Association for the defence of Protestantism, which was actually carried into effect in 1643, had formed the theme of a speech which he had made in his first parliament (27th November 1621).[1] Similar consistency marked his attitude to the King; and never by word or act did he suggest that an alternative to the monarchy as a system of government had entered his mind. That he would ever have consented to the execution of Charles, or to the establishment of a republic, is as inconceivable as that he would have submitted to the rule of the Army or the Independents.

What exactly Pym's attitude would in the end have been towards Charles cannot be stated with any certainty. If Charles had persisted in being as incorrigibly tortuous in his bargaining with Pym as he proved to be with Parliament and Army and Scots alike, even Pym might have given up the task of making terms with him. No materials exist on which we can base a judgment as to what solution he might then have attempted. Since Pym himself never envisaged, so far as we know, the problem of finding a successor to Charles I, other than Prince Charles, we cannot tell what his solution to it might have been; and to guess in the dark is futile. What we can be reasonably sure of is that his policy would have been based on the twin principle of Parliamentary Monarchy. Only through such a policy could he have applied his own political

---

[1] See above, p. 42.

philosophy, clearly enunciated fifteen years before his death : [1]
" the form of government, in any State, could not be altered without apparent danger of ruin to that State " ; yet, because " time
must needs bring alterations, . . . those commonwealths have
been most durable and perpetual, which have often reformed and
recomposed themselves according to their first institutions and
ordinance ".

This unswerving devotion to a high political ideal, combined
with a recognition of how to suit its application to the circumstances
of his own day, is Pym's supreme claim to statesmanship. John
Pym was, in brief, the statesman of the Puritan Revolution, though
he himself was neither a Puritan nor a revolutionary but was an
orthodox Churchman and a conservative.

[1] See above, p. 99.

GENEALOGICAL TABLES

THESE tables were kindly supplied to the author by H. S. Marsham-Townshend, Esq., whose father copied them from tables in the possession of Philip Pleydell-Bouverie, Esq., who, until his death in 1890, was the owner of Brymore.

Table 1. has the following certificate subjoined :

The Discent with the Armes Quarterings and Matches above mentioned and marshalled are subscribed and exemplified by William Dethick Yorke Herauld, after Garter Principall King of Armes, Ano Domini 1583. And since reviewed, enlarged and allowed by the skilfull and industrious Herald Augustine Vincent Windsor Ano Domini 1626. And now againe approved augmented and subscribed by

WILLIAM RYLEY.

LANCASTER.
Decemb : 22 ; 1643.

A further note, by the copyist in 1890, includes the following comment :

(The Pedigree from which I have made the foregoing copy cannot be William Ryley's original work, as it is brought down in the same handwriting as the rest to Sir Charles Pym's marriage to Katherine Gerrard, for which the licence was granted to the Bishop of London 24 Feb 1662/3, nearly 20 years after the date of Ryley's signature. The same handwriting gives the 8 children of Philippa and Thomas Symons, but the entries of Charles Pym and his sister Mary were made later, and that of Mary's marriage to Sir Thomas Hales later still.)

Table 2.—A copy of a table drawn up from papers at Brymore by Frances, Lady Smith, and sent by her brother William Pinney to Charles, third Earl of Romney in June 1856.

TABLE 1

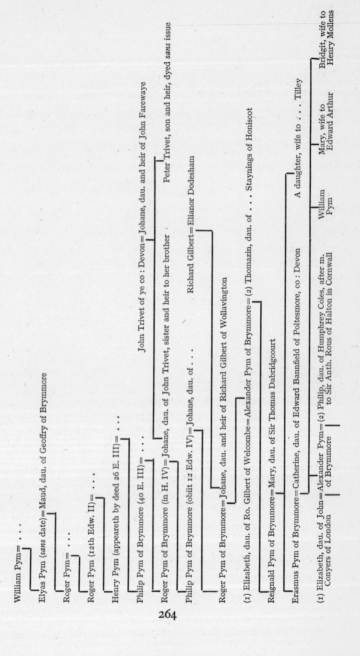

William Pym = . . .

Elyas Pym (*sans* date) = Maud, dau. of Geoffry of Brynmore

Roger Pym = . . .

Roger Pym (12th Edw. II) = . . .

Henry Pym (appeareth by deed 26 E. III) = . . .

Philip Pym of Brynmore (40 E. III) = . . .

John Trivet of ye co : Devon = Johane, dau. and heir of John Farewaye

Peter Trivet, son and heir, dyed *sans* issue

Roger Pym of Brynmore (in H. IV) = Johane, dau. of John Trivet, sister and heir to her brother

Richard Gilbert = Elianor Dodesham

Philip Pym of Brynmore (obiit 12 Edw. IV) = Johane, dau. of . . .

Roger Pym of Brynmore = Johane, dau. and heir of Richard Gilbert of Wollavington

(1) Elizabeth, dau. of Ro. Gilbert of Welcombe = Alexander Pym of Brynmore = (2) Thomazin, dau. of . . . Staynings of Honiscot

Reignald Pym of Brynmore = Mary, dau. of Sir Thomas Dabridgcourt

Erasmus Pym of Brynmore = Catherine, dau. of Edward Bannfield of Poltesmore, co : Devon

A daughter, wife to . . . Tilley

(1) Elizabeth, dau. of John = Alexander Pym = (2) Philip, dau. of Humphrey Coles, after m.
Conyers of London   of Brynmore   to Sir Anth. Rous of Halton in Cornwall

William Pym

Mary, wife to Edward Arthur

Bridgit, wife to Henry Mollens

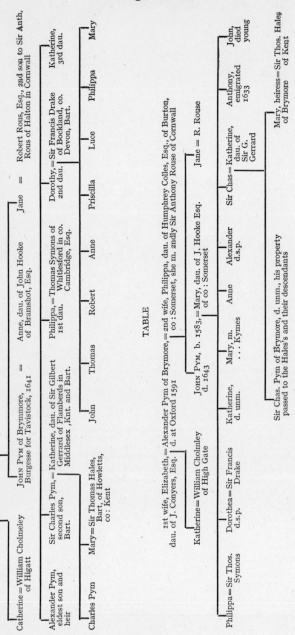

TABLE

BIBLIOGRAPHY

of works to which reference is made in footnotes

CONTEMPORARY WORKS

MSS.

Bouverie MSS.	British Museum
Brymore MSS.	Bridgwater Archives
Symonds d'Ewes	*Journal* (British Museum)
Colonial Entry Books	Public Record Office

DIARIES AND LETTERS

Baillie, Rev. Robert	*Letters and Journals* (Edinburgh, 1841)
Birch, T.	*Court and Times of James I* (1848)
„ „	*Court and Times of Charles I* (1848)
Camden Miscellanies	Vol. VIII
Warwick, Sir Philip	*Memoirs of the Reign of King Charles I* (1702–1813)

JOURNALS

House of Commons	
House of Lords	
Commons' Debates, 1621	Ed. Notestein, Relf and Simpson (Yale, 1936)
Commons' Debates, 1625	Ed. S. R. Gardiner (1873)
Commons' Debates for 1629	Ed. Notestein and Relf (Minnesota, 1921)
Journal of Sir Symonds D'Ewes, November 1640–March 1641	Ed. Notestein, 1923
Luttrell, Narcissus	*A Brief Historical Relation of State Affairs, September 1678–April 1714*
Parliamentary History	Ed. Cobbett (*1806–20*)
Proceedings and Debates of the House of Commons in 1620 and 1621, E. Nicholas	Ed. T. Tyrwhitt, 2 vols. (Oxford, 1766)
Rushworth, John	*Historical Collections* (1659–1701)
„ „	*Trial of Strafford* (1680)
Verney, Sir Ralph	*Notes on the Long Parliament*, Ed. J. Bruce (1845)
Whitelocke, Bulstrode	*Memorials of English Affairs, 1625–60* (edition 1853)

267

Bibliography

CALENDARS

Calendar of State Papers "Domestic"
Calendar of State Papers "Colonial"

PAMPHLETS

Prynne, William	*Conscientious, Serious, Theological and Legal Quaeres*
Thomason Tracts	British Museum

A Just Vindication of the Questioned Part of the Reading of Edward Bagshaw (1660)
The Diurnall Occurrences or Dayly Proceedings of Both Houses in this Great and Happy Parliament
A Speech delivered at a Conference with the Lords, January 25 1641
The Kings Majesties Message . . . With the House of Commons Humble Answer (February 7, 1641)
Two Speeches (January 1642)

FitzGeoffrey, Charles	*Death's Sermon unto the Living* (1620)

MISCELLANEOUS

Nichols, John	*The Progresses of King James I* (1828)
Wood, Anthony à	*Athenae Oxonienses* (Ed. P. Bliss, 4 vols., 1813–20)

Historical Manuscripts' Commission's Reports (H.M.C.)
Acts of the Privy Council of England (1621–3).

Clarendon, Earl of	*History of the Great Rebellion* (Ed. Macray, 1888)

SECONDARY AUTHORITIES

Black, J. B.	*The Reign of Queen Elizabeth* (1936)
Brown, Frederick	*Abstracts of Somersetshire Wills* (1889)
Buchan, John	*Oliver Cromwell* (1934)
Cokayne, G. E.	*Complete Baronetage*, 6 vols. (1900–6)
Davies, G.	*The Early Stuarts* (1937)
Dictionary of National Biography (D.N.B.)	
Forster, John	*Arrest of the Five Members* (1860)
,, ,,	*Debates on the Grand Remonstrance* (1860)
,, ,,	*John Pym* (Eminent British Statesmen, Vol. III) (1837)
,, ,,	*Sir John Eliot* (1864)
Francis, G. R.	*Scotland's Royal Line* (1928)
Gardiner, S. R.	*Constitutional Documents of the Puritan Revolution, 1625–1660* (3rd edition, 1906)
,, ,,	*History of England, 1603–1642*, 10 vols. (1883–)
,, ,,	*History of the Civil War, 1642–49*, 4 vols. (1893)
Gooch, G. P.	*English Democratic Ideas in the Seventeenth Century* (1927)

268

Bibliography

Jones, I. D.	*The English Revolution* (1931)
Lipson, E.	*The Economic History of England* (1920)
Maitland, F. W.	*Constitutional History of England* (1908)
Marriott, J. A. R.	*Life and Times of Lord Falkland*
Montague, F. C.	*Political History of England*, Vol. VIII (1907)
Newton, A. P.	*The Colonizing Activities of the English Puritans* (Yale, 1914)
Nugent, Lord	*Memorials of John Hampden* (1831)
Petrie, Sir Charles	*The Stuarts* (1937)
Pollard, A. F.	*Political History of England*, Vol. VI (1912)
Prothero, G. W.	*Statutes and Constitutional Documents, 1558–1625* (3rd edition 1906)
Ranke, L. von	*History of England* (English translation, 1875)
Savage, James	*History of the Hundred of Carhampton* (1830)
Shaw, W. A.	*The Knights of England*, 2 vols. (1906)
Tanner, J. R.	*English Constitutional Conflicts of the Seventeenth Century* (1928)
Traill, H. D.	*Strafford* (1889)
Trevelyan, G.M.	*England Under the Stuarts* (revised edition, 1925)
" "	*History of England* (1926)
Wade, C. E.	*John Pym* (1912)
Wedgwood, C. V.	*Strafford* (1935)

INDEX